Science
&
Spirituality

Those interested in the subject matter of this book are invited by the Vedic Oasis for Inspiration, Culture and Education (VOICE) to correspond at the following address :

Chaitanya Charan das
Vedic Oasis for Inspiration,
Culture and Education, (VOICE)
4, Tarapore Road, Camp
Pune – 411 001, India

e-mail : ccd.rnsm@gmail.com
web : www.voicepune.com

1st printing in India : 2,000 copies

Printed at Graphica Printers,Hyderabad.

dedicated to

His Divine Grace
A.C. Bhaktivedanta Swami Prabhupada

Founder-acharya of the International Society for Krishna
Consciousness and
the Greatest Spiritual Scientist of the Modern Times

Introduction:
My Journey Through Science and Spirituality

Science fascinated me from my childhood. The fascination was not with the technological wizardry and its products like video games, internet and cellphones, but with the prospect of the scientific spirit of enquiry unraveling the mysteries of nature, life and the universe. What secrets did the beautiful night sky with its innumerable twinkling stars hold? Where had the whole universe come from? Where had I come from? Science, with its telescopes and microscopes, promised to answer all such questions of the inquisitive mind.

My childhood fascination turned into perplexity in my teens. I had considered science to be a noble, uplifting pursuit which provided so much intellectual satisfaction as to make all grosser pleasures disdainful. Why then were the leading scientific brains delighting in the same gross pleasures that common people craved for – prestige, power, wealth and sex? Even stranger for me was the fact that many of my brilliant peers and seniors in one of the best technical colleges in India were victims of bad habits. Astrophysics had been one of my interests, but when I met a double doctorate US-returned astrophysicist and found that he was a chain smoker, I knew I had to do some serious thinking about the direction of my life.

The struggle to reconcile the lofty ideals that I cherished with the lousy reality that I observed around me prompted me turn to spirituality for answers. By my third year of engineering at the Government College of Engineering, Pune, India, I had pored over the works of several eminent Indian spiritual leaders. Although I felt that there might be something of value in their teachings, overall my scientific instincts made me look at spirituality with a healthy skepticism. Only when I heard the presentations of the devotees of the International Society for Krishna consciousness (ISKCON) did I first come across scientific evidences for the existence of God and the soul. I was stunned. I knew at that moment that my life would never be the same again; the scientist within me had discovered the spiritual dimension. The first section of this book, "Has Science Discovered God?" documents some of this evidence.

I found that the spiritual wisdom of the Bhagavad-gita and other Vedic literature answered thoroughly the very questions that had originally attracted me to science. And the life of integrity, morality and discipline that I saw among the youths living according to the Gita contrasted markedly with what I was seeing among my scientifically-educated students. Of course, I was sure that there were sincere scientists and that there were hypocritical spiritualists, but still the contrast intrigued me. While trying to make sense of this contrast, I started studying the link between science and spirituality.

It was then that I came to know the deeply spiritual, even devotional, motivations of pioneering scientists like Faraday and Kelvin; they saw scientific research as a means to better understand the glory of God. I recognized that the expulsion of spirituality from science was a recent phenomenon – and an unnatural one at that. Divorced of its spiritual purpose, science had become a servant of the materialistic modern mindset, a tool to better exploit the resources of nature. That explained to me why even scientifically brilliant people had hardly any aspirations higher than those of ordinary materialistic people. Science, bereft of its spiritual dimension, had led to the global spread of materialism. The consequences of this science-induced materialism are analyzed in the second section, "Does Science Need a Spiritual Paradigm?"

Now, I have been practicing and sharing spirituality for a dozen years. I have realized that the virtue of rational enquiry, which is fundamental to science, is also essential to distinguish genuine spirituality from pseudo-spirituality. Just as there is pseudo-science that militates against the spiritual purpose of science, there is pseudo-spirituality that does not stand the scrutiny of rational enquiry. A thorough philosophical and logical understanding of spirituality protects the spiritualist from becoming sentimental or fanatical and this is the substance of the third section, "Can Spirituality be Scientific?"

My teenage perplexity is now resolved; the bridging of the chasm between science and spirituality had also bridged the gap between my ideals and reality. I cherish the spiritual purpose and principles of my life, and I also cherish the spirit of rational, logical enquiry to understand and share my spiritual principles and practices. The global scientific and social trends that are a precursor for this harmonization of science and spirituality are discussed in the last section, "Discover the Post-Secular Synthesis."

Irrespective of whether you are a scientist or a spiritualist or are neither, this book will take you an intellectually adventurous journey. The goal of this intellectual adventure is to uncover the deepest truths of life, which is, after all, the ultimate purpose of all true science and all true spirituality.

Chaitanya Charan Das,
BE, COEP,
Spiritual Mentor,
ISKCON, Pune
11th August, 2008

Acknowledgements

My first and greatest thanks are to my foremost shiksha-guru His Grace Radheshyam Prabhu, who has guided, inspired and facilitated me in my attempts at writing.

My deep gratitude is also due to my beloved spiritual master, His Holiness Radhanath Maharaj, who has encouraged, inspired and guided me not only in writing, but also in my entire life.

I express my sincerest gratitude to His Holiness Jayadvaita Maharaj, my "writing guru" for his training, inspiration and interest.

Kundan Sud P put aside all other obligations to put his time and heart into formatting the book, designing the cover page and arranging the inside pictures.

Abhijit Toley P has been a tireless assistant who not only helped with research, proofreading and editing, but was also a constant reservoir of suggestions to improve the whole book.

My thanks to a special devotee-friend who helped extensively in proofreading.

Shuka Priya P accepted manfully the huge challenge of getting the book published within the deadline.

Shyamlila P, his good wife and his group of German devotees helped in various ways.

Nara Narayana Rishi P helped in formatting when it was most needed. And Mukundanand P arranged for his help to reach us at the right time.

Somil P helped in many ways. Manish Vithalani P gave many creative ideas and feedback, which helped shape several articles. Siddharth Reddy P helped in proofreading. Siddharth Kumar P and Gautam Kumar P helped in compiling the articles. Dhira Prashant P kept track of all the articles and helped in many timely ways Many other devotees helped in various ways.

My sincere thanks to them all.

Chaitanya Charan Das,
BE, COEP,
Spiritual Mentor,
VOICE, Pune

Contents

Discover the Post-Secular Synthesis

HAS SCIENCE DISCOVERED GOD?

The Symbiotic Factory

The Unparalleled Factory

Imagine a symbiotic factory setup, involving two hypothetical factories A and B. Suppose the two factories could be arranged such that the waste product of factory A would serve as the raw material for factory B and the waste product of factory B would serve as the raw material for factory A. Then the factory setup would be able to run perpetually with zero expenditure and unlimited profit!

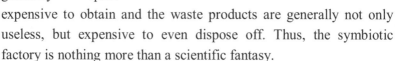

However, the raw materials for a factory are generally quite expensive to obtain and the waste products are generally not only useless, but expensive to even dispose off. Thus, the symbiotic factory is nothing more than a scientific fantasy.

Amazingly enough, a symbiotic factory setup is not only possible, but already operational in nature: respiration and photosynthesis. At every moment, we breathe in oxygen (O_2) and give out carbon dioxide (CO_2). O_2 is life-sustaining and CO_2 is life-destroying, if present in excessive quantity. Therefore, respiration by itself would diminish the supply of O_2 and increase CO_2 in the atmosphere, soon making the atmosphere and the planet inhabitable for all O_2-breathing creatures. But there is a magnificent balance system in nature, which exactly takes in the waste product of respiration CO_2 and gives out the raw material for respiration O_2 - plant photosynthesis. Isn't it remarkable that what the best scientists on the planet could do nothing more than dream about is already realized in nature. No wonder Albert Einstein remarked, "There are two ways to live life. One is to see nothing as a miracle and the other is to see everything as a miracle."

Does Nature Work Automatically?

Some people claim that nature certainly works remarkably, but its working is automatic and more or less governed by chance. They argue that seeing any divinity or God controlling nature is just a sentimental longing coming from an unscientific mentality. However, the word 'automatically' used in this context is somewhat misleading because 'automatically' doesn't indicate the absence of a controller, but rather the absence of knowledge of the controller. When we say that a machine works automatically, what it means is that the machine doesn't require continuous interaction with the operator. But still there is an operator who activates the machine and monitors its working.

For example, if you want to have fun with a child, then you might get an automatic toy. While staying out of view of the child, you release the toy and it comes moving into the view of the child. Seeing the toy moving automatically, the child becomes astounded and thinks that the toy is working by itself. But you as a wise person will never be misled into the same conclusion as this inexperienced child. For you know that even if the toy appears to be moving by itself, it is still programmed by you.

Similarly, the magnificent phenomena in nature are not occurring by themselves, as uninformed people, like the naïve child, may imagine. All natural phenomena are working under the expert, though remote and therefore invisible programming of God, as has been the conclusion throughout history of many wise people - both religious and scientific. Thus it is that the famous physicist Lord Kelvin asserted, "If you think deeply enough, you will be forced by science to believe in God."

Made Just For You

John walks into his bedroom on his tenth birthday and hey presto! The first thing that catches his eye is a new easy chair that's just the right size for him. He looks around and is elated to sees a brand new jacket that fits him exactly. Also there are shoes and stockings that are just perfect for him. To his great surprise and pleasure, he finds several new items, which are all, so to speak, tailor-made for him.

What does he conclude on seeing all this?

"That's elementary, my dear Watson. It's a birthday surprise arranged by his father."

The arrangement of John's room is an example of an acausal phenomenon. That is, knowing the effect that one wants in

advance, all the causes are adjusted to produce that effect. Acausal systems clearly need an intelligence, which understands the effect desired and then arranges the factors involved so that the effect is achieved. In the above example, the effect desired was to surprise and elate John with various birthday gifts and the intelligence that arranged them was his father's.

The Tables Have Turned

Acausal phenomena are unfamiliar to modern scientific thought, which mostly studies causal phenomena, wherein a cause produces an effect. The general agreement among the scientists till a few decades ago was that the design of life on earth was a result of aimless causal processes. Thus they seemed to have explained away the need of an intelligent designer for the universe.

But in the last few decades the tables have turned dramatically. So much so that astronomer George Greenstein noted in his book *The Symbiotic Universe,* "As we survey all the evidence, the thought insistently arises that some supernatural agency - or, rather, Agency - must be involved. Is it possible that suddenly, without intending to, we have stumbled upon scientific proof of the existence of a Supreme Being? Was it God who stepped in and so providentially crafted the cosmos for our benefit?"

What are the scientific investigations which have prompted many eminent scientists to make statements similar to these?

The Anthropic Principle

This counter-revolution began with the postulation of the Anthropic Principle by Brandon Carter in 1973. The Anthropic Principle, in its simplest form, states that we can observe in the universe only those things that are conducive to our existence as observers. It means that the entire universe, the solar system, the earth, its geology, weather, flora and fauna are all designed to make our existence possible.

On a freezing cold night, John runs trembling into his bedroom and shuts the door. To his amazement, he finds that his room is warm, cozy and fresh. On further observation, he realizes that his room has been sealed from all sides with a special material in order to be 100% cold-proof. He also notes that a room heater is the cause of the warmth. Moreover, he also sees an oxygen cylinder, which accounts for the fresh air.

Let us now see something quite similar in nature: the four remarkable properties of water, which preserve aquatic life in the water bodies throughout the long winters.

- ❦ Water has maximum density at 4 degrees centigrade. Consequently, ice has a lower density than water. During the frigid winters, ice remains on the surface, thus preventing the entire water body from freezing. This is similar to the cold-proof covering around John's room.

- ❦ Water also absorbs vast quantities of oxygen at low temperatures, which is utilized by the aquatic life under the ice sheet. This is akin to the oxygen cylinder in John's room.

♣ And water also releases large quantities of heat as it freezes, which achieves an effect similar to the heater in John's room.

The arrangement of John's room on that winter night was obviously an acausal event. Similarly the arrangement of the water bodies in winter is also an acausal event.

The same principle of benevolent design applies to all our life's necessities – air, water, food, heat, light etc.

Could all this be happening by chance? Let's consider the chances for the chance theory through an analogy.

Suppose I am playing a dice game with my life at stake. If the dice gives a '6', I live, else I die. I roll the dice and it gives '6'. "Good luck saved you", you will say. If I get '6' five successive times, you will start smelling something fishy. If I get '6' a 1,000 successive times, you will be practically sure that the dice has been designed to always fall six.

This is exactly what we see in the universe. Everything in the universe has to have a particular value for our existence to be possible and everything has exactly that value. Everything - right from the rate at which the universe expands after the big bang, the percentage of the nuclear fusion energy on the sun which is converted into starlight, the distance of the sun from the earth, the delicate ecological balance on the earth, the anomalous behavior of water.... the list goes on and on.

A Universe Designed For Life

The philosophical implications of the anthropic principle shake the very foundation of mechanistic science. British astronomer Sir Fred Hoyle in his book *The Intelligent Universe* comments, "Such properties seem to run through the fabric of the natural world like a thread of happy coincidences. But there are so many odd coincidences essential to life that some explanation seems required to account for them."

The explanation required is obvious. The universe we live in has been designed, with the express purpose of enabling our existence here. Although atheists try to do elaborate word jugglery to evade the evidence proving the existence of a benevolent designer, the theories they come up with – like parallel universes – are just flights of imagination. They are science fiction, not science.

Therefore in marketing language, it could be confidently said that the universe is "made just for you" – made by your benevolent father, God.

No wonder Noble Laureate chemist Christian B. Anfinsen declared, ""I think only an idiot can be an atheist."   ● ● ●

When Monkeys Start Typing

Typists all over the world, beware. Your jobs are in danger. You have competition....from monkeys. That's what the atheists would have us believe – at least those atheists who advocate the chance theory.

Chance is a popular word today in the world of science. And why not? It is the one- word answer to all the questions that atheists always found very disconcerting.

How did the incredibly vast universe with all its mind-boggling order come about? How did the atom with its intricate design come? Even the tiniest cell is far more complex than the biggest factory on earth. How in the wide world did it come from simple starting elements? Pat comes the reply to all these questions, with a triumphant smile, "Chance!"

The Big Dogma

That there is absolutely no empiric evidence for anything ever having come by chance doesn't really matter. In the religion of atheism, there is one unspoken dogma which practically everyone agrees upon: any theory, no matter how coherent and systematic, is unacceptable and 'unscientific' if it brings an ultimate creator into the picture. And conversely, any theory, no matter how improbable and untenable, is joyfully embraced if it helps in pushing God out. This pseudo-scientific mentality is typified by the following statement of William Bonner (pg 119, Mystery of Expanding Universe), "It is the business of science to offer rational explanations for all events in the real world, and any scientist who calls on God to explain something is failing in his job. This is one piece of dogmatism that a scientist can allow himself."

No wonder then that the chance theory has found many adherents in spite of the absence of even scanty evidence. For a mind programmed since birth to think in a mechanistic (read 'atheistic') way, 'chance' is a far more comforting word to hear than 'God' as the ultimate causative principle.

The Monkey Typist

Now let us consider whether the chance theory is possible even in principle.

In the words of the eighteenth century atheistic philosophers Denis Diderot and David Hume: given infinite time, nature would by

chance alone eventually hit on the order that we see around us. A modern version of this theory takes the form of an analogy (first introduced by Eddington): A monkey, if given infinite time, can by itself type the works of Shakespeare. To gullible minds, this analogy appears plausible – especially because the time scale involved makes it impossible to verify empirically.

The Probability

Let's first consider the mathematical probability of the monkey successfully typing at least one of Shakespeare's work, say Hamlet.

Ignoring punctuation, spacing, and capitalization, a monkey typing letters uniformly at random has a chance of one in 26 of correctly typing the first letter of Hamlet. It has a chance of one in 676 (26 × 26) of typing the first two letters. Because the probability shrinks exponentially, at 20 letters it already has only a chance of one in 2620 = 19,928,148,895,209,409,152,340,197,376 (almost 2 x 1028). In the case of the entire text of Hamlet, the probabilities are so vanishingly small they can barely be conceived in human terms. Say the text of Hamlet contains 130,000 letters (it is actually more, even stripped of punctuation), then there is a probability of one in 3.4 × 10183,946 to get the text right at the first trial. The average number of letters that needs to be typed until the text appears is also 3.4 × 10183,946.

Even if the observable universe were filled with monkeys typing for all time, their total probability to produce a single instance of Hamlet would still be less than one in 10183,800. As physicists Charles Kittel and Herbert Kroemer put it in their book *Thermal Physics*, "The probability of Hamlet is therefore zero in any operational sense of an event...", and the statement that the monkeys must eventually succeed "gives a misleading conclusion about very, very large numbers."

Common Sense Analysis

In addition to the mathematics, let's do some common sense analysis of the monkey's typing adventures. Suppose that you are told to supervise the monkey and suppose you and the monkey are told to work in 8-hour shifts.

Day 1. Both you and the monkey arrive on time and the monkey sits dutifully in front of the typewriter and starts typing (Thank goodness!) After 1 hour, what will you see? Some gibberish. Maybe 1 small word here or there. And at end of the day? Several pages of meaningless typed characters. You may find a few meaningful words - but only with great difficulty. (It is after all too much to expect the monkey to press a spacebar exactly after a meaningful word is completed!)

Day 2. Again the monkey sits down diligently and you sit behind him and he starts playing. Eight hours later, you are again looking at several printed pages struggling to find even a few meaningful words somewhere.

Day 10. "History repeats itself" You begin to realize that whoever said that knew what he was speaking about. The search for

meaningful words in streams and streams of meaningless texts is getting on your nerves.

Day 100. It is obvious to you by now that what you are looking for is never to be found. Whether it is day 10^0 or 10^2 or $10^1,000$ or $10^100000......00000...$, it really doesn't matter. The result of the monkey' typing is always going to be the same - nonsense. He is not going to learn by experience!

Now let's assume that the monkey starts working in 24 hour shifts (We won't ask you to supervise, don't worry!) Still that is not going to make any difference. A 24 hour shift is just like three 8-hour shifts with no break in between. So just as three 8-hour shifts don't give any fruitful results, one 24-hour shift will similarly bear no fruit. And just as 8-hour shifts repeated $10^1000.....$ times don't lead to any coherent text, neither will 24 hour shifts repeated $10^1000.....$ times.

The point is that the probability of a monkey typing out all the works of Shakespeare, if given millions of years, is not an infinitesimally small number; it is zero. No matter how many millions, billion, quadrillions or whatever number of years are given to the monkey (assuming he lives that long!), still the probability always remains zero.

Thus even in principle randomness does not produce order on any appreciable scale, irrespective of the time given.

The Experiment

"Even if we can't figure out in principle how a monkey can type the Hamlet, maybe it can somehow type it in practice," some diehard atheists may argue like this. Let's see what happened in a real monkey typing experiment.

In 2003, lecturers and students from the University of Plymouth MediaLab Arts course used a £2,000 grant from the Arts Council to study the literary output of real monkeys. They left a computer keyboard in the enclosure of six Celebes Crested Macaques in Paignton Zoo in Devon in England for a month, with a radio link to broadcast the results on a website. One researcher, Mike Phillips, defended the expenditure as being cheaper than reality TV and still "very stimulating and fascinating viewing"

Chance? NO chance!

Not only did the monkeys produce nothing but five pages consisting largely of the letter S, the lead male began by bashing the keyboard with a stone, and the monkeys continued by urinating and defecating on it. The zoo's scientific officer remarked that the experiment had "little scientific value, except to show that the 'infinite monkey' theory is flawed".

False Alarm

Simple common sense, isn't it? But it seems common sense is not so common, especially among atheists.

So typists, sorry for the false alarm. But don't blame us; we didn't set it on; rather we are setting it off.   ● ● ●

How Everything Began

The New Garb of Faith

Many scientists today propose the big bang theory – or some modified version of it – to explain the origin of the universe and, thus try to do away with the need for a designer.

According to the big bang theory, in the beginning (or before the beginning, if you will), all matter in the universe was concentrated into a single point (known as a singularity) at an extremely high temperature, and then it exploded with tremendous force. From an expanding superheated cloud of sub-atomic particles, atoms gradually formed, then stars, galaxies, planets and finally life.

The big bang theory, though mind-grabbing and widely-publicized, literally collapses when confronted with one gnawing question: where did the singularity come from? Here the atheists find the tables turned, for they face the same problem as the religionists whom they taunt with the question, `Where did God come from?' Just as the religionists answer that God is the cause of all causes, the scientists now have to bare their faith in their "god" – a mathematically indescribable, physically unrealizable point of infinite density and temperature, of infinitesimal size, existing before all conceptions of time and space – as the cause of all causes. Thus, the atheists stand exposed for committing the same unforgivable, intellectual crime that they charge the religionists with - making physically unverifiable, supernatural claims.

Atheists, despite all their condemnation of faith, can't do away with faith; they simply give it a new garb.

An open-minded thinker now has to choose between two options about the origin of everything - a dead, insentient, unintelligent singularity or a living, thinking, intelligent designer. Neither of these is `scientific' in the sense in which the term is presently used, for both of them take us beyond the realm of space and time, where science cannot prove anything.

What does common sense say?

All our practical experience shows that an intelligent living person can easily create a variety of things; a carpenter makes a bureau; a civil engineer makes a skyscraper; an automobile engineer makes a Mercedes Benz. There is absolutely no experience of the raw materials aligning by themselves into useful products. Just imagine what would happen to the unemployment rate worldwide if that happened!

The choice then is not between rational science and blind faith, but between blind faith garbing itself as science on one **common** side and common sense **sense** misrepresented as blind faith on the other.

Checkmated by Finetuning

But even if, for argument's sake, we accept the big bang cosmology to be true, that is, we grant that the origin and development of the universe are to be explained solely in terms of the interactions of matter and energy, still these interactions have to be so precisely adjusted as to require an intelligent designer. Indeed, so many are the parameters – the values of physical constants and ratios of natural forces – that need to have precise values that this phenomenon has been called as the 'fine-tuning' of the universe.

Consider the following examples of fine-tuning within our solar system, as explained by Dr Hugh Ross in the presentation *Where did the Universe Come from?* :

Microscopic Finetuning

1. Electromagnetism

If the force electromagnetism is weaker than what it is, there won't be sufficient electromagnetic pull to keep electrons orbiting the nucleus. If electrons cannot orbit nuclei, then electrons cannot be shared so that nuclei can come together to form molecules. Without molecules, we have no life.

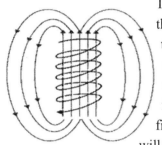 If the force electromagnetism is stronger than what it is, the nuclei will hang onto their electrons with such strength that the electrons will not be shared with adjoining nuclei and again, molecules will never form. Unless the force electromagnetism is fine-tuned to a particular value, the universe will have no molecules and no life.

2. Strong Nuclear Force

The force that holds the protons and neutrons together in the nucleus of an atom is called the strong nuclear force, which is the strongest of the four forces of physics.

If the nuclear force is too strong, the protons and neutrons in the universe will find themselves stuck to other protons and neutrons, which means we have a universe devoid of hydrogen. Hydrogen is the element composed of the bachelor proton. It's impossible to conceive of life chemistry without Hydrogen.

On the other hand, if we make the nuclear force slightly weaker, none of the protons and neutrons will stick together. All of the protons and neutrons will be bachelors, in which case the only element that would exist in the universe would be Hydrogen, and it's impossible to make life if all we've got is Hydrogen.

The value of this nuclear strong force has to be so sensitively adjusted that if it were 3/10th of 1% stronger or 2% weaker, life would be impossible at any time in the universe.

3. Mass of the Proton and Neutron

The neutron is 0.138% more massive than the proton. Because of this, it takes a little more energy for the universe to make neutrons, as compared to protons. That's why in the universe of today we have seven times as many protons as neutrons.

If the neutron were 1/10th of 1% less massive than what we observe, then the universe would make so many neutrons that all of the matter in the universe would very quickly collapse into neutron stars and black holes, and life would be impossible.

If the neutron were 1/10th of 1% more massive than what we observe, then the universe would make so few neutrons, that there wouldn't be enough neutrons to make Carbon, Oxygen, Nitrogen, Phosphorus, Potassium, etc., without which there can be no life.

4. Electrons

Gravity is the weakest among the four forces of physics. But for gravity to act on the cosmic level, the universe must be electrically neutral. That requires the numbers of the positively charged particles to be equivalent to the numbers of negatively charged particles. Else electromagnetism will dominate gravity, and stars, galaxies and planets will never form. If they don't form, then clearly life is impossible.

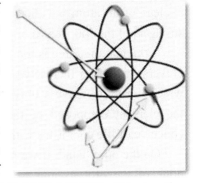

The numbers of electrons must equal the numbers of protons to better than one part of 10,000,000,000,000,000,000,000,000,000,000,000,000 (10 to the 37th power). To get an idea of this number, suppose we covered the entire North American continent from here all the way to the moon with dimes. That's a 250,000-mile high pile of dimes covering 10,000,000 square miles, and you'd have to do that with a billion North American continents from here all the way to the moon. That is   one   chance   in

10,000,000,000,000,000,000,000,000,000,000,000,000 (10 to the 37th power).

Now, imagine that in those piles of billions of dimes, there's one dime colored red. If you were to randomly shuffle your way through those billions of dimes blindfolded, and you choose one dime, the odds that you would pick up that one red dime is one chance in 10,000,000,000,000,000,000,000,000,000,000,000,000. And that's how accurately the number of electrons and protons must be balanced.

There are many more examples of such fine tuning, which, along with their implications, are well-explained in *Human Devolution* by Micheal Cremo. (He also explains lucidly the Vedic understanding of 'how everything began?')

Cosmic Finetuning

For the sake of brevity, we will just give three more examples of precise arrangements in our solar system:

1. Speed of Earth's Rotation

If the earth rotates too quickly, we will have too many storms like tornadoes and hurricanes. If it rotates too slowly, it will be too cold at night and too hot during the day.

2. The Right Size Moon

The   Earth's   moon system is that of a small planet being orbited by a huge, single moon. That huge, single moon has the effect of stabilizing the rotation axis of planet Earth to 23½ degrees. That's the ideal tilt for life on planet Earth.

The axis on planet Mars moves through a tilt from zero to 60 degrees and flips back and forth. If that were to happen on Earth, life would be impossible. Thanks to the Moon, it's held stable at 23 ½ degrees.

3. The Position of Jupiter:

It takes a super massive planet like Jupiter, located where it is, to act as a shield, guarding the Earth from cosmic collisions. We don't want a comet colliding with Earth every week. Thanks to Jupiter, that doesn't happen.

Over a 100 examples of such 'fine-tuning' (micro-precise arrangement of factors) have been documented in the technical literature and summarized in books like *The Anthropic Cosmological Principle* (1986). And more are constantly being discovered.

Where Does the Finetuning Come From?

Atheists try to explain away the fine tuning by invoking the multiple universe theory, saying that we just happen to be in the universe where everything is suitable for our existence. But parallel universes are intrinsically unproven and unprovable. They fit better the realm of science fiction than science. Sir Martin Rees, the astronomer royal of Great Britain, admits in his book *Just Six Numbers* that the multiple universe theory is simply "speculative".

All other attempts to explain the fine tuning including the grand unified theory suffer the same crippling drawback; they are simply unproven and unprovable.

To summarize the answer to the question 'how everything began?' let's hear what Nobel Laureate physicist Arthur Compton has to say, "For me, faith begins with the realization that a supreme intelligence brought the universe into being and created man. It is not difficult for me to have this faith, for an orderly, intelligent universe testifies to the greatest statement ever uttered: 'In the beginning, God...'"

● ● ●

A Scientific Examination of Evolution

Article summary.

Relevance

Why is analyzing the truth regarding evolution important? The apparently scientific nature of the theory of evolution has led to the widespread acceptance of an atheistic, materialistic worldview. So to establish that a spiritual worldview with God as the intelligent designer is not unscientific, the claim that evolution is a proven science needs to be examined.

Fossil Evidences

Scientists claim that evolution happened in the past, but does the record of the past as seen in the fossils support this? Not at all.

1. No Supporting Evidence: There are no fossil records to support the claim of transition of one species to another.

2. Suppressed contradictory evidences: There are many anomalous fossils that contradict the picture of gradual development of life on earth painted by evolution.

Other Evidences

1. Cheating proofs:

Although many so-called proofs of evolution have been disproved by scientists themselves, science textbooks worldwide keep publishing those proofs, thus misleading innocent students.

- ♣ Life in a bottle – Miller's Experiment
- ♣ Imagination in full form - Darwin's Tree of Life
- ♣ Look-alike illusions – Homology in Vertebrate Limbs

- Glue-fixed pictures – Peppered Moths
- Beaks and birds – Darwin's Finches
- Apemen or Conmen – Javaman Thighbone

1. Misinterpreted proofs:

Many proofs are offered for evolution, which on closer examination, don't prove evolution at all.

- Similarity of DNA
- Vestigial organs
- Breeding
- Playing God to disprove God
- Extinction of species

Mechanisms for Evolution

1.Natural Selection and mutation: All the mechanisms that are claimed to cause evolution – natural selection, mutation and chance – can at best cause variation within species, not variation from one species to another.

2.Irreducible complexity: Modern biochemical research has confirmed Darwin's worst fear of the existence of organs that cannot have evolved upwards step-by-step and has effectively debunked his theory.

3.Origin of life: Evolution theory has no explanation, either theoretical or experimental, as to how life originated in the first place.

Conclusion

The notion of evolution does not stand up to the standard of science; there is neither a clear, detailed theory about it, nor are there any unambiguous evidences to prove it. Therefore school education about evolution is not scientific education; it is state-sponsored indoctrination into atheism.

*****

Vision Determines Mission

Today many people accept without question the idea that man arose from lower species by the process of evolution. Others feel that whether humans had a chemical origin or a divine origin doesn't really matter; their conflicts at work, at home and in their minds appear to be of far greater importance. But could it be that most of the problems that plague us today are caused by a blunder at this first step? Our understanding of how we came about determines our goals, values and attitudes. Nobel Laureate neurobiologist Roger Sperry puts it well, "Beliefs concerning the ultimate purposes and meaning of life and the accompanying worldview perspectives that mould beliefs of right and wrong are critically dependent...on concepts regarding the conscious self."

Worldview Resulting From Evolutionary Ideas: "If I am a product of matter, there is nothing higher to life than material enjoyment. And because my predecessors survived and prospered only due to their expertise in savage competition and warfare, I too have to do the same to succeed in life."

Worldview Resulting From Spiritual Perspectives: "If my identity is spiritual and God is my eternal loving Parent, going back to His kingdom becomes the goal of my life. And I should therefore curb the animalistic instincts within me and be caring, virtuous, magnanimous and devoted to God."

Biologist Michael Denton in his book *'Evolution: Theory in Crisis'* explains the far-reaching consequences of the theory of evolution, "It was because Darwinian theory broke man's link with God and set him adrift in a cosmos without purpose or end that its impact was so fundamental. No other intellectual revolution in modern times... so profoundly affected the way men viewed themselves and their place in the universe." Once the link with God was broken, evolutionary thought set the stage for man to take the place of God, to try to become the controller of the material world or, in short, become a materialist. Biologist Douglas Futuyma's *Evolutionary Biology* states that "it was Darwin's theory of evolution," together with

Marx's theory of history and Freud's theory of human nature, "that provided a crucial plank to the platform of mechanism and materialism" that has since been "the stage of most Western thought."

The Theory

Darwin is credited with first proposing a plausible physical mechanism that would explain the variety of life forms we observe in the world around us. Evolution, as he explained it, is based on the twin principles of variation and natural selection. When members of a species reproduce, he reasoned, there is variation among individual representatives of the species. Some of these are better equipped to survive in their particular environment, and therefore their qualities are selected and passed on to their descendants. Over the passage of time, these changes in organisms are sufficient, according to evolutionary theory, to result in changes of species.

Since Darwin's time, the concept of variation has undergone some changes. Modern evolutionists believe that mutations in genes produce the variations that natural forces select for survival. (Darwin did not know about genetics.) Evolutionists have considered a number of types of genetic variations—point mutation, genetic recombination, and random genetic drift, for example—but these all fall under the broad heading of random variation. And to this day the only principle accepted as giving direction to the evolutionary process is natural selection. So Darwin's basic principles of random variation and natural selection are still the foundations of evolutionary thought.

Let's examine whether the theory of evolution is scientifically true.

Fossil Evidences

According to Darwinists, the first undisputed fossil evidence for life on earth goes back about 2 billion years. They say the first apes and monkeys appeared about 40-50 million years ago. The first ape-men (called Australopithecus) appeared about 4 million years ago. These were followed by other apemen called Homo habilis, Homo erectus, and Neanderthal man. The first human beings of modern type (Homo sapiens sapiens) appeared only 100,000 or 200,000 years ago. Civilization, according to modern scientists, is less than 10,000 years old.

However, what Darwin offered was basically "one long argument" with no proof whatsoever. He attacked the fossil record as being inaccurate, to an extreme degree and prophesied that future generations of paleontologists would fill in these gaps by diligent search. But has the diligent search of modern paleontologists fulfilled his prophesy?

No Supporting Evidence:

Here are just a few of many quotes by eminent evoloutionists about the lack of evidence supporting evolution in the fossil record.

1. Record proves prediction wrong

"One hundred and twenty years of paleontological research later, it has become abundantly clear that the fossil record will not confirm this part of Darwin's predictions. Nor is the problem a miserably poor record. The fossil record simply shows that this prediction is wrong. ...The observation that species are amazingly conservative and static entities throughout long periods of time has all the qualities of the emperor's new clothes: everyone knew it but preferred to ignore it. Paleontologists, faced with a recalcitrant record obstinately refusing to yield Darwin's predicted pattern, simply looked the other way."

Reference: Eldredge, N. and Tattersall, I., *The Myths of Human Evolution*, 1982, p. 45-46

2. Not a single example

"But fossil species remain unchanged throughout most of their history and the record fails to contain a single example of a significant transition."

Reference: - Woodroff, D.S., *Science*, vol. 208, 1980, p. 716

3. Links wanted; links missing

"Links are missing just where we most fervently desire them, and it is all too probable that many 'links' will continue to be missing."

Reference: Jepsen, L. Glenn; Mayr, Ernst; Simpson George Gaylord. *Genetics, Paleontology, and Evolution*, New York, Athenaeum, 1963, p. 114

4. Consistently missing

"The curious thing is that there is a consistency about the fossil gaps; the fossils are missing in all the important places."

Reference: Hitching, Francis, *Where Darwin Went Wrong*, Penguin Books, 1982, p.19

5. Cambrian explosion disproves darwinism

(The Cambrian explosion is the rapid appearance of most major groups of complex animals around 530 million years ago, as evidenced by the fossil record. This sudden appearance of species in the fossil record has been since the time of Darwin one of the main objections to his theory that different species evolve gradually by natural selection.)

"Paleontologists are traditionally famous (or infamous) for reconstructing whole animals from the debris of death. Mostly they cheat. ... Baffling (and embarrassing) to Darwin, this event still dazzles us and stands as a major biological revolution on a par with the invention of self-replication and the origin of the eukaryotic cell. The animal phyla emerged out of the Precambrian mists with most of the attributes of their modern descendants."

Reference: Bengtson, Stefan, *The Solution to a Jigsaw Puzzle*, Nature, vol. 345 (June 28, 1990), p. 765-766

6. Choose – theory or evidence?

"Paleontologists have paid an enormous price for Darwin's argument. We fancy ourselves as the only true students of life's history, yet to preserve our favored account of evolution by natural selection we view our data as so bad that we almost never see the very process we profess to study. The history of most fossil species includes two features particularly inconsistent with gradualism:

1.Stasis. Most species exhibit no directional change during their tenure on earth. They appear in the fossil record looking much the same as when they disappear; morphological change is usually limited and directionless.

2.Sudden appearance. In any local area, a species does not arise gradually by the steady transformation of its ancestors; it appears all at once and 'fully formed.'"
Reference: Gould, Stephen J. *The Panda's Thumb*, 1980, p. 181-182

What is special about all the above quotes is that they are from evolutionists; the verdict of the fossil record is so overwhelmingly clear that even they are forced, despite their belief in evolution, to admit the utter lack of evidence for it.

The problem is so difficult to overcome that one school of evolutionists, headed by Stephen J. Gould and Niles Eldredge, felt compelled to come up with a new evolutionary theory to account for the gaps. They propose "punctuated equilibrium" as an explanation.

The punctuated equilibrium theory makes evolution invisible in the fossil record. A supposed change from species A to species B would take place in a small population in an isolated geographic location within a geological microsecond—a period too short to allow for fossils of intermediate forms to be deposited. Then the new species B would move from its isolated place of origin and expand throughout the entire range of the old species A. On a scale of millions of years the fossils of B would suddenly replace the fossils of A, giving the impression that B had emerged without intermediate forms. According to punctuated equilibrium advocates, this lack of transitional fossils is exactly what would be expected, and therefore they can claim that any given species has in fact evolved from an ancestral form without offering any proof from the fossil record. But a theory that allows no proving or disproving on the basis of physical evidence hardly qualifies as an adequate scientific explanation.

Further, other evolutionists have pointed out the fallacious circular reasoning inherent in the model:

"The Eldredge-Gould concept of punctuated equilibria has gained wide acceptance among paleontologists. It attempts to account for the following paradox: Within continuously sampled lineages, one rarely finds the gradual morphological trends predicted by Darwinian evolution; rather, change occurs with the sudden appearance of new, well-differentiated species. Eldredge and Gould equate such appearances with speciation, although the details of these events are not preserved. The punctuated equilibrium model has been widely accepted, not because it has a compelling theoretical basis but because it appears to resolve a dilemma. Apart from the obvious sampling problems inherent to the observations that stimulated the model, and apart from its intrinsic circularity (one could argue that speciation can occur only when phyletic change is rapid, not vice versa), the model is more ad hoc explanation than theory, and it rests on shaky ground."

Reference: Ricklefs, Robert E., *"Paleontologists Confronting Macroevolution,"* *Science*, vol. 199, 1978, p. 59

II. Suppressed Contradictory Evidence:

In their book *Forbidden Archeology: The Hidden History of the Human Race*, Michael A Cremo and Richard L Thompson present scores of suppressed fossil evidences that suggest that humans have been on the earth for millions of years, in contradiction with the evolutionary idea that humans appeared only some 40,000 years ago. Here we give a few samples of their findings:

Ancient Skulls and Bones:

Reck's Skeleton

The first significant African discovery related to human origins occurred in 1913 when Pro fessor Hans Reck, of Berlin University, found a human skeleton in the upper part of Bed II at Olduvai Gorge, Tanzania. Modern dating methods give a late Early Pleistocene date of around 1.15 million years for this site. Reck said, "The bed in which the human remains were found....showed no sign of disturbance."

The skeleton was distorted by compression from the weight of substantial accumulation of sediment in the overlying strata. W. O. Dietrich, writing in 1933, stated that this feature of the skeleton argued against its being a recent, shallow burial. George Grant MacCurdy, a leading anthropologist from Yale University, considered Reck's discovery to be genuine. [pp. 630-631, Forbidden Archeology]

Castenedolo Skull

This anatomically modern human skull (Sergi 1884, plate 1) was found in 1880 at Castenedolo, Italy. The stratum from which it was taken is assigned to the Astian stage of the Pliocene (Oakley 1980, p. 46). According to modern authorities (Harland et al, 1982, p. 110), the Astian belongs to the Middle Pliocene, wihch would give the skull an age of 3-4 million years. [p. 424, Forbidden Archeology]

Anomalous Artifacts

Grooved Sphere from South Africa

A metallic sphere from South Africa with three parallel grooves around its equator (photo courtesy of Roelf Marx). The sphere was found in a Precambrian mineral deposit, said to be 2.8 billion years old. [p. 813, Forbidden Archeology]

Mysterious Letters from a Quarry

Raised letterlike shapes found inside a block of marble from a quarry near Philadelphia, Pennsylvania (Corliss 1978, p. 657; American Journal of Science 1831, vol. 19, p. 361). The block of marble came from a depth of 60-70 feet in strata dated 500-600 million years old. [p. 797, Forbidden Archeology]

Other Evidences

I. CHEATING EVIDENCE:

Consider the following five examples adapted from the article "Survival of the fakest" by Jonathan Wells published in the leading American magazine *The American Spectator* - December 2000 / January 2001

Life in a Bottle: Miller's experiment

Anyone old enough in 1953 to understand the import of the news remembers how shocking, and to many, exhilarating, it was. Scientists Stanley Miller and Harold Urey had succeeded in creating "the building blocks" of life in a flask. Mimicking what were believed to be the natural conditions of the early Earth's atmosphere, and then sending an electric spark through it, Miller and Urey had formed simple amino acids. As amino acids are the "building blocks" of life, it was thought just a matter of time before scientists could themselves create living organisms. At the time, it appeared a dramatic confirmation of evolutionary theory. Life wasn't a "miracle." No outside agency or divine intelligence was necessary. Put the right gasses together, add electricity, and life is bound to happen. It's a common event. Carl Sagan could thus confidently predict on PBS that the planets orbiting those "billions and billions" of stars out there must be just teeming with life.

There were problems, however. Scientists were never able to get beyond the simplest amino acids in their simulated primordial environment, and the creation of proteins began to seem not a small step or couple of steps, but a great, perhaps impassable, divide.

The telling blow to the Miller-Urey experiment, however, came in the 1970's, when scientists began to conclude that the Earth's early atmosphere was nothing like the mixture of gasses used by

Miller and Urey. Instead of being what scientists call a "reducing," or hydrogen-rich environment, the Earth's early atmosphere probably consisted of gasses released by volcanoes. Today there is a near consensus among geochemists on this point. But put those volcanic gasses in the Miller-Urey apparatus, and the experiment doesn't work – in other words, no "building blocks" of life. What do textbooks do with this inconvenient fact? By and large, they ignore it and continue to use the Miller- Urey experiment to convince students that scientists have demonstrated an important first step in the origin of life. This includes the above-mentioned Molecular Biology of the Cell, co-authored by the National Academy of Sciences president, Bruce Alberts. Most textbooks also go on to tell students that origin-of-life researchers have found a wealth of other evidence to explain how life originated spontaneously – but they don't tell students that the researchers themselves now acknowledge that the explanation still eludes them.

Imagination in Full Form: Darwin's Tree of Life

Darwin's theory claims to account for the origin of new species – in fact, for every species since the first cells emerged from the primordial ooze. This theory does have the virtue of making a prediction: If all living things are gradually modified descendants of one or a few original forms, then the history of life should resemble a branching tree. Unfortunately, despite official pronouncements, this prediction has in some important respects turned out to be wrong. The fossil record shows the major groups of animals appearing fully formed at about the same time in a "Cambrian explosion," rather than diverging from a common ancestor. Darwin knew this, and considered it a serious objection to his theory. But he attributed it to the imperfection of the fossil record, and he thought that future research would supply the missing ancestors. But a century and a half of continued fossil collecting has only aggravated the problem. Instead of slight differences appearing first, then greater differences emerging later, the greatest differences appear right at the start. Some fossil experts describe this as "top-down evolution," and note that it contradicts the "bottom-up" pattern predicted by Darwin's theory. Yet most current biology textbooks don't even mention the Cambrian explosion, much less point out the challenge it poses for Darwinian evolution. Then came the evidence from molecular biology. Biologists in the 1970's began testing Darwin's branching tree pattern by comparing molecules in various species. The more similar the molecules in two different species are, the more closely related they are presumed to be. At first this approach seemed to confirm Darwin's tree of life. But as scientists compared more and more molecules, they found that different molecules yield conflicting results. The branching-tree pattern inferred from one molecule often contradicts the pattern obtained from another. Canadian molecular biologist W. Ford Doolittle doesn't think the problem will go away. Maybe scientists "have failed to find the 'true tree'," he wrote in 1999, "not because their methods are inadequate or because they have chosen the wrong genes, but because the history of life cannot properly be represented as a tree." Leading evolutionist Stephen J Gould admitted, "The evolution tree that adorns our text books have data only at the tips and nodes of their branches, the rest is all inference, however reasonable, not the evidence of fossils."

Nevertheless, biology textbooks continue to assure students that Darwin's Tree of Life is a scientific fact overwhelmingly confirmed by evidence. Judging from the real fossil and molecular evidence, however, it is an unsubstantiated hypothesis masquerading as a fact.

Look-alike Illusions: Homology

Most introductory biology textbooks carry drawings of vertebrate limbs showing similarities in their bone structures. Biologists before Darwin had noticed this sort of similarity and called it "homology," and they attributed it to construction on a common archetype or design. In The Origin of Species, however, Darwin argued that the best explanation for homology is descent with modification, and he considered it evidence for his theory. Darwin's followers rely on homologies to arrange fossils in branching trees that supposedly show ancestor descendant relationships. In his 1990 book, Evolution and the Myth of Creationism, biologist Tim Berra compared the fossil record to a series of Corvette models: "If you compare a 1953 and a 1954 Corvette, side by side, then a 1954 and a 1955 model, and so on, the descent with modification is overwhelmingly obvious." But Berra forgot to consider a crucial, and obvious, point: Corvettes, so far as anyone has yet been able to determine, don't give birth to little Corvettes. They, like all automobiles, are designed by people working for auto companies, or in other words, designed by an outside intelligence. So although Berra believed he was supporting Darwinian evolution rather than the pre-Darwinian explanation, he unwittingly showed that the fossil evidence is compatible with either. Law professor (and critic of Darwinism) Phillip E. Johnson dubbed this : "Berra's Blunder." The lesson of Berra's Blunder is that we need to specify a natural mechanism before we can scientifically exclude designed construction as the cause of homology. Darwinian biologists have proposed two mechanisms: developmental pathways and genetic programs. According to the first, homologous features arise from similar cells and processes in the embryo; according to the second, homologous features are programmed by similar genes. But biologists have known for a hundred years that homologous structures are often not produced by similar developmental pathways. And they have known for thirty years that they are often not produced by similar genes, either. So there is no empirically demonstrated mechanism to establish that homologies are due to common ancestry rather than common design. Without a mechanism, modern Darwinists have simply defined homology to mean similarity due to common ancestry. According to Ernst Mayr, one of the principal architects of modern neo-Darwinism: "After 1859 there has been only one definition of homologous that makes biological sense: Attributes of two organisms are homologous when they are derived from an equivalent characteristic of the common ancestor." This is a classic case of circular reasoning. Darwin saw evolution as a theory, and homology as its evidence. Darwin's followers assume evolution is independently established, and homology is its result. But you can't then use homology as evidence for evolution except by reasoning in a circle: Similarity due to common ancestry demonstrates common ancestry. Philosophers of biology have been criticizing this approach for decades. As Ronald Brady wrote in 1985: "By making our explanation into the definition of the condition to be explained, we express not scientific hypothesis but belief. We are so convinced that our explanation is true that we no longer see any need to distinguish it from the situation we were trying to explain. Dogmatic endeavors of this kind must eventually leave the realm of science." So how do the textbooks treat this controversy? Once again, they ignore it. In fact, they give students the impression that it makes sense to define homology in terms of common ancestry and then turn around and use it as evidence for common ancestry.

Glue-fixed Pictures: The Peppered Moths

Darwin was convinced that in the course of evolution, "Natural Selection has been the most important, but not the exclusive means of modification," but he had no direct evidence of this. The best he could do in The Origin of Species was give "one or two imaginary illustrations." In the 1950's, however, British physician Bernard Kettlewell provided what seemed to be conclusive evidence of natural selection. During the previous century, peppered moths in England had gone from being predominantly light-colored to being predominantly dark-colored. It was thought that the change occurred because dark moths are better camouflaged on pollution-darkened tree trunks, and thus less likely to be eaten by predatory birds. To test this hypothesis experimentally, Kettlewell released light and dark moths onto nearby tree trunks in polluted and unpolluted woodlands, then watched as birds ate the more conspicuous moths. As expected, birds ate more light moths in the polluted woodland, and more dark moths in the unpolluted one. In an article written for Scientific American, Kettlewell called this "Darwin's missing evidence." Peppered moths soon became the classic example of natural selection in action, and the story is still retold in most introductory biology textbooks, accompanied by photographs of the moths on tree trunks. In the 1980's, however, researchers discovered evidence that the official story was flawed – including the pertinent fact that peppered moths don't normally rest on tree trunks. Instead, they fly by night and apparently hide under upper branches during the day. By releasing moths onto nearby tree trunks in daylight, Kettlewell had created an artificial situation that does not exist in nature. Many biologists now consider his results invalid, and some even question whether natural selection was responsible for the observed changes. So where did all those textbook photos of peppered moths on tree trunks come from? They were all staged. To expedite things, some photographers even glued dead moths to trees. Of course, the people who staged them before the 1980's thought they were accurately representing the true situation, but we now know they were mistaken. Yet a glance at almost any current biology textbook reveals that they are all still being used as evidence for natural selection.

Beaks and Birds: Darwin's Finches

A quarter of a century before Darwin published The Origin of Species, he was formulating his ideas as a naturalist aboard the British survey ship H.M.S. Beagle . When the Beagle visited the Galapagos Islands in 1835, Darwin collected specimens of the local wildlife, including some finches. Though the finches had little in fact to do with Darwin's development of evolutionary theory, they have attracted considerable attention from modern evolutionary biologists as further evidence of natural selection. In the 1970's, Peter and Rosemary Grant and their colleagues noted a 5 percent increase in beak size after a severe drought, because the finches were left with only hard-to crack seeds. The change, though significant, was small; yet some Darwinists claim it explains how finch species originated in the first place. A 1999 booklet published by the U.S. National Academy of Sciences describes Darwin's finches as "a particularly compelling example" of the origin of species. The booklet cites the

Grants' work, and explains how "a single year of drought on the islands can drive evolutionary changes in the finches." The booklet also calculates that "if droughts occur about once every 10 years on the islands, a new species of finch might arise in only about 200 years." But the booklet fails to point out that the finches' beaks returned to normal after the rains returned. No net evolution occurred. In fact, several finch species now appear to be merging through hybridization, rather than diverging through natural selection as Darwin's theory requires. Withholding evidence in order to give the impression that Darwin's finches confirm evolutionary theory borders on scientific misconduct. According to Harvard biologist Louis Guenin (writing in Nature in 1999), U.S. securities laws provide "our richest source of experiential guidance" in defining what constitutes scientific misconduct. But a stock promoter who tells his clients that a particular stock can be expected to double in value in twenty years because it went up 5 percent in 1998, while concealing the fact that the same stock declined 5 percent in 1999, might well be charged with fraud. As Berkeley law professor Phillip E. Johnson wrote in The Wall Street Journal in 1999: "When our leading scientists have to resort to the sort of distortion that would land a stock promoter in jail, you know they are in trouble."

Here is one more example from *Forbidden Archaeology*

Apemen or Conmen – Javaman Thighbone

In August 1892, Eugene Dubois discovered a fossilized humanlike femur on the bank of the Solo River in central Java, near the village of Trinil. 45 feet from this location he found a skullcap and molars. Dubois believed the molars, skull, and femur all came from the same being. However, the fact that these bones were found 45 feet from the place where the skull was unearthed, in a stratum containing hundreds of other animal bones makes doubtful the claim that both the thighbone and the skull actually belonged to the same creature or even the same species. In 1895 Dubois presented his findings to the Berlin Society for Anthropology, Ethnology, and Prehistory. The president of the society, Dr. Virchow declared that the femur was human and the skull belonged to an ape. Late in his life, Dubois concluded that the skullcap belonged to a large gibbon, an ape not considered by evolutionists to be closely related to humans. But this concept of the "missing link" is still widely promoted today! [pp. 464-465, Forbidden Archeology]

Sheer Speculation

The extent of speculation especially regarding human origins is evident from the following statement by a leading archaeologist, "I shall discuss the broad patterns of hominoid evolution, an exercise made enjoyable by the need to integrate diverse kinds of information, and use that as a vehicle to speculate about hominid origins, an event for which there is no recognized fossil record. Hence, an opportunity to exercise some imagination." [American Anthropologist, Distinguished Lecture; Hominoid Evolution and Hominoid Origins, by David Pilbeam. Vol. 88, No. 2 June 1986. p. 295.]

According to paleoanthropologist Misia Landau, theories of human origins "far exceed what can be inferred from the study of fossils alone and in fact place a heavy burden of interpretation on the fossil record – a burden which is relieved by placing fossils into pre-existing narrative structures." In 1996, American Museum of Natural History Curator Ian Tattersall acknowledged that "in paleoanthropology, the patterns we perceive are as likely to result from our unconscious mindsets as from the evidence itself." Arizona State University anthropologist Geoffrey Clark echoed this view in 1997 when he wrote: "We select among alternative sets of research conclusions in accordance with our biases and preconceptions." Clark suggested that "paleoanthropology has the form but not the substance of science." Biology students and the general public are rarely informed of the deep-seated uncertainty about human origins that is reflected in these statements by scientific experts.

Instead, they are simply fed the latest speculation as though it were a fact. And the speculation is typically illustrated with fanciful drawings of cave men, or pictures of human actors wearing heavy make-up.

II. Misinterpreted Evidences

Let's analyze some other common examples of evidence that people uncritically assume to be supporting the idea of evolution. (The following section is adapted from the *Origins* magazine published by BBT Science):

Similarity of DNA

In recent years, geneticists have discovered that in species of similar form the DNA and other proteins have similar molecular structures. So just as evolutionists have deduced ancestral relationships among species from similarities in physical form, some of them now deduce such relationships from the genetic similarities. It is not, however, very surprising that similar species would have similar genetic materials. But the main point is that such similarities show nothing definite about how the organisms originated and cannot be used as proof of Darwinian-style evolution.

Further, talks about genetic similarities can be quite deceptive, considering the level of complexity of genetic structures. For example, some evolutionists argue that since humans and chimps have 98.4% similar DNA, it's clear that they have an evolutionary linkage. But Dr. Barnay Maddox, leading genome and genetic researcher, points out that the 1.6% difference in DNA amounts to a difference of 48 million nucleotides. And a difference of only 3 nucleotides proves fatal to an animal.

Vestigial Organs

It can be reasonably argued that vestigial organs may be the result of design rather than evolution. The embryo of the baleen whale, for example, is said to possess what appear to be vestigial teeth. In the process of embryonic development, these are reabsorbed and replaced in the adult form by baleen (long, fringed structures in the mouth of the whale used to strain tiny organisms from seawater for food). Evolutionists take the vestigial teeth as evidence that the baleen whale evolved from a whale species that had teeth.

But there is another possible explanation. Let us suppose that an intelligent creator wanted to design a large number of whalelike forms in the most efficient way. He might start with genetic coding for a basic body plan that included teeth. When he arrived at the plan for the body of the baleen whale, he could alter the genes to suppress the growth of teeth and add genetic information to cause the growth of the baleen strainers. In this version, you would also expect to see embryonic teeth. Altogether the design hypothesis is as reasonable as the evolutionary hypothesis, and perhaps even more so, because the evolutionists have no step-by-step explanation for the origin of baleen. They can only assert that it happened by a kind of evolutionary magic. Despite all this they reject outright any argument in favor of design, a possibility they refuse to consider because it violates their unproven belief that everything in the universe can be explained by unaided physical laws and processes.

Breeding

Ever since the time of Darwin, the changes resulting from breeding have been put forward as evidence for evolution. If man can produce limited changes in plants and animals over a few generations, then just imagine the possibilities of change over the course of millions of years. So goes the reasoning.

But evolution by natural selection and inducing changes in plants and animals by breeding are not at all comparable. In breeding there is a deliberate intent to obtain specific results—a bigger apple, a cow that produces more milk—but in the process of natural selection there is no intelligent directing plan.

Also, all available evidence shows that there are limits to the changes that can be brought about by breeding. The French zoologist Pierre-P. Grassi points out in his book *Evolution of Living*

Organisms, "The changes brought about in the genetic stock [by breeding] affect appearances much more than fundamental structures and functions. In spite of the intense pressure applied by artificial selection (eliminating any parent not answering the criterion of choice) over whole millenia, no new species are born. ... Ten thousands years of mutations, crossbreeding, and selection have mixed the inheritance of the canine species in innumerable ways without its losing its chemical and cytological [cellular] unity. The same is observed of all domestic animals: the ox (at least 4,000 years old), the fowl (4,000), the sheep (6,000), etc."

The process of breeding is something like stretching a rubber band. It stretches only so far—and then it either breaks or snaps back. For example, during the nineteenth century, domesticated rabbits were brought into Australia, where there were no native rabbits. When some of these domesticated rabbits escaped, they bred freely among themselves, and very quickly their descendants reverted to the original, wild type.

In short, it may be possible to induce changes in the existing form by breeding (making the creature smaller or bigger, for example), but it does not appear possible to generate entirely new complex structures in the organism in this way. If this cannot happen by man's conscious efforts, why should we assume it could happen by blind natural processes?

Playing God To Disprove God

As we have many times suggested, this leaves open the possibility of an intelligent designer. Yet many evolutionists feel that the particular way organisms are structured rules out such an intelligent designer. Harvard paleontologist Stephen J. Gould writes, "Odd arrangements and funny solutions are the proof of evolution— paths that a sensible God would never tread." As an example, he cites the Panda's thumb. The Panda bear has a thumb it can use to grasp the bamboo shoots that form the mainstay of its diet. This thumb, however, is not one of the five fingers of the normal mammalian paw. Rather this extra digit is constructed from a modified wrist bone, with appropriate rearrangement of the musculature.

In essence Gould claims, "God would not have done it that way. Therefore it must have happened by evolution." But this negative theological reasoning is invalid on many counts. The first point is that it is inappropriate for the evolutionists to introduce in their favor a concept they have completely excluded from their account of reality—namely God. Secondly, we might ask from where they have obtained such explicit information about how God would or would not create things if He existed? How do they know He might not produce new features in organisms by modifying existing ones?

In the case of the Panda's thumb, we note that although Gould rejects design by God as an explanation, he fails to provide an adequate explanation by evolutionary processes. He simply states that a single change in a regulatory gene, which controls the action of many structural genes, was responsible for the whole complex development of bone and muscle. But he does not specify which regulatory gene changed, nor does he explain how a change in the regulatory gene would orchestrate this remarkable transformation. He offers nothing more than the traditional vague magic-wand explanation.

Extinction of Species

Sometimes, the extinction of species like dinosaurs is presented as the proof of the working of natural selection as an evolutionary agent.

Extinction of species due to a hostile environment or some similar external cause does nothing to prove evolution's claim that one species changes into another just by natural selection. Some bacteria can be killed by antibiotics, but that doesn't prove that bacteria evolved into different species.

Evolutionist Stephen Jay Gould refers to this impasse of natural selection as follows, "The essence of Darwinism lies in a single phrase: natural selection is the creative force of evolutionary change.

No one denies that selection will play a negative role in eliminating the unfit. Darwinian theories require that it create the fit as well."

That requirement of Darwinian evolution – to create new fit species – is not proven at all by the extinction of dinosaurs.

Sometimes fossils like those of Archaeopteryx, a dinosaur that had feathered wings, like birds as well as teeth, which no bird has, are portrayed as showing that birds evolved from dinosaurs. Let's see what scientist Luther D. Sunderland (1984) has to say on this in his book Darwin's Enigma, "Is Archaeopteryx the ancestor of all birds? Perhaps yes, perhaps no: There is no way of answering the question. It is easy enough to make up stories of how one form gave rise to another, and to find reasons why the stages should be favored by natural selection. But such stories are not part of science, for there is no way of putting them to the test."

This "evidence" doesn't at all prove that species can change – and it certainly doesn't prove that natural selection can cause that change of species. All that it proves is that a particular creature that existed in the past no longer exists. Period.

Mechansims for Evolution

I. Natural Selection and Mutation:

Natural selection, a process originally proposed by Darwin, favors (selects) organisms with traits that best enable them to cope with the struggle for existence amidst the pressures exerted by the environment. In this struggle, the strongest organisms, the ones most suited to natural conditions, survive. For example, in a herd of deer under threat from predators, the deer that can run fastest will naturally survive. Consequently, the herd of deer will eventually consist of only fast-running individuals.

Evolutionists like to ascribe almost mystical powers to natural selection and they claim that it has resulted in the "illusion of design" (Richard Dawkins) that we see all around the world. Indeed, natural selection is the evolutionists's substitute for God. But observation as well as logic shows that natural selection has its limits.

Continuing with the deer example, no matter how long natural selection continues, it will not transform deer into another species. The weak deer will perish, the strong will survive, but, since no alteration in their genetic data takes place, no transformation of a species occurs.

The same applies for all species. Natural selection does not produce new species, new genetic information, or new organs. That is, it cannot cause anything to evolve.

Problem of Incipient Stages of Organs

Stephen Gould points out in *Natural History*, October, 1985, that among the difficulties of Darwinian theory "one point stands high above the rest: the dilemma of incipient stages." He further explains, "We can readily understand how complex and full developed structures work and owe their maintenance and preservation to natural selection---a wing, an eye, the resemblance of a bittern to a branch or of an insect to a stick or dead leaf. But how do you get from nothing to such an elaborate something if evolution must proceed through a long sequence of intermediate stages, each favored by natural selection? You can't fly with 2% of a wing or gain much protection from an iota's similarity with a potentially concealing piece of vegetation. How, in other words, can natural selection explain these incipient stages of structures that can only be used (as we now observe them) in much more elaborated form?"

Problem at microbiological level

Genetics (which Darwin knew nothing about as that branch of science was not developed at his time) further exposes the impracticality of natural selection. as seen from the following quote: "No matter what phraseology one generates, the basic fact remains the same: any physical change of any size, shape or form is strictly the result of purposeful alignment of billions of nucleotides (in the DNA). Nature or species do not have the capacity for rearranging them, nor adding to them. Consequently no leap (saltation) can occur from one species to another. The only way we know for a DNA to be altered is through a meaningful intervention from an outside source of intelligence: one who knows what it is doing, such as our genetic engineers are now performing in their laboratories." - Cohen, I.L. (1984), *Darwin Was Wrong: A Study in Probabilities*

Darwin himself admitted the limitation of natural selection, "Natural selection can do nothing until favorable individual differences or variations occur." Neo-Darwinism tries to deal with this problem by adding mutation as the mechanism genetic information to the concept of natural selection.

Radiation and chemical effects result in breakages and dislocations in the DNA molecule, carrying genetic data, that's located in the cell nucleus. Mutations are accidental and either damage the nucleotides that make up DNA or else dislocate them. They typically give rise to irreparable damage and alterations in the cell. For that reason, the mutations that evolutionists depend on for biological development are not, as is popularly thought, some magic wand that transports living things to a more advanced and perfect state. A few mutations may be beneficial – they may lead to slight improvement within a species, like increased immunity from a particular disease. But their net effects are harmful and they have never led to the formation of anything close to a new species.

Prof. Richard Goldschmidt, a zoologist at the University of California, admits, "It is true that nobody thus far has produced a new species or genus, etc., by macromutation [a combination of many mutations]; it is equally true that nobody has produced even a species by the selection of micromutations [one or only a few mutations]. In the best-known organisms, like Drosophila, innumerable mutants are known. If we were able to combine a thousand or more of such mutants in a single individual, this still would have no resemblance whatsoever to any type known as a [new] species in nature."

Stephen Jay Gould, evolutionary theorist at Harvard University, admits even more bluntly, "You don't make new species by mutating the species. . . . A mutation is not the cause of evolutionary change."

II. Irreducible Complexity

Michael Behe in 1996 in his book *Darwin's Black Box: The Biochemical Challenge to Evolution* explains, "By irreducibly complex I mean a single system composed of several well-matched, interacting parts that contribute to the basic function, wherein the removal of any one of the parts causes the system to effectively cease functioning."

Natural selection has no intelligence. It does not possess a will that can decide what is good and what is bad for living things. As a result, natural selection cannot explain biological systems and organs that possess the feature of "irreducible complexity." These systems and organs are composed of a great number of parts cooperating together, and are of no use if even one of these parts is missing or defective. (For example, the human eye does not function unless it exists with all its components intact).

Therefore, the will that brings all these parts together should be able to foresee the future and aim directly at the advantage that is to be acquired at the final stage. Since natural selection has no consciousness or will, it can do no such thing. This fact, which demolishes the foundations of the theory of evolution, also worried Darwin, who wrote: "If it could be demonstrated that any complex organ existed, which could not possibly have been formed by numerous, successive, slight modifications, my theory would absolutely break down."

III. Origin of Life

Darwin stated that the original life was breathed into one or a few forms by the creator, but neo-darwinists claim that the first living molecule originated spontaneously from chemicals.

Concerning the question of the origin of such a molecule, Biologist Andy Pross said, ". . . one might facetiously rephrase the question as follows: given an effectively unknown reaction mixture, under effectively unknown reaction conditions, reacting to give unknown products by unknown mechanisms, could a particular product with a specific characteristic . . . have been included amongst the reaction products?" (Pross Addy. 2004. *Causation and the origin of life. Metabolism or replication first? Origins of Life and Evolution of the Biospheres* 34:308)

In *Evolution from Space*, noted British astronomers Sir Fred Hoyle and Chandra Wickramasinghe assert that the chances of life's arising from some ancient random mixing of chemicals are so "outrageously small" as to be absurd "even if the whole universe consisted of organic soup." The incensed authors are amazed that although the situation is well known to geneticists, evolutionists, and paleoanthropologists, nobody seems concerned enough to "blow the whistle decisively on the false theories."

Nonetheless, Richard Dawkins (1986, pp. 47-49), in his book *The Blind Watchmaker*, still proposes that chance and natural selection (represented by a simple computer algorithm) can yield biological complexity. To demonstrate that the process is workable, he programmed a computer to generate random combination of letters and compare them to a target sequence that forms an intelligible grammatically correct sentence. Those combination of letters that come closest to the meaningful target sequence are preserved, whereas those that depart from the target sequence are rejected. After a certain number of runs, the computer produces a target sequence. Dawkins takes this as proof that random combination of chemicals could by natural selection gradually produce biologically functional proteins. The reasoning is, however, faulty. First, Dawkin assumes the existence of a complex computer, which we do not find in nature. Second, he assumes the presence of a target sequence. In nature there is no target sequence of amino acids that is specified in advance, and to which random sequences of amino acids can be compared. Third, the trial sequences of letters that are selected by the computer do not themselves have any linguistically functional advantage over other sequences, other than that they are one letter closer to the target sequence. For the analogy between the computer algorithm and real life to hold, each sequence of letter chosen by the computer should itself have some meaning. In real life, an amino acid leading up to a complex protein with specific function should itself have some function. If it has no function, which can be tested for fitness by natural selection, there is nothing on which natural selection can operate. Meyer (1998, p. 128) says, " In Dawkin's simulation, not a single English word appears until after the tenth iteration.... Yet to make distinctions on the basis of function among sequences that have no function whatsoever would seem quite impossible? Such determinations can only be made if considerations of proximity to possible future functions are allowed, but this requires foresight that molecules do not have." In other words, Dawkin's result can only be obtained because of the element of intelligent design embedded in the whole experiment.

(The above refutation of chance is taken from *Human Devolution*)

Conclusion

Thus, if the evidence is objectively examined, there is practically no proof for the theory of evolution in the fossil record. Worse still, fossils that contradict the theory, despite being present in significant numbers, have been systematically neglected and suppressed by a process of knowledge filtration. Worst of all, evolutionists, desperate to present some proof for their faith in evolution, foist on gullible school students all over the world evidences that have long been disproved.

Not only is there no clear evidence, but there is also no clear mechanism explaining how evolution could have taken place. This utter absence of any scientific basis for the theory of evolution is what made British author Malcolm Muggeridge write in his book The End of Christendom. "I myself am convinced that the theory of evolution, especially the extent to which it's been applied, will be one of the great jokes in the history books in the future. Posterity will marvel that so very flimsy and dubious an hypothesis could be accepted with the incredible credulity that it has."

Once the facts become clear to us, not only posterity, but even we will be prompted to marvel at how such a dubious theory has gained such widespread acceptance in our times. The answer is: propaganada. Adolf Hitler expressed this mechanism of making lies appear truths, "If you tell a big enough lie and tell it frequently enough, it will be believed." Evolution has gained acceptance only due to the misleading propaganda of the evolutionists, among the people who are not very well-versed about the intricacies of science, but are impressed by the technological wizardry accomplished by science. The extent of unquestioning faith people have in science was pointed out by Albert Einstein when he said, ""Tell a man that there are 300 billion stars in the universe, and he'll believe you.... Tell him that a bench has wet paint upon it and he'll have to touch it to be sure." Evolutionists abuse this scientific credibility to assert their baseless claims about their theory.

No wonder that Dr W R Thompson, former Director of the Commonwealth Institute of Biological Control, Ottawa, stated:

"The success of Darwinism was accompanied by a decline in scientific integrity." (Thomson WR "Introduction," *Origin of Species*, by Charles Darwin (Dutton: Everyman's Library, 1956, p. xxii.))

The extent to which scientific integrity declined is quite shocking and is documented in the movie Expelled: Intelligence not allowed. (Visit expelled.com for more info) In their desperation to protect their pet theory, evolutionists have:

1. Suppressed contradicting evidence
2. Persecuted scientists opposing evolution
3. Censored papers presenting problems in evolution from being published in scientific journals
4. Use bombastic word jugglery to make evolution appear 'scientific'.

By actions like these, evolutionists stand convicted of the same crime that they accuse religionists – being fanatical about one's own views and intolerant about opposing views.

This religious nature of evolution was noted by physicist HS Lipson, "Evolution became in a sense a scientific religion. Almost all scientists have accepted it and many are prepared to 'bend' their observations to fit in with it. To my mind the theory does not stand up at all." (Lipson HS, "*A Physicist Looks at Evolution*" *Physics Bulletin*, vol. 31 (May 1980), p. 138.)

Harvard Paleontologist Richard Lewontin's statement reveals the bias toward atheism that is inherent in the modern scientific mindset, "We take the side of science in spite of the patent absurdity of some of its constructs because we have a prior commitment, a commitment to Materialism [naturalism]. Materialism is absolute, for we cannot allow a Divine Foot in the door." (Harvard Paleontologist Richard Lewontin, Quoted in "*Billions and Billions of Demons*," The N.Y. Review of Books, January 9, 1997)

Thus evolution is not science; it is a religion, an unproven, unreasonable, absolutist religion. Everyone has a right to believe in one's own religion. So evolutionists too can believe in their religion if they choose. But they have no right to impose it on others as if it were scientific education. An irrational faith that makes absolute claims and has absolutely no evidences cannot be allowed to masquerade as science, especially when that masquerade misinforms and misleads entire generations into godlessness and immorality. Abraham Lincoln stated poignantly the crucial role of education in shaping the future, "The philosophy of the classroom in one generation becomes the philosophy of the government in the next."

Fortunately for the future of the world, there are still scientists with intelligence and integrity, scientists who are ready to fight against this atheistic tyranny of thought. For example, Dr. Colin Patterson, senior paleontologist at the British Museum of Natural History and editor of its journal, as well as author of the book Evolution, explains how he came out of the spell cast by evolutionary ideas, "Question is: Can you tell me anything you know about evolution, any one thing that is true? I tried this question on the geology staff at the Field Museum of Natural History and the only answer I got was silence. - - Then I woke up and realized that all my life I had been duped into taking evolutionism as revealed truth in some way." - Dr. Colin Patterson, *Evolution and Creationism*, Speech at the American Museum of Natural History, New York (November 5, 1981), pp. 1,2.

Dr Patterson is far from being the only scientist opposing evolution. As of June 2008, over 700 scientists from all over the world, all with doctorate degrees in science, have made a joint declaration entitled 'A Scientific Dissent from Darwinism', with the statement: "We are skeptical of claims for the ability of natural selection and random mutation to account for the complexity of life. Careful examination of the evidence for Darwinian theory should be encouraged." (The list of scientists with their degrees and designations is available at www.dissentfromdarwin.com) The intelligent design movement, an international group of scientists, is increasingly challenging and exposing the dogma of evolutionists.

Srila Prabhupada, the founder of ISKCON, was among the pioneer spiritual leaders in exposing the fallacies of the theory of evolution. Not only did he himself speak strongly against it and inspire his followers to counter it in the language of science, but he also presented the Vedic alternative to evolution. One of Srila Prabhupada's leading scientist-disciples, Dr Michael Cremo, has scientifically postulated this alternative in his book, '*Human Devolution: The Vedic alternative to Darwinian Evolution.*' He explains that human beings comprise of matter, mind and consciousness and we as conscious beings have devolved down from the realm of pure consciousness (the spiritual world) to the material realm. He concludes that the real evolution is not of bodily form, but of consciousness, and that evolution of consciousness back to the spiritual realm can be affected by the sonic technology of mantra meditation. (More information is available at www.humandevolution.com)

As vision determines mission, we hope that this article will help share the vision that evolution is far from a scientific truth and that an alternate explanation is seriously needed, which is offered competently by the authoritative Vedic texts.   ● ● ●

The Greatest Scientists on God

"Little science takes you away from God but more of it takes you to Him."

- Louis Pasteur,
Founder of Microbiology

"All things are indeed contrived and ordered with singular providence, divine wisdom, and most admirable and incomprehensible skill. And to none can these attributes be referred save to the Almighty."

- Sir William Harvey,
Founder of Modern Medicine

"In God there is Power, which is the source of all, also Knowledge, whose content is the variety of the ideas, and finally Will, which makes changes or products according to the principle of the best."

- Wilhelm Leibniz,
Founder of Infinitesimal Calculus

"For me the idea of a creation is inconceivable without God. One cannot be exposed to the law and order of the universe without concluding that there must be a divine intent behind it all"

- Wernher Von Braun,
Founder of Astronautics

"We feed our Bodies; our Souls are also to be fed: The Food of the Soul is Knowledge, especially Knowledge in the Things of God."

- John Ray,
Founder of Modern Biology

"When I reflect on so many profoundly marvelous things that persons have grasped, sought, and done, I recognize even more clearly that human intelligence is a work of God, and one of the most excellent"

Galileo Galilei,
Founder of Experimental Physics

"There are two books laid before us to study, to prevent our falling into error; the first, the volume of the Scriptures, which reveal the will of God; then the volume of the creatures, which express His power."

Sir Francis Bacon,
Founder of the Scientific Inductive Method

"I believe in God. It makes no sense to me to assume that the Universe and our existence is just a cosmic accident, that life emerged due to random physical processes in an environment which simply happened to have the right properties.

Antony Hewish
1974 Nobel in Physics

"And thus I very clearly see that the certitude and truth of all science depends on the knowledge alone of the true God, insomuch that, before I knew him, I could have no perfect knowledge of any other thing.

Rene Descartes,
Founder of Analytical Geometry

"The more we learn about creation — the way it emerged — it just adds to the glory of God."

Joseph Murray,
Nobel Laureate in Medicine and Physiology

"I saw in it (the atom) the key to the deepest secret of nature, and it revealed to me the greatness of the creation and the Creator."

Max Born
Nobel Laureate in Physics

"For religion, God is at the beginning; for science, God is at the end."

Max Planck
Nobel Laureate in Physics

"An equation for me has no meaning, unless it represents a thought of God."

Srinivasa A. Ramanujan
Pioneering Indian Mathematician

There is a higher power, not influenced by our wishes, which finally decides and judges."

Werner Heisenberg
1932-Nobel Laureate in Physics

I have endeavored to gain for human reason, aided by geometrical calculation, an insight into His way of creation...may He cause us to aspire to the perfection of His works of creation by the dedication of our lives...

Johannes Kepler
Founder of physical astronomy & modern optics

"We ought to value the privilege of knowing God's truth far beyond anything we can have in this world."

Michael Faraday
Founder of .electromagnetism

"'Almighty God, who has created man in Thine own image, and made him a living soul that he might seek after Thee, and have dominion over Thy creatures, teach us to study the works of Thy hands, that we may subdue the earth to our use, and strengthen the reason for Thy service.

James Clerk Maxwell
Founder of statistical Thermodynamics

"'Those to whom God has imparted religion by intuition are very fortunate and justly convinced. But to those who do not have it, we can give it only by reasoning, waiting for God to give them spiritual insight."

Blaise Pascal

"Through steady observation and a meaningful contact with the divined Order of the world's structure, arranged by God's wisdom, - who would not be guided to admire the Builder who creates all!"

Copernicus
Founder of heliocentric cosmology

"The wonderful arrangement and harmony of the cosmos would only originate in the plan of an almighty omniscient being. This is and remains my greatest comprehension."

Isaac Newton
Founder of classical physics

"Overwhelming evidences of an intelligence and benevolent intention surround us, show us the whole of nature through the work of a free will and teach us that all alive beings depend on an eternal creator-ruler."

Lord Kelvin
Founder of thermodynamics

"For me, faith begins with the realization that a supreme intelligence brought the universe into being and created man. It is not difficult for me to have this faith, for an orderly, intelligent universe testifies to the greatest statement ever uttered: 'In the beginning, God...'"

Arthur Campton

"The principle of divine purpose... stares the biologist in the face wherever he looks. ...The probability for such an event as the origin of DNA molecules to have occurred by sheer chance is just too small to be seriously considered."

Ernst Boris Chain
Nobel Laureate in medicine

"When confronted with the marvels of life and the universe, one must ask why the only possible answers are religious. ... I find a need for God in the universe and in my own life."

Arthur L. Schawlow
Nobel Laureate in physics

"Those who say that the study of science makes a man an atheist must be rather silly people."

Maxborn(1882-1970)
Nobel Laureate in physics

"Overwhelming evidences of an intelligence and benevolent intention surround us, show us the whole of nature through the work of a free will and teach us that all alive beings depend on an eternal creator-ruler."

Lord Kelvin
Founder of thermodynamics

"For me the idea of a creation is inconceivable without God. One cannot be exposed to the law and order of the universe without concluding that there must be a divine intent behind it all.

Von Braun
Founder of aeronautics

"I only trace the lines that flow from God."

Albert Einstein
Nobel Laureate in physics

"So many of my colleagues are Christians that I can't walk across my church's fellowship hall without tripping over a dozen physicists."

William D. Phillips
Nobel Laureate in physics

"The more I work with the powers of Nature, the more I feel God's benevolence to man"

Guglielmo Marconi, 1909
Nobel Prize in Physics

DOES SCIENCE NEED A SPIRITUAL PARADIGM?

Happy New Year

This new year greeting mostly remains a wish. Can this sincere wish be transformed into a reality? As we live in the age of science, let us first analyze this greeting from the perspective of science.

What's A Year?

Let's begin with the word 'year'. A year is a unit for measuring time. And what is time? Though the reality of time, especially in the form of its effect on us, is undeniable, time is one among the many fundamental truths of life that defy scientific definition. Be that as it may, we measure time by the movement of the cosmic bodies. As per current scientific understanding, one year is the time in which the earth completes one revolution around the sun. For an object orbiting continuously in a circular path, no point on the orbit can be considered special. So scientifically there's nothing "New" about the new year; the earth is going to continue in its same old path!

What's New?

Let's consider the word 'new'. All of us have an inherent attraction for new things. Why? Is it not because the old is, in some way or the other, unsatisfactory? The old lifestyle, the old relationships, the old job – all these leave us feeling incomplete and unfulfilled. And the fond hope is that the new will change that same old story.

But what's actually going to be new? People change their externals to make things better. But from a scientific viewpoint, everything is just atoms! The astounding variety around us results from sub-microscopic variations in the atomic and molecular structures, such as a different number of electrons orbiting within the atom of a particular element. Now what is the most dramatically 'new' thing that a person can do? Maybe get a new girlfriend or boyfriend. But that just means getting someone whose skin pigments have a slightly different atomic arrangement! (Talks about personality are, after all, "unscientific"!) So changing the atomic arrangement around you (new house, new car, new job, new spouse and the like) or the atomic arrangement inside you (mundane "new year resolutions") and hoping that that will make the "new" year "happy" doesn't make much scientific sense.

What's Happiness?

And what about "happy"? Happiness is another fundamental reality of life that is beyond the realm of science. Noble Laureate Physicist Erwin Schroedinger pointed out that the entire world of emotions remains inaccessible to science, "Science cannot tell us a word about why music delights us, of why and how an old song moves us to tears." Though the situation remains the same today, reductionistic scientists have faith in their belief in reductionism, despite having no proof for it. For them, pleasure or pain is nothing more than certain C fibers or Delta fibers firing in certain parts of the body. Ironically, such scientists postulate theories claiming that all emotions including happiness are illusions to win Nobel prizes in order to ultimately become happy!

The sweet greeting "Happy New Year!" is often expressed with genuine good wishes. Does it have no meaning? Reductionistic science certainly strips this greeting (and in fact all greetings and even life at large) of all meaning.

Anyway, can everything in life be "scientific"? Would a chemist give his wife a bunsen burner as a wedding gift? If a neurologist found that his wife was upset with him, would he do a brain scan to find out what was wrong?

Philosopher of science Karl Popper puts this limitation of science as follows, "Science may be described as the art of systematic oversimplification." The point is that though science is a useful, even powerful, tool to understand reality, but we should not forget that what science shows is a map of the complete reality; it is not the complete reality.

Explore The Spiritual Dimension

Therefore let us be open to all branches of knowledge – including the spiritual – that can help us to get a more complete understanding of reality.

Vedic wisdom explains that each one of us is a sentient, eternal and blissful spiritual personality having inherently the nature of befriending and loving God and all living beings. The Vedic scriptures also wish us a genuinely felt "Happy New Year." In fact, they wish that every moment of our life be happy and new. Not only that, they go much further and delineate a practical process by which this wish can be transformed into a reality. Let's investigate.

The Vedas agree with the common understanding that to become happy something new has to be done. But the understanding of new as given in the Vedic wisdom is significantly different from the general understanding.

The Vedic scriptures explain that all living beings eat, mate, sleep and defend. In fact, the subhuman beings do nothing but these four activities. And modern man is also doing just these four activities, although in a sophisticated way. Even most scientific advancement is impelled by these four fundamental drives. Let's see how.

Among the first things that man did after unraveling the mysteries of the atom is to use the atomic bomb; that's defending in the most horrendous form seen in the contemporary times. A major result of the advent of the information age is the internet, which has sex (and its related words) as the top search object on google; that's mating. The leaps in genetic engineering have mostly been actuated by the desire for better meat and other foodstuffs; is that anything higher than eating? Dunlop beds, nowadays water beds and what not; they are all obviously for sleeping. So a little thought will reveal how all the "advanced" activities done by the modern man eventually boil down to eating, sleeping, mating and defending. And there's nothing new in them, no matter how we do them externally. The Srimad

Bhagavatam (7.5.30) describes this in graphic terms: *punah punas carvita carvananam* "Chewing the chewed,"

But humans are not meant to live the same old life of eating, sleeping, mating and defending; they is meant to something new. And that brings us to the realm of spirituality. A hog cannot understand the difference between its body and soul; a human being can. A dog cannot practice meditation; a human being can. Spirituality is not just a different ability that we humans have; it is our defining privilege, that we have been granted due to possessing a higher intelligence that accompanies the human body.

Therefore the Vedic scriptures encourage us to sublimate our attraction for the new by directing it to the realm of spirit. *athato brahma jijnasa* This starting aphorism of the Vedanta-sutra means: "Therefore, inquire about the higher dimensions of life." Why does a start with the word "therefore"? Because implied is a clarion call, "Now, O spirit soul, who has acquired a human body, cease from the animal business of eating, sleeping, mating and defending. Now you are endowed with a higher intelligence in the human form. Therefore inquire about the higher truths of life."

The Real Happy New Year

This higher enquiry is not a fruitless armchair speculation. The answers to it constitute a practical way of life which bestows upon the seeker unlimited happiness from the spiritual stratum. This in fact is the Vedic mission: *sarve janah sukhino bhavantu* -- Let everyone be happy – not superficially and temporarily by success in the rat race for sense gratification, but deeply and eternally by absorption in loving service to God.

Spiritual life culminates in the development of love of God, Krishna. Love of God, the Universal Father, precipitates love for all living beings as one's own brothers. This selfless love completely satisfies the self and also makes the lover of God the topmost welfare worker for all living beings.

Love of God is our original and real nature, but due to prolonged and excessive contact with matter, it has become completely obscured and is now misdirected towards various material objects. All genuine spiritual practices are meant to revive this love of God, which is presently dormant in our hearts. Among all such practices, the most potent in the present age is the process of mantra meditation - chanting of the maha mantra Hare Krishna Hare Krishna Krishna Krishna Hare Hare Hare Rama Hare Rama Rama Rama Hare Hare.

God being infinite is eternally new (*nitya navanavayamana*) and so loving Him is an eternally new and happy experience. Hence, revival of our love of God is the ultimate fruition of the wish "Happy New Year!"   ● ● ●

Guided Missiles, Misguided Men

Martin Luther King, Jr, stated in his *From Strength to Love*, "The means by which we live have outdistanced the ends for which we live. Our scientific power has outrun our spiritual power. We have guided missiles and misguided men." Little did he know how prophetic his words would be in a literal sense several decades later.

A Comfortable State Of Misery

In the modern times, we have achieved considerable ability to manipulate our external environment with the help of science and technology. Technological gadgets have, to a large extent, helped make life comfortable and easy, relieving us of many of the discomforts and inconveniences associated with a traditional way of life. The ads go so far as to claim that the world can now be in our grip *(kar lo duniya muthi mein)*

Yet, have all these comforts made us more peaceful or happy? People in the past hardly ever complained of stress or depression, but these have become almost synonymous with the modern way of life. The World Health Organization (WHO) has declared that mental diseases will be the greatest health challenge of this century.

❖ With the rapid rise in promiscuity in modern times, the family, the basis of a steady and sustainable society, is breaking apart. A survey showed that two out of three marriages in the US end in divorce within three years of marriage. Marital rupture is traumatic for the spouses and devastating for their children.

Statistics show that divorced people as well as children of divorced parents are more likely to succumb to addictions than their married counterparts. Even if they don't succumb to addictions, the agony that comes from the rupture of relationships leaves lifelong scars.

♣ Worldwide addictions are on the rise. WHO statistics indicate that tobacco alone kills nearly 10,000 people worldwide every day. There are  around 1.1 billion smokers in the world (about one-third of the global population aged 15 and over). By 2020 it is predicted that tobacco use will cause over 12% of all deaths globally. This is more deaths worldwide than HIV, tuberculosis, maternal mortality, motor vehicle accidents, suicide and homicide put together. And, to make matters worse, smoking is a relatively mild form of addiction as compared to alcoholism and drug abuse.

With the children of today's disturbed, ruptured and addicted generation being the leaders of tomorrow, the future of the world becomes a matter of deep concern. The school massacres in US from Littleton to Virginia Tech may well be an ominous precursor of things to come.

So, despite the bluff and the bravado of a comfortable life, most modern people find themselves in mental misery. They thus live in a comfortable state of misery. And the tragic irony is that most of this misery is self-inflicted. For example, no one needs to smoke to survive but still people smoke and bring disease and suffering upon themselves.

Thus modern society may have succeeded in guiding missiles but has failed utterly in guiding human beings. What is the cause of this unfortunate, indeed tragic, state of affairs - guided missiles and misguided men? The Vedic texts offer valuable insights into this. Let's explore.

The Enemies Within

The Vedic texts explain that within the human psyche are six formidable forces which misguide a person constantly and impel him to self-destructive behavioral patterns. These forces are lust, anger, greed, pride, envy and illusion. Among these, lust, greed and anger are the most dangerous and are declared in the Bhagavad-gita to be "the three gates to hell". Let us see how these relate to the problems plaguing the present-day world.

Lust:

It is the source of all kinds of sexual drives. While regulated sex is necessary for procreation, lust tends to create uncontrollable sexual urges within a person. While modern media - and practically

the entire modern society - portrays passionate lust as a gateway to unlimited bodily pleasures, such a conception is in reality short-lived and treacherous; it is individually frustrating and socially disastrous. Enamored by erotic fantasies, a person tries to enjoy in newer ways and with newer partners. But each successive experience leaves him increasingly disappointed - and craving for more. Why? Because the highest pleasure the body can offer is heartbreakingly brief. Frustrated in his quest for erotic enjoyment, such a person turns in despair to perverted sources of pleasure like smoking, drinking and drug abuse.

As far as the family is concerned,

uncontrolled lust in either or both of the spouses wreaks havoc in the lives of both of them as well as of their children, as discussed earlier.

Deadly sexually transmitted diseases (STDs) like AIDS, which result from uncontrolled lust, have devastating individual and social consequences, which need no elaboration.

Greed:

Greed makes one crave for far more than what one needs. A person victimized by greed does not find satisfaction no matter how much he accumulates. At the same time, his greed forces him to exploit others and strip them of even their basic needs in order to achieve his selfish ends.

During a morning walk through a slum area, Srila Prabhupada noticed some stout people jogging along the road. He poignantly commented that in the huts people did not get enough to eat, while the wealthy tended to overeat and were therefore forced to jog to decrease their weight.

Consider the following UNICEF statistics about the world hunger problem:

- ✤ Hunger kills a person every 3.6 seconds and over 15 million children every year.
- ✤ To satisfy the world's sanitation and food requirements would cost only US$13 billion- what the people of the United States and the European Union spend on perfume each year.
- ✤ Nearly one in four people, 1.3 billion - a majority of humanity - live on less than $1 per day, while the world's

358 billionaires have assets exceeding the combined annual incomes of countries with 45 percent of the world's people.

The irony with greed is that the greedy person watches others die of starvation without helping them and can't save himself from dying of anxiety.

Anger:

Anger arises when one's lusty desires are frustrated. Anger leads to all forms of violence ranging from petty quarrels to world wars. The modern media with its vivid depiction of violence portrays anger as a heroic quality. This is a major cause of the spiraling rates of violent criminality in modern societies. While most people recognize that in real life anger is not a desirable emotion, they savor the violent scenes in the movies. And then strangely enough they wonder why they themselves, in fits of anger, speak such words and do such deeds which break the hearts of their loved ones and which they themselves bitterly regret later. Anger destroys relationships and ruins lives.

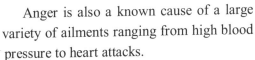

Anger is also a known cause of a large variety of ailments ranging from high blood pressure to heart attacks.

This brief analysis gives us an idea of how the three internal enemies - lust, greed and anger are the root cause of a large variety of problems in modern society. If we were to extend this analysis to include pride, envy and illusion, (which we will leave to the readers so as to maintain the brevity of the article), we would find that every problem, individual or social, local or global, has its origin in these six misguiding forces.

The Vedic texts not only point out the root problem, but also describe the lasting solution. The means to counter the internal enemies is spiritual technology.

Spiritual Technology

Just as material technology enables us to control the world around us, spiritual technology helps us to control the world within us, that is, to control the lust, anger and greed within us. The Vedic society was oriented to make people expert in spiritual technology. This spiritual expertise was achieved through a harmonious combination of education, culture and devotion. Let us compare Vedic society and modern society on these three counts:

Education:

In Vedic society, education did not mean just learning some technical skills to earn a living. It focused on acquiring spiritual knowledge, which gave the student a clear vision to see the deadly nature of the internal enemies. Vedic education also provided the student with the knowledge and the training to fight and conquer these enemies when they attacked. Overcoming lust, anger and greed did not however mean being condemned to live a dry life without any desires or ambitions. Vedic education enabled the student to utilize his desires and talents positively in pursuance of his enlightened self-interest so as to achieve lasting happiness.

In modern society, education focuses mainly on acquiring technical or other knowledge to earn a living. It leads only to the development of the intellect (the ability to recollect and manipulate information), not the development of the intelligence (the ability to discriminate between the right and the wrong, the beneficial and the harmful). It does not emphasize inculcating ethical, moral or spiritual values. Those educated in this way are able to control the world around them with material technology but fail miserably in controlling the world within them as they have no knowledge of spiritual technology. The result is tragic - a world with guided missiles and misguided men.

Culture:

Vedic culture was based on the implicit understanding that human happiness came not by external aggrandizement meant to satisfy one's lust, anger and greed, but by inner realization that gradually freed one from these internal enemies. Life in Vedic times was therefore not a rat race for wealth, but was arranged to enable one to utilize one's inherent material abilities in satisfying and productive service to society. Simultaneously the social environment provided abundant facilities and encouragement for one to develop oneself spiritually and thus find happiness within oneself.

Modern culture, on the other hand, glamorizes as success stories the icons of lust (sexually appealing movie-stars), anger (action heroes) and greed (exploitative businessmen). The modern media with its undisguised promotion of a consumer culture and the entire society with its emphasis on material success both fuel and fan the lust, anger and greed within people. Thus, modern culture far from discouraging lust, greed and anger encourages them as the signs of success.

Devotion:

In Vedic society devotion to God was inculcated right from birth. Due to their firm devotion, people experienced sublime non-material satisfaction that gave them inner spiritual strength. Being content within, they could resist the otherwise irresistible pushings of lust, greed and anger. (Modern social studies have confirmed the power of spiritual practices as the

best insurance from self-destructive behavioral patterns) In the Vedic times, genuine devotion to God did much more than protect people from addictions; it made them honest, kind, considerate, loving and selfless and thus facilitated a peaceful and harmonious society.

In modern times, many people don't believe in or don't care for God. Even those who profess to be believers do so mostly out of social custom or fear of the unknown. They have very little scientific understanding of God and are therefore not serious about their devotion. When lust, greed and anger attack them, they just don't have the inner strength to fight and so they become easily victimized. This is all the more true for those who are openly atheistic or materialistic.

Modern society thus gives a free play to the misguiding forces of lust, anger and greed. It's only natural therefore that the modern world, despite its expertise in guiding missiles, is filled with misguided men.

Is there a way out of this predicament?

Healing a Wounded World

Lust, anger and greed are like diseases afflicting the minds of people. The variety of problems bedeviling the world today - poverty, starvation, violence, disease and pollution, to name a few – are the symptoms of these diseases.

Dealing with these symptomatic problems through social service will not bring about a lasting solution. As long as people are not freed from slavery to their internal enemies, they cannot be peaceful or happy. And as long as they are not peaceful and happy, they will inevitably indulge in activities that will perpetuate the symptomatic problems.

ISKCON is among the very few organizations in the world arming people with the spiritual technology to conquer the internal enemies. ISKCON provides education, culture and devotion, which is based on the Vedic texts and is suitably presented for the modern times. This empowers ISKCON devotees to protect themselves from the insidious influences of lust, greed and anger and live a pure life filled with peace and joy.

Consider for example the four principal activities of an individual misguided by lust, anger and greed - intoxication, gambling, illicit sex and meat eating. Intelligent people can easily recognize the harmful nature of these activities and can also understand that a world free from these activities would be a much better place. Most people unfortunately indulge in these activities either voluntarily or involuntarily, being impelled by lust, greed and anger. Serious ISKCON devotees however refrain from these activities as a basic regulative principle for spiritual advancement. That they are able to do so in a world that is slave to these activities is itself eloquent testimony of the protection through wisdom that ISKCON offers.

ISKCON is, of course, working at a humanitarian level to mitigate suffering and distress; it runs the world's largest vegetarian food relief program - Food for Life. But the highest service that ISKCON offers to the people of the world is its tireless attempts to provide them protection from their internal enemies and to enable them to find lasting peace and happiness within themselves. ● ● ●

Is Something Missing in Modern Education?

"We have controlled machines and uncontrolled men," declares a slogan depicting the potential threat of global disaster due to the misuse of technology. It catches the tragic irony of modern society. The last century has seen amazing advances in science and technology, by which, "the world is at your finger-tips", as some ads put it. Yet statistics expose the twentieth century as the most violent century in known human history. The book *Ending Violent Conflict* by Michael Renner states that three times more people died in wars in of the twentieth century than in the entire history of warfare between A.D. 1 and 1899.

Therefore, the question begs itself: where has modern society gone wrong? Despite extensive attempts at mass education, why has the advancement of knowledge not made people peaceful? Illiteracy can no longer be considered a reason since the best schools in the world have also witnessed violence in the last decade. The foundation of American society has been rocked by the repeated massacres by school children of their own peers and teachers for no good reason whatsoever. In many schools, metal detectors now screen every child before he enters 'the modern temple of learning'.

Immorality Originates In Spiritual Bankruptcy

The Vedic texts, a vast body of profound knowledge coming down from ancient India, provide thought-provoking insights into this sorry state of affairs. In the Vedic paradigm, knowledge is exalted for its transformational power. "What you know" is not considered as important as "'What is the effect on you of what you know". In marked contrast, modern education swamps students with information, but sadly the information brings hardly any transformation in the students. It scarcely leads to the strengthening of character; many of the students indulge in self-destructive habits like smoking, alcoholism and drug abuse; and even the best of them consider earning maximum money as their most important value. "Information, information, information, but no transformation" is the plight of the modern educational system.

Of course, many curricula worldwide do have some sort of value education, but that value education mostly serves a cosmetic purpose; it is ineffectual in actually building the character of the students. The Vedic texts assert unequivocally that morality has to be founded on spirituality; otherwise it soon becomes a mere lip-service.

Unless one has an understanding of God and His laws, the call to ethics has little weight. After all, what is there in an atheist's worldview to impel him to stick to morality, especially if he thinks that the primary goal of life is the pursuit of bodily pleasure and that he can get away with whatever he does, provided he just does it cleverly enough?

Further, if a person doesn't understand his real identity as an eternal soul, if he thinks that this life is all that he has for enjoyment, what will stop him from sacrificing morality at the altar of bodily

pleasure? "Beg, borrow, steal, kill, but enjoy" - that will become the motto of such a spiritually bankrupt person.

State-Funded Atheistic Indoctrination

Modern scientific (read 'atheistic') education is significantly responsible for this spiritual and social decay. Eminent scientists like Newton, Copernicus, Faraday, Kelvin, Max Planck, Maxwell and Einstein, to name a few, have stated that their scientific study has led them to the conclusion that, behind the marvels of nature, is a super-intelligent being, God. Many influential leaders of the West including US Presidents like Benjamin Franklin and John Adams, philosophers like Socrates and Ralph Waldo Emerson, business magnates like Henry Ford, psychologists like Carl Jung and C P Dupey, and Nobel-Prize winning authors like Herman Hesse and Isaac Bashevis Singer have expressed their belief in the reincarnation of the soul. Even those scientists, who are not spiritually-minded, readily admit that spiritual subjects such as the existence of the soul and God are simply beyond their scope. But unfortunately science textbooks worldwide portray dubious theories such as the big bang theory and evolution theory as proven facts, thus forcing the naïve and innocent students to embrace atheism as the only "scientific" way of looking at the world. Many eminent scientists have openly challenged the scientific validity of these theories. When such theories are far from being truths, presenting them to students in textbooks as truths is not scientific education, but atheistic indoctrination. It's not just ordinary indoctrination, but state-funded indoctrination. If we let our children be taught that they have come from monkeys, how can we expect them to not behave like monkeys? The notion that life is a result of chemical combination breeds a murderous mentality toward both subhumans and humans:

- ♣ "If life is just a product of chemicals, then why can I not cut a bag of chemicals (an animal) and eat it, if it tastes good?
- ♣ "If there is nothing more to life than chemical activity, then why can I not destroy the lump of chemicals (a human being) if it obstructs my path to success?"

When entire generations grow up with such perverted conceptions, is it strange that peace eludes humanity?

Empowerment by Spiritual Education

If we want our children to inherit a peaceful world, we have to teach them the spiritual truths that will engender that peace - within and without. To this end, the following universal spiritual principles need to be incorporated into the syllabus worldwide:

5. God is the Supreme Father of everyone and the Supreme Owner and Controller of everything.

6. We are accountable for all our actions to God (As you sow, so shall you reap).

7. We are spirit souls, eternal children of God and our real happiness is not in material acquisition, but in spiritual realization, in lovingly harmonizing ourselves with nature and God.

These spiritual precepts do not contradict the principle of secularism because secularism should not be misunderstood or misinterpreted as atheism. Secularism basically implies impartiality toward different religions and the above precepts are the common underlying teachings of the major religions of the world. It will be most unfortunate if, in the name of secularism, we force people to stay in spiritual ignorance and thus court global disaster.

Srila Prabhupada, the founder-acharya of the International Society for Krishna Consciousness (ISKCON), practically demonstrated the efficacy of spiritual education as a means to individual and social transformation during the period of the counterculture in the USA in the 1960s. Empowered by this divine knowledge, thousands of youths were able to break free from the shackles of all self-destructive habits and become selfless spiritual activists, dedicated to the holistic service of God and all living beings. Even today, it is a globally repeated and repeatable phenomenon that when an individual adopts genuine spirituality, he concomitantly develops character and compassion, which are the pre-requisites for sustained world peace.

Srila Prabhupada succinctly states the missing spiritual dimension of modern education – and of modern society at large,

"Without the awakening of divine consciousness within the individual, there is no use of crying for world peace."   ● ● ●

awaken the divine consciousness

Foolososphy

Pascal's Wager

The famous mathematician and philosopher Blaise Pascal offers an interesting 'thought experiment' concerning religious belief. The scriptures state that if we follow God, we will dwell with Him in the realm of eternal happiness. And if we refuse to follow Him, we are making future appointments with suffering. Taking an agnostic position, Pascal states that revelation (the word of God as given in the religious scriptures) is intrinsically beyond experimental scientific verification; we can't know in advance what actually happens to us after death.

With this premise, he proposes that our life is a wager. (This is one wager which no one can avoid) If God exists and we bet for God, then we rejoice eternally. If God exists and we bet against Him, suffering awaits us. If God doesn't exist and we bet for God, we still are not the losers because everything is anyway going to be finished at death!

"That's too much"

The controversial issue here is the sacrifice of carnal pleasures by those who follow God. If God doesn't exist, then have His followers not been cheated of bodily delights in the pursuit of an illusion? Pascal agrees that the religious have to, in his own words, "curtail" their "passions", but he points out that the purely rational benefits of a life in accordance with standard moral principles outweigh the restrictions that may be imposed by scriptures: "Now what harm will you come by in making this choice? You will be faithful, honest, humble, grateful, generous, a sincere friend, truthful.

Certainly, you will not enjoy those pernicious delights - glory and luxury, but will you not enjoy others?"

The atheistic attack on Pascal has been that he has unduly minimized the sacrifice end of the bargain; the carnal delights of a "free life" are too much to give up. Indeed that is the reason why many people shy away from spirituality, "It will obstruct my enjoyment of life now." This has become the essence of most modern philosophical thought: the pleasures that the world offers are the ultimate goal of life. The atheistic leaning of modern science can also be traced to this fundamental belief. The principal thrust of contemporary technology in all its diverse fields has been to enhance the quality and the quantity of material pleasure that man can enjoy in this life.

The Myths vs. the Facts

The upsurge in atheism in the West from the 1960s onwards fuelled the free sex revolution or what was in euphemistic terms called, "value-free living". Self-restraint was dubbed as pleasure-denying, stifling, dogmatic, unreasonable and unnecessary and was thrown to the winds. All kinds of sexual perversions became the vogue; everything that one could imagine (and even that which one couldn't imagine) was attempted in order to maximize bodily pleasure.

This free sex culture has now spread its wings even to India, especially through the media –newspapers, magazines, TV, movies etc. Before we embrace it, being enamored by its promise of extraordinary erotic enjoyments, let us see what has been its consequence for the West.

In *The New Harvard Guide to Psychiatry*, the editor Armand M Nicholi, Jr, a Harvard Medical School psychiatry professor, makes these remarkable observations:

Many who have worked closely with adolescents over the past decade have realized that the new sexual freedom has by no means led to greater pleasures, freedom and openness; more meaningful relationships between the sexes; or exhilarating relief from stifling inhibitions. Clinical experience has shown that the new pemissiveness has often led to empty relationships, feelings of self-contempt and worthlessness, an epidemic of venereal disease, and a rapid increase in unwanted pregnancies. Clinicians working with college students began commenting on these effects as early as 20 years ago. They noted that students caught up in this new sexual freedom found it "unsatisfying and meaningless".....A more recent study of normal college students (those not under the care of a pyschiatrist) found that, although their sexual behavior by and large appeared to be a desperate attempt to overcome a profound sense of loneliness, they described their sexual relationships as less than satisfactory and as providing little of the emotional closeness they desired....They described pervasive feelings of guilt and haunting concerns that they were using others and being used as "sexual objects"

That's an insider's version of the unpalatable reality behind the smiles, the hugs..... the freedom portrayed in Santa Barbara and other Western soap operas.

This report is not an exception; rather it is typical of the trend in psychology these days. There is a growing body of evidence that licentious behavior and unhappiness have a strong correlation.

Free Sex or Free Shocks?

Little needs to be said about the menace that sexually transmitted diseases (STDs), especially AIDS, pose to humanity. The dreaded AIDS epidemic, if unchecked, is feared to be likely to devour a large portion of the entire human population by the middle of the next century. Unbelievable, but true. Medicine doesn't seem to offer much hope; a cure seems as far away as ever. And even if AIDS is cured, medical history shows that a new even more deadly disease is waiting to take over as soon its predecessor subsides.

And the social consequences of divorce (a common result of sexual promiscuity) are ominous, to put it mildly. The Costly Consequences of Divorce: Assessing the Clinical, Economic and Public Health Impact of Marital Disruption in the United States, a National Institute for Healthcare Research publication, shows that divorced and separated people are more likely to suffer serious physical and mental health problems and are at significantly higher risk for alcohol abuse, premature death and suicide. The effects on the children from broken homes are even more disastrous, extending from poorer school performance to higher rates of juvenile delinquency and teen suicide.

The Crowning Irony

Who could ever have thought that science, and that too psychology and psychiatry (with their libido concepts), would one day end up confirming the fundamental injunction of all religions: sin breeds misery?

What then is the verdict of science vis-a-vis Pascal's wager? Is the pleasure of an unrestricted life too much to give up? Patrick Glynn, Associate Director at the George Washington University, in his book *God: The Evidence* answers unambiguously, "Modern research in psychology makes clear that the morally unrestrained life is not worth living. The crowning irony is this: Even if their beliefs were to be proved illusions, religiously committed people lead happier and healthier lives, as numerous studies show." For example, a study reported in the *Readers*

Digest Sep-Oct 2001 issue showed that people who prayed regularly lived on an average seven years longer than those who didn't pray.

Patricide and Suicide

From an emotional point of view, atheism is patricide; the atheist is by his intellect and reason, murdering his own father, God. Of course, God is not going to die just because of the atheist's disbelief. (Remember "the fox and the sour grapes" story?) But his belief has disastrous consequences on the atheist himself. Rather than being a loved, cared and protected son of the omnipotent Supreme Father, he makes himself a lonely, destitute, fearful orphan. Such a life full of uncertainty and anxiety with the crushing intellectual burden of dogmatic atheism is hardly worth living. Though breathing like the bellows of a blacksmith externally, his heart is dead like a stone internally. Thus, his atheism leads to his committing virtual suicide.

There is one difference between a person who is dead within and a person who is physically dead. A physically dead person can do no harm to anyone, but the frustrated atheist tries to fool the gullible masses with the venomous idea that athiesm is a scientific belief, whereas in actuality there is no scientific basis for atheism. As misery loves company, the miserable atheist makes it his life's mission to make others similarly athiestic and thus miserable. When the blind lead the blind, all of them fall into a ditch.

Why?

Atheism is not beneficial at any level - whether emotional, mental, physical or sociological. There is no reason, no logic, no justification, no intelligence to an atheistic world view.

So the weight of the available evidence makes atheism a doctrine devoid of any sense of rationality at all; if atheist were denounced as mad, it would be difficult to give any scientific evidence to refute the denunciation. Atheism is not a philosophy; it is a foolosophy (the sophistry of fools) The facts show that the atheists and their followers are on the way to MAD (Mutually Assured Destruction).

But there's still hope. If atheists open their minds to the facts and harmonize with God, their destiny can change.   ● ● ●

Where Technology Falls Short

We live in the age of technology. We commute by automobiles and airplanes and communicate by emails and mobiles. The media and the Internet provide us the latest information from all over the world. Movies filled with hi-tech special effects entertain us. Air conditioners and room heaters keep our life comfortable despite climatic inconveniences....The list goes on. Technology has transformed almost every aspect of our lives. Of course, a few of us may have concerns about the pollution and environmental problems that technology has led to. But overall most people feel that technology has benefited us immensely.

Where Is Technology Taking Us?

The razzle-dazzle of comforts, luxuries and hi-tech gadgets make it appear that technology has led to progress in human society. But has the quality of life of people in the modern technology-centered society improved?

* In the past people would leave the doors of their homes open and still be fearless. Now moderns lock, bolt, chain and buzzer-alarm their doors and are still fearful. Is this progress?

* Most moderns are proud of their posh houses, fast cars, smooth roads and skyscraper offices, but they can't even sleep without a pill. Can a society be considered progressed if it makes its people struggle to get the simple and essential pleasure of sleeping, a pleasure that the "primitive" villager gets effortlessly?

- The technological worldview being materialistic gives rise to selfishness, competition and exploitation. Most moderns, despite the show of romantic love, can't trust their own spouses - what then to speak of parents and children or bosses and colleagues. Do alienated, suspicious people comprise a progressive society?

- Mechanized factories can never offer as much employment as the farms did in the past. So a large number of people have to suffer or fear unemployment. For subsistence some of the unemployed turn to begging and others to crime. And overall the modernized industrial environment is so agitating to the mind that self-destructive addictions become the only solace for most people. Are unemployment, criminality and addictions indicators of progress?

- Technology provides comforts, but the high-speed high-stress technology-centered lifestyle takes away the peace of mind necessary to enjoy the comforts. A software engineer has an AC in his office, but still he sweats - not due to heat, but due to tension. Thus technology makes us comfortably miserable.

- Medical technology may have eradicated a few diseases and may offer cures to some more. But far more people need medical attention today than in the past due to unhealthy congested city living, sedentary lifestyles and polluted air, water and food. This is evident from the ever-increasing number of clinics, hospitals and medicine shops. Moreover many of the sophisticated medical treatments, unlike the traditional herbal cures, are prohibitively expensive.

- Most moderns can hardly imagine life without television, movies and myriad other forms of hi-tech entertainment.

And they pity their ancestors who did not have all this enjoyment. But people in the past knew how to find joy in the simple things of life - like sharing and caring in joint families, observing and learning from nature and hearing and chanting the names and glories of God. Consequently they did not find life boring. On the contrary it is we who have divorced ourselves from simple natural pleasures by our infatuation with technology. And so, despite our much-touted entertainment, we still find ourselves constantly bored. The entertainment industry may use sophisticated technology, but is the dependence on entertainment - and the serious inner emptiness that it symptomizes - a sign of progress?

* Technology intoxicates us with the feeling of being the controller. Just by pressing a switch, we can cause huge machines to perform complex actions. Just by clicking a key, we can summon information from any part of the world. By constantly working with machines, we become habituated to controlling them and expect everything and everyone to be similarly controlled. When people refuse to be controlled like machines, we end up with all sorts of relationship conflicts ranging from domestic cold wars to marital ruptures, from quarrels to murders. And in life when things don't go the way we want them to, we end up suffering from a wide range of mental problems, from depression to addiction, from stress to suicide.

Technology – Ancient and Modern

Many of us may have been led to believe that we moderns possess the most advanced technology in the history of our planet. However, the pyramids in Egypt, the Stonehenge monoliths in the

UK and the non-rusting iron pillars in India are some telltale products of an ancient technology that was amazingly superior to our modern technology. In fact, the Vedic texts describe even more intriguing technologies. Vimanas (pollution-free airplanes), brahmastras (precise and powerful missiles activated by mystical sound incantations) and astonishingly potent and swift healing by techniques involving medicinal herbs, empowered mantras and Ayurvedic surgeries are a few examples.

These examples of ancient technology show that the Vedic attitude is not opposed to technology per se. But it cautions us about infatuation with material technology leading to neglecting or forgetting the spiritual goal of life.

Imagine a doctor who prescribes only a painkiller to a seriously sick patient. The patient is happy because he gets relief. The doctor is happy because he gets his fees. Happy end of story, isn't it? The problem is - the story doesn't end there. The patient's pain is not cured, but covered. Soon it will recur and worsen.

All of us are like the patient. From the moment of birth, we have a death sentence on our heads. Time forces us to helplessly grow old, get diseased and die. Our journey through life is not only doomed, but also distressful. Miseries from our own bodies and minds (e.g. fever, indigestion, stress, depression), miseries from other living beings (e.g. mosquitoes, competitors, superiors, relatives), and miseries from nature (e.g. extreme heat or cold, floods, earthquakes) periodically torment us throughout our life.

The Vedic texts explain the cause and cure of our suffering. We are spiritual beings entrapped in material bodies. We belong, not to this temporary and miserable material world, but to an eternal and blissful spiritual realm, where we live forever in loving harmony with God. Due to our desire to enjoy independent of God, we are placed in this world, which is an arena for experimentation and rectification. In this material world, we transmigrate through different species of life, searching for pleasure by experimenting with matter in various ways, but getting only misery and death. In the human species, we are given advanced human intelligence to recognize our unfortunate predicament. For such intelligent humans, the Vedic texts offer a systematic program of spirituality that enables them to re-harmonize with and return back to eternal life with God.

This spiritual program is based on recognizing our intermediate position in the cosmic hierarchy. As spiritual sparks we are superior to matter but subordinate to God, who is the controller of both matter and spirit. In our natural harmonious state in the spiritual world, we live in loving harmony with God and have nothing to do with matter. And when we are in the material world, the Vedic scriptures recommend that we focus on devotion and service to God - and take care of the body only as much as is required for it to serve as an efficient vehicle for our service to God and our spiritual journey back to Him. This life of simple living and high thinking will permanently free us from our present entanglement in material miseries and help us to easily and swiftly re-achieve our rightful eternal happiness. Thus spirituality offers the real cure for our suffering. In this program for spiritual reclamation, material technologies were used mainly to assist in achieving the ultimate goal of life.

In our modern times, the human intelligence has been used primarily to develop materially - especially technologically. Technology gratifies our senses, inflates our ego and makes us feel comfortable and proud. However, technology provides entertainment, not peace; comforts, not happiness; medicines, not health; cosmetics, not youth; life support systems, not life. Thus technology is like the painkiller that covers, but doesn't cure, our suffering in material existence. Worse still, it creates an illusory sense of well-being, which makes people feel that a spiritual solution is unnecessary. Instead of simple living and high thinking, people start simply living and hardly thinking. Infatuated by promises of a hi-tech paradise, people don't even think about the spiritual purpose of life, erroneously considering it to be unscientific and outdated. Thus technology steals our opportunity to attain eternal life and condemns us to stay on and suffer in this world of birth and death.

Therefore the basic difference between ancient technology and modern technology is that the former helped people to achieve the goal of life, while the latter causes people to forget the goal of life. Srila Prabhupada explains the regrettable direction of modern technological advancement: the intelligence that is meant for solving all problems permanently is misused to convert a castor oil lamp into an electric lamp.

Spiritualizing Modern Technology

A question may therefore arise, "Do we have to give up technology and return back to village life?"

We don't have to give up technology; but we do have to give up the illusion that technology can make us happy. If we are diseased, we don't have to give up the painkiller; but we do have to give up the illusion that the painkiller can cure our disease. We have to adopt the cure of spirituality for attaining real happiness.

And as the modern world is almost completely pervaded by technology, we can use the Vedic principle of yukta vairagya, devotional renunciation: without being attached to material things for personal enjoyment, use them for the service of God as required.

Srila Prabhupada gives an analogy to explain the application of this principle with respect to technology.

Suppose a gang of thieves have robbed a bank and are fleeing in a car at the speed of 80 kmph on a road with a speed limit of 40 kmph. What are the policemen chasing the thieves to do? Stick to the speed limit and let the thieves escape? Or break the speed limit, drive faster than the thieves, arrest them and retrieve the stolen wealth?

In our modern times, the wealth of spiritual knowledge of people is being stolen away by hi-tech propaganda of atheism, materialism, consumerism and hedonism. Therefore it is incumbent on all genuine spiritual scientists to use the same technology to spread knowledge of spirituality and harmonious living and help people reclaim their wealth of spiritual wisdom and happiness. Thus the   principle of yukta-vairagya enables us spiritualize modern technology, as can be seen in the following examples.

- ❖ ISKCON is constructing splendid temples equipped with state-of-the-art animatronics, robotics and multimedia theaters to kindle the interest of people in the message of the Bhagavad-Gita.

- ❖ At many of its major festivals, sophisticated lasers shows offer breathtaking glimpses of beautiful Deities being worshiped all over the world to inspire devotion to God amongst the people.

ISKCON

- ❖ ISKCON is offering children a positive alternative comprising of devotionally-oriented toys, games and movies, which engender virtue and nobility, instead of the vice-producing media images of violence and sensuality.

* ISKCON's faculty members give presentations using slides shows, VCDs and other state-of-the-art technology. Even the article you are reading is an example of the yukta-vairagya principle in action.

This spiritual utilization of technology is attracting millions of people towards the service of God, and helping them to find inner fulfillment and achieve their right to eternal life and happiness.

But much more remains to be done, if we want to steer our planet out of the mess we have landed it into by our indiscriminate adoption of technology. For our modern times, Srila Prabhupada envisioned an East-West synthesis; spreading Indian spiritual wisdom with Western material technology. He compared the coming together of Vedic spirituality and modern technology to the coming together of the proverbial blind man and the lame man. But for this synthesis to take place, the technologically advanced West has to recognize that it is lacking in spiritual vision. And the financially-crippled India has to shed its deeply-ingrained inferiority complex arising from material poverty and recognize its wealth of spiritual knowledge. If we acknowledge our respective endowments and deficiencies, we can become pioneers in bringing about an international spiritual revival. In our sadly misled modern world, this may be the only hope to usher in a new era of harmony and happiness. Are we ready?   ● ● ●

Smiling Faces, Crying Hearts

Meet Mr. Befooled. He has a broad smile on his face. He is thinking, "Just see how clever I am! I have outwitted my doctor." Sometime ago, he was afflicted by a severe pain. His doctor prescribed an expensive medicine and a cheap painkiller. After he started the treatment, his pain subsided. A few days ago, he accidentally discovered that taking just the painkiller was enough to keep the pain away. The discovery delighted him, "I don't have to spend so much money on the antibiotic after all."

Poor Mr. Befooled. Little does he know what's in store for him. The painkiller has just created an illusion of health by deadening him to the sensation of pain. Unknown to him, the disease is worsening within. And soon it will become so aggravated that the painkiller will no longer work. By then it may be too late for even the medicine to act.

The Empty Heart

Our present existence can be likened to a heart disease; we find ourselves in a situation where our innate longing for happiness is inevitably frustrated. Our heart longs for love and the happiness that it brings. Loving relationships give meaning and joy to life; indeed they make life, filled as it is with hardships, worth living. Ironically enough, intimate relationships, which have the potential of bringing the highest happiness, often become the source of the greatest anxiety and agony. Being an extremely intense emotion, love builds for the object of love such a lofty tower of expectations, hopes and dreams that it is practically impossible for any human being to ascend and stay in that tower. Love is almost always blind and marriage is almost always an eye-opener. Even if somehow a somewhat satisfying relationship is formed, it is invariably severed by the inexorable sword of time. And the stronger the relationship, the more agonizing is its summary termination.

Fearing disappointment, betrayal or ultimate devastation, most people do not dare to love. But a heart that does not love is profoundly empty. And an empty heart makes for a dry life, bereft of purpose and thrill. Without the satisfaction of loving reciprocation, life becomes at best boring and at worst agonizing. If there is nothing worth dying for in one's life, there is nothing worth living for either. Thus most people live with a heart disease; their heart's longing finds no lasting fulfillment.

Advancing In Emptiness

In the modern times, advancement in science and technology has led to a considerable increase in physical comforts and luxuries. Hi-tech gadgets now relieve us of many of the routine daily chores, which were thought to be making life repetitious, boring and burdensome. Also for most people, the worldview created by science makes religion appear outdated, sentimental and unscientific. They thus feel themselves free to enjoy fully the sensual pleasures that were earlier restricted or prohibited by religion. Therefore being pampered by technology and freed from religion, most modern people consider themselves far superior to the people of the past.

However scientific advancement provides no help whatsoever in filling the empty hearts of people; on the contrary, it

tends to increase the void in the heart. The mechanistic approach of modern science reduces sentient human beings to machine-like humanoids. It further reduces human behavior and personality to an interaction of lifeless particles governed by impersonal laws. Cherished human emotions like love become nothing more than electrochemical signals coursing through nerves and neurons. Such a conception appears shocking when stated so bluntly, but it is precisely what the scientific worldview implies and what most people unconsciously accept by embracing a technology-centered lifestyle. Of course, love is a much-bandied word in the modern times, especially in the media, but what is portrayed as love is basically lust.

Lust Is Not Love

About so-called love, Montaigne remarks, "Love is nothing save an insatiable thirst to enjoy a greedily desired object." Love and lust are as different as gold and iron. Just as iron can be easily made to look like gold by an external coating, similarly lust can be made to look like love by an external show. But lust is an animalistic drive resulting from the craving of the flesh, whereas love is a sublime outward flow of oneself meant exclusively for the pleasure of the

beloved. Lust is primarily selfish, whereas love is essentially selfless. And selfishness ruins relationships, whereas selflessness nourishes them. That is why relationships formed on the basis of lust – the so-called 'love' marriages - tend to be highly volatile, as is evident from the spiraling divorce rates in cultures encouraging sexual permissiveness.

Statistics show that in the USA every third marriage ends in rupture within three years. About pre-marital sexuality, 'The New

Harvard Guide to Psychiatry' notes: Students caught up in this new sexual freedom found it "unsatisfying and meaningless".....A more recent study of normal college students (those not under the care of a pyschiatrist) found that, although their sexual behavior by and large appeared to be a desperate attempt to overcome a profound sense of loneliness, they described their sexual relationships as less than satisfactory and as providing little of the emotional closeness they desired. Thus modern culture degrades love to a frantic search for carnal gratification, a search that soon becomes an exercise in meaninglessness; it therefore aggravates and perpetuates the void in the heart.

The Boredom Industry

Modern society has devised ingenious ways of attempting to somehow forget this emptiness of the heart. Typical is the multi-billion dollar entertainment industry. Dubbed as the boredom industry, it provides people an escape-way from the frustrating grind of daily life to an imaginary world. There, they vicariously become a dream character, who speaks smartly, behaves flawlessly, fights heroically, wins invariably and enjoys erotic fantasies unlimitedly. But all that the entertainment provides is a temporary feeling of well being, which cannot and does not last. Worse, the grandiose and fantastic settings for bodily enjoyment that it depicts, fuel lust, greed and anger. These irrational and irresistible passions can never be satisfied in actual life. This further cripples the ability of people to experience and exchange love in their real lives and thus the emptiness of the heart deepens. And the vicious cycle – emptiness of heart leading to artificial enjoyment and the vicarious enjoyment resulting in further emptiness of the heart - perpetuates itself. The consequent desperation results in the maniac frenzy that surrounds sports, movies and similar forms of entertainment.

Sophisticated Painkillers

Thus for the disease of the empty heart, artificial pleasures are nothing more than sophisticated painkillers. Just as a painkiller creates an illusion of health that only worsens the actual disease, artificial enjoyment creates an illusory state of stimulation and excitement that just cannot be maintained in actual life. Even when the body is young and healthy, no one can actually enjoy as much as the media portrays. The resulting unfulfilled passions lead to enormous frustration even in youth. And as the body ages and dwindles, nature forcibly strips away all abilities to enjoy. By then the sense of loneliness and emptiness, which was somehow numbed through extravagant sensual indulgence in youth, becomes so pervasive that life becomes an hellish, unlivable ordeal. Thus artificial enjoyment in youth sentences one to a condemned existence in middle age and senility.

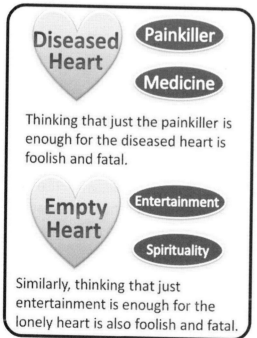

Thinking that just the painkiller is enough for the diseased heart is foolish and fatal.

Similarly, thinking that just entertainment is enough for the lonely heart is also foolish and fatal.

At this point a question may arise: accepting that artificial enjoyment is just a painkiller, what is the harm if it provides some much-needed relief in a stressful life? Returning to the starting analogy, Mr. Befooled's blunder is not that he takes the painkiller, but that he rejects the actual medicine, thinking that he is more intelligent in taking just the painkiller. He thus cheats himself of the chance to be cured. Similarly, modern society, being infatuated with the analgesic of artificial enjoyment, has rejected the cure of genuine spirituality, which can lead to an eternal life of real enjoyment. So the foregoing critique of artificial enjoyment is meant to serve as a necessary prelude to an introduction to the Vedic paradigm of real enjoyment.

Endless Love

The Vedic texts assert that our loving propensity is not meant to be forgotten or frustrated, rather it is meant to be completely and eternally fulfilled. Our longing for love is integral to our being and it remains strong even after our body dwindles. This indicates that our longing for love belongs to a setting that is different from and independent of our present bodily situation. The Vedic texts therefore posit that our actual existence is spiritual, that is, beyond the constricting confines of space (our material body) and time (our present lifespan). We are eternal spiritual beings, known in Sanskrit as atman (soul), and our real life is in a deathless spiritual realm. There we relish and rejoice in an everlasting loving relationship with the supreme spiritual being, God. When a person is beautiful, wealthy, intelligent, strong, famous or renounced, that person attracts our love towards him. Being supreme by definition, God possesses all these cherished attributes in full eternally; He is thus supremely beautiful, supremely wealthy, supremely intelligent, supremely strong, supremely famous and supremely renounced. He is therefore universally attractive and is hence best described by the name Krishna, which in Sanskrit means all-attractive. *sarva akarshati it krishna* "The Supreme Being who attracts everyone is known as Krishna." Over and above these six attractive qualities, Krishna also has an especially endearing seventh opulence – a most loving nature. In the spiritual realm, He personally and individually reciprocates with the love of each soul. In one of his songs, the renowned Beatle, George Harrison, has described Krishna as "the Lord who loves those who love Him." Krishna is thus the perfect object of love and the soul's longing for love, when reposed in Krishna, finds everlasting fulfillment.

In the spiritual realm each soul is endowed with a free will to enable him to choose to love Krishna and thus experience the ecstasy of endless love. By causeless misuse of his free will, when a soul refuses to love Krishna, he is sent from the spiritual realm to the material world. Here he tries to find a substitute object of love, but the temporal nature of all material objects frustrates him inevitably and repeatedly. Krishna being a most magnanimous lover does not forsake those souls who turn away from Him. He arranges to provide for their essential material needs – light, heat, air, water and food - through nature. He further provides a systematic program of spirituality to enable them to return to the spiritual realm.

Recognizing Genuine Spirituality

In the modern times, due to lack of spiritual education, almost any practice meant for any purpose passes as 'spiritual'. Actual spirituality however is a divinely delineated path meant specifically to re-unite us with the lost love of our heart. Love necessitates regulated behavior. For example, when a boy wants to develop a loving relationship with a girl, he very carefully does the things that will please her and he scrupulously avoids doing the things that will displease her. The same principle holds true in spiritual life, wherein an aspiring transcendentalist desires to develop a loving relationship with Krishna. Hence so-called spirituality that does not demand regulated behavior can be safely rejected as bogus. Of course the regulations expected in spiritual life are not meant to stifle our enjoyment in life, rather they are a necessary requisite to awaken our dormant love for Krishna, by which we can experience in full our original joyful nature.

Divine Sound

The positive program for spiritual rediscovery given by Krishna is centered on divine sound. Spiritual sound vibration is fundamentally different from material sound vibration; it is much more than a mere carrier of information. Divine sound contains within itself the potency to free the hearer from vicious material desires and to enable him to experience higher realms of reality. Therefore the Vedanta-sutra, the condensed essence of all Vedic wisdom, concludes with the aphorism: *anavrttiih shabdat* "The

uncovering of pure consciousness takes place through divine sound."

Divine sound is most effective when received from those living according to spiritual principles. Therefore it is vital for an aspirant on the spiritual path to associate regularly and submissively with advanced spiritualists. In such holy association, he can have his consciousness purified by receiving spiritual knowledge and by molding his life accordingly. Divine sound is also easily and universally accessible through the medium of the Holy Name, especially the maha mantra Hare Krishna Hare Krishna Krishna Krishna Hare Hare Hare Rama Hare Rama Rama Rama Hare Hare. Krishna and His name are non-different. Therefore chanting of the Holy Names brings us immediately in contact with Krishna. This sublime contact provides us a glimpse of our spiritual joyful nature and thus stimulates the awakening of our original love for Krishna. Hence another essential principle for progressive spiritual advancement is regular mantra meditation.

A serious spiritualist also eschews activities that impede the swift awakening of his love for Krishna. The most detrimental of such activities are meat eating, gambling, intoxication and illicit sex. All living beings – whether human or subhuman – are the children of God. So if a so-called spiritualist satisfies his palate by gorging on the flesh of his own brothers in the family of God, his spirituality is just a charade. Gambling agitates and preoccupies the mind with false hopes of future prosperity and thus takes away the impetus for striving to attain the platform of real happiness. Intoxication creates a further illusion within the illusion of material life and thus propels one in a direction opposite to that desirable for spiritual realization. Illicit sex perverts the soul's divine longing for love into an animalistic hunt for sensual titillation. It dulls the spirit, quickens the senses and rivets one's consciousness to flesh. The Bhagavad-gita (3.41) therefore warns that lust is "the destroyer of knowledge and self-realization."

Abstaining from these four self-destructive behavioral patterns – meat eating, gambling, intoxication and illicit sex – is not however a necessary pre-requisite for embarking on the spiritual path. From any position in life, one can adopt the positive principles of spirituality. Contact with divine sound provides spiritual happiness, purifies the heart and elevates one to a higher level of consciousness, at which stage following the negative injunctions becomes easier.

The Cure for the Heart

Those who adopt this process of reawakening their dormant love for Krishna can very soon experience Krishna and His love in their lives. Countless people throughout history have had these spiritual experiences. And even today ISKCON (The International Society for Krishna Consciousness) is freely distributing this cure for the soul to anyone and everyone all over the world. Thousands are experiencing the joy of Krishna consciousness in their lives. Seeing the medicine of Krishna consciousness working in their lives, they no longer need the analgesic of artificial enjoyment. For them, self-restraint is not a source of mental and physical torture, but a gateway to higher happiness.

It is unfortunate, nay tragic, that most of the modern society has placed itself in the position of Mr. Befooled. Most people have rejected the cure of spirituality and embraced the analgesic of artificial enjoyment. And they think of themselves as very advanced and intelligent in doing this. But the passage of time is showing that neither is a life of artificial enjoyment satisfying, nor is a society espousing artificial lifestyles sustainable. Despite the best facilities for bodily enjoyment, Western and westernized societies are witnessing an alarming rise in divorces, criminality, addictions and suicides. Stress, a disease unheard of in earlier times, is now synonymous with the modern lifestyle. All these are symptomatic of hearts that are profoundly and desperately empty. The disease of the empty heart has worsened so much that in many cases even the painkiller of artificial enjoyment is no longer working.

But still it is not too late. The cure of genuine spirituality is easily available. It is safe, simple and sublime. And it works for those who give it a sincere try. The process of filling what theologian Michael Novak has called "the empty shrine" at the heart of modern existence is the most exciting and glorious of intellectual, and human, adventures. The onus is on the bold and the intelligent to take up the challenge. ● ● ●

The One-Eyed Modern Guru

It is television that we are talking about. Television has become an integral part of every modern house. It is thought by most modern people to be an indispensable necessity that offers them a much-needed break from the tension and boredom of modern, high stress life-style. Although a few whispers are often heard here and there about the detrimental affects of TV, they are generally drowned out by the overwhelming uproar of those wanting the enjoyment offered by television.

Television is not run by social workers interested in the welfare of the audience. TV is run by businessmen who are ready to do anything and everything to maximize their profits. Although people eagerly savor the various programs on television, little do they know the deadly effect it is having on their minds. Most TV programs show levels of opulence and enjoyment that are unattainable for common people. Such programs, coupled with the alluring advertisements of various luxury products that are periodically aired between all programs, ensures that the audience's hearts become filled with uncontrollable and most often insatiable desires for wealth and pleasure. This inevitably results in people behaving like programmed robots working hard to try to earn money - by hook or by crook - to enjoy life the way it is portrayed on TV. TV doesn't offer harmless, innocent entertainment; it determines the values and goals of people.

Television is becoming the guru of the modern man; it teaches him how to dress, how to walk, how to talk, how to eat. However, TV is a treacherous guru.

Consider the following facts and figures about the TV habit in America compiled by the Washington-based Realvision, a project of the global TV-turnoff network:

I. TV Undermines Family Life

Television has proved that people will look at anything rather than each other. -Ann Landers

1. Amount of television that the average American watches per day: over 4 hours
2. Time per week that parents spend in meaningful conversation with their children: 38.5 minutes
3. Percentage of 4-6 year-olds who, when asked, would rather watch TV than spend time with their fathers: 54

II. TV Harms Children and Hampers Education

I wish there were a knob on the TV to turn up the intelligence. There's a knob called "brightness," but that doesn't work. -Author Unknown

1. Number of hours recommended by the American Pediatric Association for children two and under: 0
2. Average daily time American children under age two will spend in front of a screen: 2 hours, 5 minutes
3. Average time per week that the American child ages 2-17 spends watching television: 19 hours, 40 minutes
4. Hours of TV watching per week shown to negatively affect academic achievement: 10 or more
5. Hours per year the average American youth spends in school: 900
6. Hours per year the average American youth watches television: 1,023

III. TV Promotes Obesity

Television has changed a child from an irresistible force to an immovable object. -Author Unknown

1. Factor by which men who watch more than 21 hours of TV a week increase their risk of Type 2 diabetes: 2
2. Economic cost of obesity in the United States in 2000: $117 billion

IV. TV Promotes Overconsumption

Television is simply automated day-dreaming. -Lee Lovinger

1. Number of TV commercials viewed by American children a year: 40,000
2. Age by which children can develop brand loyalty: 2
3. Percentage of American children age six and under who have products based on characters from TV shows or movies: 97

V. TV Promotes Violence

"If everyone demanded peace instead of another television set, then there'd be peace." -John Lennon

1. Number of violent acts the average American child sees on TV by age 18: 200,000
2. Number of murders witnessed by children on television by the age 18: 16,000
3. Percentage of youth violence directly attributable to TV viewing: 10
4. Percentage of Hollywood executives who believe there is a link between TV violence and real violence: 80
5. Percentage of children polled who said they felt "upset" or "scared" by violence on television: 91

When the children are exposed to ghastly violence, it's natural that some of these children go with guns to schools and shoot their teachers and co-students. Many intelligent Americans including eminent film stars, social activists and national leaders have joined hands in forming a "no TV" campaign group. They and their children have minimized TV viewing to the barest minimum necessary. Their concern is mostly material; excessive TV viewing inhibits creativity, creates lethargy and wastes time.

TV – The Culture-Killer

But from the point of India, which has the most glorious cultural and spiritual heritage in the world, the effects of TV are far more insidious.

The Vedic scriptures explain that we are spiritual beings, souls. It is our eternal birthright to rejoice in divine love with the all-attractive Supreme Person, Krishna. The philosophy and practice of the eternal love between the soul and the Supersoul is the greatest legacy of ancient India not only for India, but for the whole world.

Indians are meant to lead the world through the spiritual wisdom and culture. Srila Prabhupada would lament that Indians are sitting on jewels but are begging for broken glass. Instead of being victimized by the bombardment of Western culture though TV, Indians have the opportunity to find the treasure of divine love and happiness that lies dormant within their own heart and share it with the whole world. The original television meaning 'vision from a distance' was when Sanjaya observed from the court in Hastinapura the events on the battlefield of Kurukshetra and narrated them to Dhritarashtra. Thus the message of the Bhagavad Gita is India's ancient TV program and it was this – and similar - program that Indians have been relishing for millennia.

What 700 years of Mogul rule could not accomplish, what 200 years of British rule could not do, television has done in just 30 years. Television has attacked and damaged severely the very foundation of Vedic culture. In the past, everyone in India would gather every evening as a family in a local temple or under a nearby banyan tree to sing bhajans, kirtans and hear the glorious stories of Lord Rama and Lord Krishna and the timeless message of the

Bhagavad-gita -- of the soul and its loving relationship with God. Their minds and hearts saturated with these divine vibrations, people would sleep happily, wake up enthusiastically and joyfully advance towards the ultimate goal of life -- to return back to the kingdom of God. Unfortunately, nowadays instead of coming together to glorify God, people come together in front of the modern deity -- TV. There they sit together united in a stupor of illusion, burning with passion and desire, dissatisfied and frustrated, imagining happiness in the vicarious, inane pleasures offered by the idiot box. The insipidity of the entertainment on TV is well-expressed by Frank Lloyd Wright, who dubbed TV as "chewing gum for the eyes."

That's why Fred Allen put the growing popularity of TV as "the triumph of machine over people."

The Better-Than-TV Option

But we don't have to live lifelong with second-hand pleasures.

That same ancient cultural and philosophical legacy has been made accessible to the whole world by Srila Prabhupada through the Krishna consciousness movement, ISKCON. ISKCON offers fulfilling and uplifting engagements like practical and powerful

meditation techniques, joyful spiritual chanting and dancing programs, enlightening discourses and books that can strengthen and sharpen our intelligence and various services for making humanity happier and more harmonized with the Lord. When all these activities fill their lives, devotees have no struggle in giving up TV addiction. In fact, they don't even miss TV; they feel that those who are giving up the sublime devotional pleasure for the inane TV pleasures are missing so much.

Maybe we should give the better-than-TV option a try?   ● ● ●

The Tea Quake

The British Legacy

The British may have left India, but every morning brings a jarring reminder of their continued rule over India. It's tea; the 'slow poison' drink that is their post-independence legacy.

Tea is alien to the original Vedic culture. The British started extensive tea-fields in India to meet the demands of the Western market. Once the Western demand was met, they realized that their profits could be multiplied manifold if they could generate a local market. So through economic coercion (the government held all the tax strings)

Is it tea time?

and false propaganda (the innate inferiority complex of the Indians of that time made them only too ready to imitate anything Western), they hooked the Indians to tea. And the vested interests of the tea barons have ensured the perpetuation and proliferation of this useless addiction.

In this article, let us take the example of this almost ubiquitous beverage and analyze what it represents.

"My Dear Tea "

Mr. Armchair Critic sits on his easy chair in the morning, sipping a cup of tea and reading the newspaper, "O my God, 5,000 people killed and 1000 crore worth property destroyed in Gujarat earthquake!" In the same breath, he calls out, "Ramu, get one more cup of tea; make sure it's hot and sweet."

Here's hypocrisy at its best (or worst, depending on how you look at it). How? Let's do a simple analysis.

Statistics indicate that the population of India exceeds 100 crores. At least 25 crore people drink 2 cups of tea everyday. If each cup of tea costs Rs 2.5, India spends Rs 125 crores just on tea everyday. So if Indians stop drinking tea for just 8 days, it can compensate for the entire quake loss. In other words, the seemingly harmless tea cup causes a devastating quake in the national revenues that takes a toll of Rs 1000 crores every 8 days.

If some prefer coffee instead of tea, that's even more expensive. And if its soft drinks, that hurts the economy even more.

Apart from the loss of money, just imagine if all the hundreds of acres of land now devoted to cultivation of tea, coffee and the like were utilized for cultivating food-grains; our hunger and starvation problem could be eliminated from the root.

And there's more in store - the health costs involved. The injurious effects of nicotine present in tea, caffeine present in coffee and several ingredients present in soft drinks have all been well-documented by health experts. And needless to say, they have been equally well pushed under the carpet and kept away form the public eye by the powers that be.

Our financial woes explained in a nutshell: "A tea cup a day keeps economic health away."

The foregoing analysis may be quite startling for some of you, but the point to note here is that often our casual indulgences end up causing as much scarcity and suffering as do devastating natural calamities. Tea is just a representative of our many apparently harmless indulgences, which on a little analysis turn out to be not just superfluous, but also dangerous.

"It Peps Me Up"

Just about everyone who drinks tea knows that it has hardly any nutrition value. And yet everyone keeps drinking it. Why? "It stimulates my brain to work better. In a day full of dreary, burdensome work, the tea-break is practically the only thing to look forward to. It helps me cope with problems better. So what's wrong?" Not only for tea, but for many such obviously superfluous activities like smoking, drinking, etc., and even for most of the hobbies that people nurture like gardening, stamp collecting, reading mundane fiction literature, watching movies, listening to mundane music, and so on and on, this is the typical answer one generally gets.

The Vedic scriptures propose a radically different approach to problem management: "Instead of temporarily forgetting the problems in a tea-induced hallucination, find out fundamentally why the problems are there and tackle them at the root level." Tea doesn't solve the problem; it only puts people into a temporary illusion of forgetfulness. And as the clock ticks on inexorably, both their problems and their bodily systems worsen. Undaunted, they keep gulping down tea and keep trying to forget the reality – till death destroys the illusion.

When Painkillers Replace Medicines

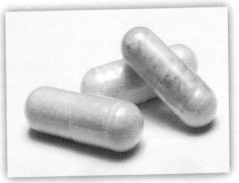

An analogy from medicine will make the pernicious effects of tea and the like more clear. When a patient has acute pain, the medicines alone may not provide immediate relief; they may take time to cure the disease. So the patient is given some painkillers to numb himself to the pain. Now suppose he thinks, "The painkillers are what relieve my pain; the medicines do nothing." And he starts taking just the painkillers and avoids the medicines. What is the result? Due to the temporary cessation of pain, he lives happily in an illusion of good health. But without his knowledge, the disease is devouring him from within. And one day, even the painkillers stop working. But by then it's likely to be too late.

The Vedic scriptures explain that:

❖ The disease of all living beings in the material world is ignorance of their real identity. The direct symptom of this disease is the feeling of incompleteness, the feeling of a lack of real happiness that everyone in the world experiences time and again.

❖ The process of devotional service is the medicine for this disease; it awakens the living being to his actual identity as a spiritual being - a beloved child of the Supreme Lord. Once he is reinstated in his original identity, the soul relishes eternal ecstasy in loving service to God. That is his healthy state.

❖ Material enjoyment is the painkiller, which helps to temporarily cover the pain of the disease of ignorance. So it is allowed by the scriptures; but only in a strictly regulated way so that it does not interfere with the real treatment of devotional service.

But the modern intelligentsia declares that taking the painkiller (material enjoyment) is the goal of life! And that taking the medicine (performing devotional service) is an unnecessary waste of time, meant for those sentimentalists who can't do anything better!

A tragically myopic view of life, to say the very least. What is its consequence? The masses, being addicted to bodily pleasures of which tea is a mild representative, live in the illusion of well-being. They sip their cups of tea and think themselves much more intelligent than the genuine spiritualists who engage in devotional service. And they drag on in a meaningless, mundane, vegetable-like

existence. Till they are tortured by old age, tormented by disease and finally terminated by death. Only to take birth again - to continue drinking tea and suffering old age, disease and death. And the cycle goes on.

The Cover-Up

"But the tea industry provides much-needed employment to so many people." That's like saying that pick-pocketing provides employment to so many people. The pick-pocketing industry plunders people of their hard-earned money. The tea industry basically does the same. Once the people in the tea industry understand the great harm they are doing to society, they will naturally look for and find other forms of employment.

Of course, the ad industry by its awesome power fools people into thinking that they are being modern and trendy while they are actually being stripped of their hard-earned money. An inside secret of the ad industry - the key to successful advertising: "The best ad is that which can sell a refrigerator to an Eskimo." Nice to hear and laugh, but in simple language, it means that the best ad is the one which cheats the most. Cheating - isn't that what the ad industry is mostly about? Are there any ads for rice, wheat and other necessities? Rarely, if at all. The things that are advertised most aggressively are those which no one actually needs. Through a series of moving optical illusions, the masses are made to think that they can't live without such things. And thus they are plundered - willingly. The entire tea business is a glaring example of such open robbery.

Why don't we learn all these things in our schools and colleges? Could it be because the powers that be want us to stay in ignorance so that they can continue exploiting us? Although in one sense this entire racket is so obvious, the whole system programs us to think in such a way that we just can't perceive the obvious. Common sense thus becomes conspicuously uncommon.

Is there any way out of this whole mess?

A Recipe For Wisdom

The world's greatest masterpiece of philosophical wisdom, the Bhagavad-Gita (10.10) gives a remarkably simple recipe for getting both pragmatic common sense and profound philosophical wisdom.

The Lord is the source of all common sense (aned all uncommon sense and all super sense too). When a living being engages in the devotional service of the Lord, the Lord gives him intelligence from within. Equipped with this intelligence, the living being can see things as they are. He thus becomes a genuine intellectual acting for the true welfare of his own self and of the whole world.

In the present age, devotional service can be performed very easily through mantra meditation - through the repeated chanting of the maha-mantra (the great chant for deliverance).

> Hare Krishna Hare Krishna Krishna Krishna Hare Hare
> Hare Rama Hare Rama Rama Rama Hare Hare

The Holy Name is the inner light which opens the eyes of the chanter to the reality of the world he is currently living in. It also reveals the higher realms of reality where he actually belongs. And, most importantly, it bestows him with the dynamic intelligence by which he can live in this world as a champion of truth and ultimately achieve the ultimate truth - the kingdom of God.

Mantra Meditation has worked for countless millions of people throughout history. And it is working for millions of people all around the globe even today. Why not give it a try?   ● ● ●

Bad habits – Causes and Cures

The trout is lured by the worm on the hook of the fisherman, the mouse by the cheese in the mouse-trap. A tragic irony of the struggle for existence is that living beings are often destroyed by what they desire. But at least the fish and the mouse have excuses: the bait and the cheese look like sustenance. Also, the fish and the mouse do not know in advance that they will be trapped. Humans seldom have either of these excuses. The temptations that wreck their lives are quite often pure indulgences known to be dangerous. For example, no one has to smoke for survival and all smokers are aware that smoking is dangerous.

Tragically Trapped

Consider the following World Health Organization statistics:

♣ Tobacco kills nearly 10,000 people worldwide every day.

♣ By 2020 it is predicted that tobacco use will cause over 12% of all deaths globally. This is more deaths worldwide than HIV, tuberculosis, maternal mortality, motor vehicle accidents, suicide and homicide combined.

♣ Half of those who start smoking in adolescence will die in middle age, losing around 22 years of normal life expectancy.

Consider further the following facts:

♣ An average cigarette contains 401 poisons and 43 cancer-causing chemicals.

♣ There are around 1.1 billion smokers in the world (about one-third of the global population aged 15 and over).

Thus, we have quite a sobering picture of the world around us. The statistics about other self-destructive behavioral patterns – alcoholism, substance abuse and suicide - are equally, if not more, alarming. And even among so-called normal people, practically everyone is victimized by some form of self-destructive behavioral pattern - unwarranted expressions of anger that turn out to be disastrous, unintentional use of caustic words that break hearts and so on.

A question naturally arises: how does an intelligent human being embark on such a destructive course? Most people know that when they start, say, smoking, they are treading into a danger zone. But the media, their friends circle and the peddlers persuade them to experiment just once. Seeking a break from the humdrum daily life with its inane pleasures, they acquiesce. The impression of instant pleasure gets embedded in their mind and in future whenever they face a reversal, they tend to seek immediate relief through smoking. Every successive experience of smoking reinforces the earlier impressions, strengthens the tendency to seek momentary relief and weakens the voice of intelligence and conscience. Smoking becomes an irresistible demand, a compulsive need, an addiction. Smokers turn into helpless victims, driven again and again to the instant relief offered by the puffs.

Current Solutions

Here are some methods now in use for breaking addictions:

1. Knowledge: If people were better educated about the dangers involved, would that deter them from addictive indulgences? Maybe sometimes, but not generally. In fact, knowledge sometimes has the opposite effect. For example, in most countries, after governmental regulations made it mandatory to display the statutory warning, "Cigarette smoking is injurious to health" on every cigarette ad and pack, cigarette sales increased; the warning tended to evoke a daredevil spirit in smokers.

2. Emotional Support: People often turn to addictions when emotionally let down or betrayed by loved ones. Emotionally neglected adolescents are especially susceptible to addictions. Providing emotional support through personal counseling is a potential solution. But professional counseling often leads to chronic dependence on the counselor. And for many, professional guidance costs too much. Friends can help, but in our fast-paced modern life, few people can invest the time and energy needed to consistently provide intensive emotional support.

3. Sublimation: Sublimation involves replacing a gross physical drive with a more refined substitute. For example, an alcoholic might try to seek refuge in music instead of alcohol. But this can work only if he has a strong liking for music and if his addiction to alcohol is not overpowering. Due to the alcoholic's recent mental impressions of indulgence in alcohol, that urge generally appears far more attractive than its substitute.

4. Willpower: Seeing the physical and emotional pain that he is inflicting upon himself and his loved ones, an addict may sometimes by sheer determination decide to give up his perverted habit. Unfortunately few people are able to muster such strong willpower. Even if successful, they face the grim prospect of an entire lifetime of constant inner struggle with the fear of succumbing at any moment. And failure often brings with it intolerable feelings of guilt, making living itself an agony.

5. Substitution: Addicts often try to switch their addiction to a less harmful substitute - smokers try patch or nicotine gum (which give small doses of the drug), heroin addicts try methadone and so on. While this may make the addiction less debilitating, the addict is still not freed from his emotional craving and mental dependence on external substances. Also the substitute drug continues to take its toll on the health and the wealth of the addict. Thus substitution leads at best to lessening of the evil and at worst to its perpetuation, never to its elimination.

6. Religion: Statistical surveys have shown that the religiously committed are less likely to succumb to seeking perverted pleasures. Adopting religious principles rigorously also sometimes helps addicts to free themselves. Dr Patrick Glynn writes in his book God: The Evidence, "It is difficult to find a more consistent correlative of mental health, or a better insurance against self-destructive behaviors, than a strong religious faith."

While each of these methods has had some small success, the real solution to self-destructive behavior lies in understanding its roots.

Let's consider the problem from the Vedic perspective.

The Vedic Paradigm

In the Bhagavad-gita (3.36), Arjuna asks Lord Krishna, "By what is one impelled to sinful acts, even unwillingly, as if engaged by force?" Lord Krishna replies, "It is lust only, Arjuna, which is born of contact with the mode of passion and later transformed into wrath, and which is the all-devouring sinful enemy of this world."

The background to this dialogue is the fundamental teaching of the Bhagavad-gita. The source of life in the material body, the actual self, is a non-material particle of spirit, known as the atman or the soul. The essential need of the soul is to love and be loved and to experience unbounded happiness through loving exchange. Being spiritual by constitution, the soul belongs to a higher dimensional milieu, the spiritual world. There the loving propensity of the soul finds complete fulfillment in the supremely lovable all-attractive person, who personally reciprocates with his love. In fact, the Vedic texts state: eko bahusyam. The Supreme has expanded into infinite subordinates for the purpose of loving reciprocation. The Vedanta Sutra explains: raso vai sah. The Supreme is the reservoir of all divine loving emotions. The Srimad Bhagavatam confirms that this Supreme Person is all-attractive and is therefore best known by the name Krishna, which means all-attractive in Sanskrit. In the spiritual world, Krishna is the pivot of all relationships and the soul continually relishes ever-intensifying and ever-expanding ecstasies of love in relationship with Him there.

Love necessitates freedom; only when the object of love freely chooses to reciprocate one's love does the experience of love becomes truly satisfying and fulfilling. The soul is therefore endowed with a minute free will to enable him to experience the joy of loving Krishna. But when the soul misuses his free will and becomes causelessly unwilling to love Krishna, he has to find a substitute in whom he can repose his loving propensity. Of course, by definition, there can be no substitute for the Supreme. And, by his very constitution, the soul cannot find happiness in loving anyone other than the Supreme. But for those souls who insist on making that attempt, the world of matter (where all of us currently reside) provides the necessary arrangement for experimentation and rectification.

The Enemy Within

As soon as the soul comes to the material world, his love for Krishna becomes perverted into lust. Lust is a formidable illusory force that offers the soul various surrogate objects of love to experiment with. Lust creates and perpetuates the misidentification of the soul with the material body that he is given. Lust causes within all living beings the overpowering drive for gross sexual enjoyment in specific, and all forms of material enjoyment in general.

Modern civilization with its media, social environment, culture and overall values aggravates lust disproportionately. Especially the celluloid promises of unending sexual bliss provoke wild erotic fantasies. But the actual experience of sexual enjoyment is heartbreakingly brief; dreams cherished for years vanish within moments. Though what people experience is so pathetically little as compared to the hype, the media blitz goads them on. Sexual enjoyment, especially illicit, is a complicated affair; it involves money, time, intense emotions, interpersonal relationship dynamics, risk for prestige and so on. And the attempt for such enjoyment, even if somehow successful, leaves one feeling disappointed and cheated - and craving for more. And if unsuccessful it creates great anger. Either way the victims are soon so enslaved by lust that the more they try, the more they get frustrated, and yet the more they become impelled to keep trying. Eventually, the accumulated enormous frustration makes instant relief a desperate necessity. Such people easily fall prey to the lure of quick pleasures offered by addictions.

Lust is thus the internal enemy, which causes all self-destructive behavioral patterns. The Gita (18.39) describes vividly the nature of all perverted pleasures: they appear to be like nectar at first but poison at the end. Srila Prabhupada comments, "While one enjoys sense gratification, it may be that there is some feeling of happiness, but actually that so-called feeling of happiness is the ultimate enemy of the sense enjoyer." Why? Because it reinforces the illusion that true happiness can be found in this world.

Lust is present in everyone in varying degrees. That is why everyone, no matter how materially successful he may be, has some tendencies towards self-destructive behavior. People generally become concerned about such tendencies only when it exceeds socially acceptable limits. But actually lust throttles the ability of everyone to make meaningful contributions toward society and even towards their own future; the difference is only in degree. From the spiritual point of view, lust is inherently self-destructive; it strips the soul of the unlimited spiritual happiness that is his birthright and forces him to labor for paltry material sensations of pleasure that can never satisfy his immortal longing.

The Only Way to Conquer Lust

Lust being a perversion of our original, essential nature, cannot possibly be annihilated, suppressed, repressed or even sublimated. But it can be reverted to its original nature by redirecting our loving propensity back to Krishna through the scientific process of devotional service. Action on the spiritual platform is what Lord Krishna recommends to Arjuna as the key to overcoming lust, "Therefore knowing oneself to be transcendental to the material senses, mind and intelligence, O mighty-armed Arjuna, one should steady the mind by deliberate spiritual intelligence (Krishna consciousness) and thus – by spiritual strength – conquer this insatiable enemy known as lust." (Bhagavad-gita 3.43)

The channeling of consciousness from matter back to Krishna is most easily and effectively executed through the medium of divine sound. The Supreme Person Krishna being omnipotent is fully present in His Holy Names. Chanting of the Holy Names therefore connects one immediately with Krishna, who is the supreme pleasure principle. Regular meditation on the Holy Names enables one to experience happiness streaming down from the spiritual dimension. This spiritual pleasure is so satisfying that it soon frees one from the craving for perverted mundane pleasures like drugs, alcohol etc.

Millions of people all over the world have experienced the purifying potency of the Holy Names of God. During the period of the counterculture in the US in 1960s and 1970s, Srila Prabhupada propagated the congregational chanting of the Holy Names and saved thousands of young people from a condemned life of drug addiction. All over the globe ISKCON devotees who practice mantra meditation – chanting of the maha mantra Hare Krishna Hare Krishna Krishna Krishna Hare Hare Hare Rama Hare Rama Rama Rama Hare Hare - everyday for two hours are easily able to eschew intoxication (of all forms), gambling, meat-eating and illicit sex, which are the primary self-destructive activities impelled by lust. Because these four activities greatly obscure the original consciousness of the soul, abstaining from them helps to accelerate the purification of the chanting. However chanting is so powerful that, even if one is initially unable to give up these activities, if one just continues chanting, soon one will experience spiritual pleasure and get the inner strength to get rid of them. When many people in the modern times are so captivated and enslaved by lust that they consider life without these activities an impossibility, devotees lead lives that are natural, peaceful, satisfying, meaningful and constructive, protected as they are by their mantra meditation.

But the benefits of chanting do not stop at freedom from addiction, nor is chanting meant only for those victimized by self-destructive behavioral patterns. Chanting the Holy Names of God is a universal, time-tested, non-sectarian method of bringing about the blossoming of consciousness to its highest bloom of pure love for God and all living beings. Chanting frees one from all selfish desires, which throttle the flow of the fullness of life. It enables one to experience within oneself continuous happiness, which is absolutely independent of the state of the body and the external world. Chanting thus heralds the advent of a life of selfless spiritual service to God and all His children. This selflessness within individuals alone can form the basis of lasting world peace and harmony.

The world-famous Beatle, late George Harrison, a diligent practitioner of mantra meditation, sings:

If you open up your heart,
You will know what I mean
We've been polluted so long
But here's a way for you to get clean
By chanting the name of the Lord and
You'll be free
The Lord is awaiting on you all to awaken
And see.

- 'Awaiting On You All'
From the album '*All Things Must Pass*'

● ● ●

CAN
SPIRITUALITY
BE SCIENTIFIC?

The Spiritual Dimension of Life

10 friends lived together on top of a 100-storied building. Once when they returned after an outing, they found, to their dismay, that the lift was not working. Having no alternative, they decided to lighten the arduous climb by narrating a humorous story each. By the time it was the turn of the last person, they had almost reached the top floor. The tenth person said, "I am sorry, but my story is really tragic. Hearing it will break your hearts to pieces. Its only a one-line story though. I have forgotten the key downstairs!"

The Dead End

Right from our early childhood, its drilled into us that the way to becoming happy is to make it big in life. And accordingly, we roll back our sleeves and get down to work. Slowly, painfully we struggle up the ladder of material success. School, SSC, HSC, Engg / Medical, MBA / MS, Project Leader, Manager?.Managing Director. The dream career growth chart. Assuming that one succeeds (a big assumption), what next?

Just take a look at the life of any of the supposedly successful people around you. Big money, big cars, big houses. And big enemies, big underworld dons?.?big tensions, big terrors. You don't have to be a Sherlock Holmes to understand that they are not happy. But wasn't happiness their goal when they started off? What went wrong?

Just as the ten friends forgot about the key while hearing anecdotes, the modern man also forgets the goal of happiness while working hard for achieving his goals. He gets so caught up in the struggle for success (or at least survival) that he forgets that he is not getting any happiness. And it goes on till the 100th floor?death. "I forgot the key to happiness. I foamed and fumed? in vain." But by then its too late.

Lets look at our own lives. Till whatever rung we have climbed on 'the ladder of success', have we become happy? "Its there. Grab it" ??"Hey! Where did it go?" No matter how much we achieve, happiness eludes us. "Its just one step away", but that's the way it always stays no matter how many steps we take. "Try but don't cry", exhort the diehard materialists. But an intelligent person will think, "Just a minute. Is it intelligence to believe that which has not materialized for me or for anyone else despite years of diligent pursuit?"

What's Missing?

The Vedic scriptures explain that each one of us is an eternal, individual being - atman or soul. Our fundamental need is love. And as we are eternal, we need an eternal object of love - the Supreme Person. The ecstasy of this endless love completely satisfies all the innermost desires of our heart.

Everyone implicitly recognizes that love alone can make him happy. But the big mistake that almost everyone falls prey to is to search for that eternal love in the temporary realm of dead matter. People think that by giving more and more wealth to their loved ones, they will get more and more love. But that just doesn't work. People love the wealth, not the wealthy. And finally the separating sword of time is there to ruthlessly cut off even the wealthiest people from all their loved ones.

The Vedic scriptures do not negate our loving propensity; rather they redirect it to the right person. When we learn to love the Supreme Father, then automatically we develop true love for all living beings (including our loved ones). And this love is truly the wealth of the heart; it can never be thwarted; it conquers all limitations of space and time.

"Spirituality? I Can Do Without It"

Let's see what Chemistry Nobel Laureate Richard R Ernst has to say: "Science and technology alone cannot solve the problems of the new millenium. We need additional guidelines for our actions?

These guidelines have to do with ethics, with philosophy and with faith."

A person may be able to live without a spiritual dimension to his life, but then he will also have to live without direction, purpose, meaning, happiness and love.

"Spirituality? That's Unscientific"

Eminent Mathematician Jagadish N Srivastava, CNS Research Professor, Colorado State University refutes this categorically, "Spirituality is not just a bunch of emotions and fantasy. It is the Reality of our existence. Physics lives inside it only."

A possible doubt, "Most religions worldwide have degenerated to a set empty rituals, which the masses are told to follow without understanding. Isn't this the cause of the disillusionment of the intelligent and inquistive younger generation with orthodox religion?"

That may be true, but it is important to understand that bad application of a thing does not make the thing itself bad. Actual spiritual life is a higher dimensional science with authorized universities and textbooks. The aspiring spiritual scientist is carefully guided by an expert professor of spiritual science along the path to success in the experiment in spirituality.

"Spirituality? My Life Is Too Fast for It"

Once when a plane was in flight, the co-pilot made an announcement, "I have good news and bad news. The good news is that we are going very fast and the bad news is that we don't know where we are going!"

For most people, life is like a 100 meter (or rather 100 year) sprint. No time for thinking. But its a strange sprint. Everyone - the gold medallist, the silver medallist,.. the last runner - gets the same prize – de ath.

If someone still insists that he just wants to come first in such a sprint and that he doesn't care for anything else, what can be said? "Where ignorance is bliss, it is foolish to be wise."

Spirituality? That's Too Dry for Me."

Can love ever be dry? The love of the material world dries up quite fast. "Love is blind, but marriage is an eye-opener."

Spiritual life is however the ultimate love. Actual spirituality is not inane inactivity, it is dynamic adventure for the pleasure of the beloved. A real spiritualist sings, dances, travels, works, jokes a

nd rejoices - all in service to God. In fact, he alone enjoys life to the fullest. Spirituality is not self-abnegation, it is self-fulfillment.

"Spirituality? That's Escapism"

A true spiritualist does not run away from the world; rather he lives in the world and actively fulfils all his responsibilities in such a way as to also achieve the ultimate goal of life-- love of God. Being a satisfied, happy, dynamic and responsible individual, he is a beacon light for the whole world.

He differs fundamentally from a materialist because he has received the highest education (raj-vidya), by which he knows how to add God to everything in his life. Thus he lives without becoming entangled in the selfish intrigues of this world. His principle is "Be in this world, but not of this world."

Spiritual life is an education. Teachers are needed to teach spirituality, but that does not mean that everyone who learns it has to become a teacher. Even in the Vedic times, only a tiny percentage of the population renounced the world and became full-time spiritual teachers. The greatest text of spirituality, Bhagavad-gita, exhorts its student, Arjuna, not to renounce work, but to do work for the Lord.

Thus spirituality can bring happiness into the life of anyone who accepts it. But only the intelligent will take to spiritual life and become happy - now and forever.   ● ● ●

Does Religion Cause War?

Many people feel that the world would be better off without religion. We can understand their sentiments when we consider that modern times have seen large-scale violence in the name of religion. But is religion the only cause of violence? If it were, then parts of the world dominated by atheistic views should have been absolutely peaceful. But history shows that violence has touched all parts of the world more or less equally, independent of the theological beliefs of the people. In fact, most of the wars throughout history, including World Wars I and II, were fought for purely secular political, economic, or ideological reasons; religion was not an issue at all.

Not only that, more human beings were persecuted, murdered, tortured and dehumanized as a direct result of atheistic Marxism in the twentieth century alone than have been harmed in all of the world's religious wars combined since the very beginning of human history. Whenever wars were fought in the name of religion, the real issue was the same: the increase of wealth and power. Religion was just a convenient scapegoat for the powers that be to mask their grossly materialistic motives. And even such "religious" violence has been only a tiny fraction of the secular violence witnessed by the world in recent times.

Is Religion Dispensable?

The protest that religion leads to violence implies that religion is bad and should be rejected. But can the human being do without religion? The universally accepted goal of life is the quest for happiness. When man neglects or rejects religion, consciously or unconsciously his conception of his own self becomes "a lump of chemicals that has by chance come alive." The quest for happiness then degenerates into a savage struggle for carnal enjoyment. Wealth, wine, and women become the only goals of life. Such a conception of life is individually frustrating and globally disastrous. The fundamental need of the individual is love; everyone wants to love and be loved. But in the material conception of life there can be no such thing as real love. People put up a façade of love for another person as long as they get sensual pleasure in return. When that stops, they dispose of their object of "love" just as fast as they would dump a broken TV. In their heart of hearts, people know that no one loves them, no one cares for them. Naturally they feel lonely, rejected, insecure, and frustrated. These feelings are the root of stress, depression, addictions, delinquency, hypertension, criminality, and even suicide. Studies in psychology have confirmed that there is no better insurance against self-destructive behavior (including drinking, substance abuse, and suicide) than strong religious faith. At a global level the rejection of religion leads to a setting wherein love, ethics, morality, and selflessness become meaningless. Although the anti-religionist may feebly urge the masses to "be good," such an appeal has no substance. "If the goal of life is to enjoy and I'm here for who knows how long and there is no life after death, then why wait? I should just enjoy. Beg, borrow, steal, or even kill, but enjoy." By making religion dispensable, we court global disaster.

The Vedic Definition of Religion

What is this mysterious phenomenon known as religion--a phenomenon that causes millions of people to congregate annually at Jagannatha Puri, Tirupati, Badrinath, Mecca, and the Vatican, braving the weather, the crowds, and all the other troubles of a pilgrimage? The Vedic texts of ancient India give an understanding of religion quite different from the common understanding. (To avoid the negative connotations the word religion inevitably brings, I'll use the word spirituality to designate the Vedic understanding of what is commonly called religion. I'll discuss the difference between the two terms later.)

According to the Vedic texts, spirituality imparts the vision to see the cosmos in the proper perspective and to live in harmony with it. The basic teaching of the Vedic texts is that the cosmos is not just matter; it has a spiritual dimension. The Bhagavad-gita (13.27) states,

"Know that whatever you see in existence, both the moving and the nonmoving, is only a combination of the field of activities [matter] and the knower of the field [spirit]." Modern scientific research in fields such as past-life memories, near-death experiences (NDEs), and consciousness studies also strongly suggests a spiritual part of our being that continues to exist even after bodily death. The Vedic texts explain that our real self is not material; a spiritual particle called the atma, the soul, animates our material body. The supreme spiritual being who animates the entire cosmos is called the Paramatma, or the Supersoul. And the relationship between the two --the soul and the Supersoul--is loving service, like the relationship between a parent and a child. This loving relationship exists eternally in the highest realm, called the spiritual world. The soul's refusal to harmonize with the will of the Supreme temporarily obscures the relationship. The soul is then placed in the realm of matter, where we all now reside.

The Vedic texts further explain that genuine spirituality is meant to awaken us to our original spiritual identity through a harmony of philosophy and religion, the two rails on which spirituality runs. The philosophical aspect of spirituality involves the study and understanding of matter, spirit, and the controller of both--the Supreme Lord. And the religious aspect involves following rules and regulations that bring about realization and experience of the spiritual realm (This definition of spirituality and the approach of modern science are strikingly similar, as explained in the article The Respirtualization of Science).

The genuine spiritualist, by dint of systematic practice of both philosophy and religion, understands the nature of the cosmos and learns to live in harmony with it. Having realized his own identity as an eternal spiritual being and his loving relationship with the Supreme Being, a mature spiritual scientist sees all living beings as his brothers. His vision of universal brotherhood leads him to spontaneous, selfless, and holistic service to all living beings. About such a spiritual welfare activist, the ˆsopanisad (Mantra 2) states, "One may aspire to live for hundreds of years if he

continuously goes on working in that way, for that work will not bind him to the law of karma. There is no alternative to this way for man." Thus genuine spirituality, far from being the cause of violence, is the source of harmony--within and without. A true spiritualist is self-satisfied and helps others become self-satisfied. There is no question of violence in a society of self-satisfied persons.

The Real Cause of Violence

What then, from the Vedic perspective, is the cause of violence?

Imbalance occurs in the cosmic order when humankind lives in disharmony with either of the energies of the cosmos. When the material concept of life prevails over the spiritual, dharmasya glanih, the decline of spirituality, results. Spirituality may decline when one neglects its religious aspect, its philosophical aspect, or both. Srila Prabhupada remarks, "Religion without philosophy is sentiment, or sometimes fanaticism, while philosophy without religion is mental speculation." And the absence of both religion and philosophy marks the degeneration of the human species to the animal platform.

When humanity degenerates to the animal platform, the law of the jungle--survival of the fittest--prevails. And just as peace is impossible in a jungle, peace remains a utopian dream in the concrete jungles of today, despite all sorts of "landmark summit meetings." Therefore violence is caused not by spirituality but by the perversion of spirituality, which has divested the human being of his humanity. So the way to restore peace is not by rejecting spirituality but by reforming it. This will pave the way for humanity to once again develop human qualities such as love, contentment, continence, selflessness, and humility, which alone can engender lasting peace. We can compare the defects that have crept into spirituality to a cataract in the eye. To cure the eye, we must remove the cataract, not pluck out the eye. Similarly, we have to arrest the decline in spirituality, not reject spirituality itself. Just as plucking out the eye causes blindness, rejecting spirituality will rob humanity of the precious eyes of divine wisdom, resulting in disharmony and disaster. The spiraling rates of crime and violence all over the globe give us a glimpse of the anarchy in store if humanity continues to neglect spirituality.

Correcting the Iron-Age Chaos

When cosmic disorder occurs, the Supreme Being descends to the material realm to reestablish spirituality, by which humankind can once again learn to live in harmony with the cosmos.

In the present age, dharmasya glanih prevails, since all the aspirations and achievements of most of humankind are within the realm of matter. Most people have no interest in philosophy. And those with some interest pursue it mainly as a means to an academic career or for intellectual growth and not as a zealous search for the Truth. Unable to understand the truths of the cosmos, they mislead others. Similarly, most people are not religiously inclined. The somewhat religious are mostly ritualistic and mechanical in their religious practices; they have little scientific understanding of what they are doing or why. People often claim to be fighting to protect their religion, but if questioned they don't even know its fundamental tenets. And even if they know them, they're not interested in following them. Such pseudo religionists are interested only in their own profit and use religion as a tool to promote it. Thus the present age of iron is characterized by an almost total decline in spirituality or a perversion of it. To correct the enormous disorder prevalent in the modern times, the Supreme Being descends in a form that transcends all restrictions of time and space. He descends in His holy names, which always stay with us, irrespective of time, place, and circumstance. That is why we see that the major religions of the world enjoin their followers to chant the holy names of God. Chanting is the universal religion for the current age. And among the innumerable names of God, the Vedic scriptures assert that the most potent is the maha-mantra, "the great chant for deliverance": Hare Krsna, Hare Krsna, Krsna Krsna, Hare Hare/ Hare Rama, Hare Rama, Rama Rama, Hare Hare.

The Supreme Being has also given a concise yet complete manual for the present age in the form of the Bhagavad-gita, the essence of Vedic wisdom. It is the ideal textbook for the aspiring spiritual scientist. About the Bhagavad-gita, Ralph Waldo Emerson wrote, "I owed a magnificent day to the Bhagavad-gita. It was the first of books; it was as if an empire spoke to us, nothing small or unworthy, but large, serene, consistent, the voice of an old intelligence which in another age and climate had pondered and thus disposed of the same questions which exercise us."

A Call to the Youth of India

Eminent thinkers throughout the world, including leading scientists such as Nobel Laureate Richard R. Ernst, peace workers such as Nobel Laureates Oscar Arias Sanchez and Betty Williams, and spiritualists such as Nobel Laureate the Dalai Lama, firmly believe that only a synthesis of science and spirituality can lead the world out of the present troubled times.

The youth of India have a unique position in the world. By virtue of birth in the holy land of India, they inherit the priceless wealth of spiritual knowledge expounded in the Vedic texts. And by virtue of their education and training, they have developed the scientific spirit of rational inquiry. Thus they are best suited to bring about the much-needed synthesis of science and spirituality that thinkers all over the world are searching for. The late Professor Arthur Ellison, a mechanical and electrical engineer, stated, "Surely the great and unique contribution that India has made and must continue to make to the world's progress is in the field of religion--of truth and reality.... India can most certainly help the West to find the spiritual way back towards reality, which is essential for all real progress." Unfortunately, most young Indians today are enamored by the razzle-dazzle of Western culture--blue jeans, supermarkets, Big Macs, Disney "fun," rock music, Hollywood movies, and the like. But before embracing Western culture, wouldn't it be worthwhile to study the condition of those who have lived with it their whole lives? Statistics show that in the U.S.A. a thousand teenagers attempt suicide every day. Seventy percent of all high-school seniors have attempted or seriously thought about suicide. Thirty-three percent of American adults have serious mental health problems. Psychiatry and psychology are the most lucrative professions in America, and among all professionals, the highest suicide rate is found among psychiatrists and psychologists. Yet for most Indians, America is the land of their dreams. Srila Prabhupada would lament that modern Indians are sitting on jewels and begging for broken glass. Let the intelligent youth of India become selfless spiritual scientists dedicated to saving the world from its suicidal course. Let them, in the true spirit of science, study the theory of spirituality with all seriousness and at the same time perform the experiment of mantra meditation. Those who take up this challenge will become living spiritual scientists and will help usher in an era of peace, harmony, and understanding.   ● ● ●

Karma's Flawless Justice

"Why me! What did I do to deserve this?" cries the outraged person who feels unfairly singled out by cruel providence. Why bad things happen to good people is a question that may haunt us when we see virtuous people victimized by painful reverses in life. The "problem of evil" has been the bane of Western theologians and thinkers for centuries. Simply stated, the problem is, Why does evil exist in the world despite the presence of an almighty God?

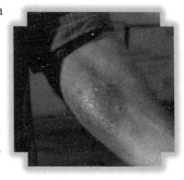

The Vedic scriptures give a clear understanding of the problem of evil. They explain that evil comes upon us because of our own bad acts. That's called karma. But when our due suffering reaches us, we've forgotten the wrongs we did in the past. Hence the indignant outburst, "Why me?"

Karma: Not So Unfamiliar

Ralph walks into his house and sees an ugly burn on his father's right hand. Shocked, he cries out, "Dad, what happened?"

Early one morning, Mrs. Choy calls her family physician. "Doctor, my stomach really hurts." The doctor promptly asks, "What did you have for dinner last night?"

Rahul is having respiratory problems. After examining him, the doctor asks, "At what age did you start smoking?"

These simple, everyday incidents imply acceptance of an idea similar to the concept of karma. On seeing a particular effect, we want to know its cause. This is what the law of karma is about: for every action there is a reaction. The law of karma is similar to Newton's third law, except that it involves, not the physical level, but subtler concepts like higher powers and cosmic justice. Nonetheless, just as Newton's law is not a belief but a principle of physical science, the law of karma is a principle of higher-dimensional science.

The Mystery of the World

Karma is a simple, logical, and satisfactory explanation for suffering, but often our observations don't seem to confirm it. Corrupt politicians amass fortunes without being punished; criminal rogues live in style as underworld dons; shady businessmen who earn millions illegally are considered the success stories of the times. On the other hand, the upright crusaders of truth are sidelined, the innocent are punished, and the honest languish in poverty. Where is justice? Reincarnation forms an integral part of the Vedic explanation for the seeming contradictions in karma. The first point to understand is that we're eternal; our life doesn't begin with birth or end with death. Lord Krishna says in the Bhagavad-gita that just as a person gives up old and worn out clothes and puts on new ones, we souls give up old and worn out bodies and accept new ones at the time of death. That's reincarnation.

We souls, as the active principle in the body, are responsible for all our good and bad acts. Therefore, we have to reap the fruits, either in this life or in a subsequent one. So an apparently virtuous person suffering greatly is reaping the effects of bad activities performed in this or previous lives. Conversely, a bad person may enjoy temporary prosperity now because of past good acts.

An analogy may help clarify the workings of the law of karma. In villages, grain is often stored in huge vertical containers; fresh grain is poured into the top, and old stored grain is taken out from the bottom. A farmer may have produced poor quality grain of, say, brand Z for the past four years and stocked it in his container. This year he produces high quality grain of, say, brand A and stores it at the top. He is therefore exasperated when he finds grain of brand Z coming out from the bottom. This illustrates how seemingly innocent people suffer in this life.

Do Bad Things Happen to Good People?

What makes the workings of karma difficult to appreciate is that most people have a karmic record that is neither white nor black, but shades of gray. That mixed record leads to reactions that often appear arbitrary. A question that vexes many when they see bad things happening to good people is, If these people were really so bad in their earlier lives as to deserve a severe reversal in this life, then wouldn't they have continued with their lower nature from their previous life into this one? If they were sinful in their past lives, how could they have been virtuous in this life for so long?

There are several possible answers. We often see even upright people occasionally succumbing to temptation and perpetrating abominable misdeeds. Of course, their virtuous nature rectifies them quickly, but still the fact remains that they did commit a greatly sinful act and are therefore liable for a reaction. So the wrongdoing, like an ugly black spot on their otherwise clean karmic slate, will result in a severe reaction in an otherwise happy future life. Shift this scenario one lifetime backwards and we have the answer to the above question. The harsh affliction coming to a good person may thus be due to an occasional but grave transgression in the previous life.

Also, one's behavior in this life is not determined only by one's tendencies in the previous life; upbringing and association in this life also play a significant role. So if a person with bad inclinations is born into a good family because of some good karma, his congenial upbringing and surroundings may empower him to shed his baggage of sinful propensities. Thus he may become a moral person in this life, but his sins from his previous lives will make him suffer despite his rectified conduct now.

Moreover, most sinful desires and tendencies manifest in adolescence, when lust starts making its presence felt. So a child may appear innocent in this life, but may have a very dark karmic record in the previous life. And the consequent sinful proclivities, though strong, may remain dormant in seed form in the heart till the teenage years. Owing to the past sins, the seemingly innocent child may even undergo a traumatic victimization, which may appear totally unwarranted from the limited perspective of this life, but which is not undue when seen from the perspective of the total karmic account. (This does not, of course, absolve their abusers of guilt. Just because the child is due to suffer does not give the perpetrators the right to take the karmic law into their own hands. They too are accountable for their actions and so will have to suffer grievously for victimizing the child.)

Thus the principles of reincarnation allow us to view life with a much broader perspective—not from the standpoint of one brief lifetime, which is nothing more than a flash in time, but from the standpoint of eternity. With this broader vision we can understand how each of us individual souls is alone responsible for our own karma. Understanding this universal and infallible system of justice is the basis of lasting peace and real happiness.

The writer W. Somerset Maugham got it right when he wrote in The Razor's Edge, "Has it occurred to you that transmigration is at once an explanation and a justification of the evil of the world? If the evils we suffer are the result of sins committed in our past lives, we can bear them with resignation and hope that if in this one we strive towards virtue, our future lives will be less afflicted."

Ignorance Is No Excuse

Implicit in the above discussion is the idea that certain things are wrong because they're against God's rules and that doing them gives bad reactions. But people sometimes ask, "What if I didn't know they were wrong when I did them? Why should I suffer now for doing what I didn't know was wrong?"

In the court of divine justice, a human being cannot claim innocence on the grounds of ignorance. The laws of nature are impartial and inescapable. Fire is going to burn anyone who puts his hand into it, even an ignorant child.

Consider this story: Once a traveler going through a forest saw a light a short distance away. When he reached there, he found, to his pleasant surprise, a magnificent palace. As no one seemed to be around, he ventured inside. He found himself in an elegant hall with furniture, cushions, fans, and other luxuries. He also saw a dining table full of delicacies. Seeing no one around, he ate, relaxed on the sofa under the fan, and had a good time.

One doesn't have to be an expert moralist to figure out that the traveler was not doing the right thing. The amenities were not his to enjoy. Although the owner might not be immediately visible, it was the traveler's duty to find out about the owner and act according to whatever rules the owner might have formulated for visitors. The owner has every right to punish a trespasser.

Similarly the world we live in is like the palace: all our needs—air, water, heat, light, and so on—are provided for. So before using these gifts, every human being must inquire about the maker and the owner of the world—God—and the rules according to which he expects the inhabitants of the world to operate. Action without such basic common sense invites trouble. A human being cannot presumptuously exploit everything around him, harm others for his own selfish interests, and then claim protection from the law of karma on the grounds of ignorance.

Moreover, our being ignorant about the laws of karma is not accidental or arbitrary; it is a result of past bad acts. We may be born in an environment where we get little or no opportunity or encouragement to know about God, and so we may be ignorant about karma. But we may get such a birth because in our previous life we had the chance to hear about God but we didn't care. Therefore, in response to our past desire to avoid God, we are now born into a situation where we don't have to hear about him.

Still, irrespective of our past acts, God does not want us to be victimized by ignorance. Therefore he gives us scriptures, which are like the manual for life, and he sends his devotees to spread awareness about the scriptural principles. Krishna explains in the Gita (15.10–11) that the transmigration of the soul under the laws of karma is visible for the wise, who see with the vision of scriptural knowledge, but is invisible for the deluded, who insist on seeing with material vision.

Good Without God?

"Of course I believe in karma," someone may say. "But I don't bother myself with doubtful sectarian religious concepts like God. I just believe in being good and doing good to others, in living honestly and not harming others. I don't deserve to be punished."

Here's another story: Once a gang of thieves robbed a bank and fled to the forest, where their leader turned to the others and spoke with utmost gravity, "We should all be honest, principled gentlemen. So let's not try to cheat each other, but share this money equally among ourselves."

Obviously, such honesty among thieves has no value. Similarly, we have not created even one of the things in the world we reside in, not even the bodies we live in. The Ishopanishad (Mantra 1) asserts, "Everything animate and inanimate within the universe is owned and controlled by the Supreme Lord." So when we neglect God, claim his property as our own, and decide to be "good" among ourselves without even acknowledging God, how are we better than the "honest" thieves? In the eyes of the universal government, we are thieves and will be penalized by the inexorable law of karma.

Thus goodness without God will not save us from the clutches of karmic reactions. It is important to understand the definition of sin in this connection. Sin is more than just activity that harms others. From the absolute standpoint, Srila Prabhupada explains, "the root of sin is deliberate disobedience of the laws of nature through disregarding the proprietorship of the Lord." (Ishopanishad, Mantra 1, Purport). So even goodness without God is sinful.

Beyond Karma

One might correctly conclude at this point, "Okay, I'll learn all of God's rules, follow them strictly, and guarantee myself a future with no suffering."

Well, that's easier said than done. There are so many rules that it's impossible to not break any of them. For example, Krishna doesn't want us to kill any living being. But just by walking, driving, chewing—living!—we end up killing germs, insects, and other living beings. And even if we manage to live a largely sinless life, we still have to suffer the inevitable miseries of material existence: birth, death, old age, and disease.

So what's the solution? We have to act only for Krishna, under the guidance of a genuine spiritual master. That not only frees us from karmic reactions, but it gradually awakens our innate love for Krishna. We are all his beloved children, and when we learn to love him we become entitled to live an eternal, enlightened, and joyful life in his abode, the kingdom of God. And that's the real goal of life, not trying to make ourselves comfortable through repeated births in the material world. Therefore Krishna concludes the Gita (18.65–66) by urging us to go beyond ordinary good acts to pure devotion and assuring us that we will then not only be saved from all sinful reactions, but will also return to him to live happily forever.   ● ● ●

The Science of Karma

What is karma? How does it act? Questions like these are much more common today than a few decades ago. This is evident not only from the fact that the word 'karma' has a place in the English dictionary, but also from the fact that Gallup polls show an increase in percentage of people, not only in the eastern world, but also in the western world, who believe in karma. However, karma is not just a belief system; it is a precise science. Even more important is that it is a science of consequences, consequences that we ourselves have to bear in our lives. Therefore it's vital to understand this science..

The Logic of Karma

1. All of nature obeys laws

The law of karma is: For every action there is equal and opposite reaction. In the Bible, it is phrased as: As you sow, so shall you reap.

Science has discovered that all of nature obeys laws. From the microscopic to the macroscopic, for any interaction of any kind, nature follows laws. In fact, science is nothing but a study and application of nature's laws. If all of nature is governed by laws, why should we humans be an exception to such laws?

There is a saying: we can never break God's laws; we can only break ourselves against God's laws. If somebody says, "I don't believe in the law of gravity" and jumps from the top of a ten-storied building, what will happen? He will definitely not break the law of gravity, but surely he will break himself against the law. He will fall down and break his leg, or he may even break his head. Similarly, we can never break any of the laws of God. Just as the law of gravity is impartial and inexorable and acts on all physical objects indiscriminately, the law of karma is impartial and inexorable and acts on all living entities indiscriminately.

2. Normal training system

If the students study well, their parents appreciate them and give them some gifts. If they don't study nicely, the parents chastise them and reduce their pocket money. Wherever there is a superior supervisor, the normal way of training is punishment for the bad and reward for the good. Similarly, since God is the most benevolent parent and the most intelligent trainer, he also follows the same system. He uses the law of karma to train us.

Doubts About Karma

1. Why not action-reaction in one life?

Somebody may ask, "Why should I suffer now for my actions in a previous life? Why so much delay?" Different seeds fructify after different time durations. Grains harvest after two or three months, some fruit seeds produce fruits after twenty years and some seeds may even take hundred years to fructify. Every action that we do is like a seed sown. The seed will fructify and we cannot escape the result. One may say, "I don't like this fruit, I don't want it." But one will be forced to eat the fruit, even if it is thorny. The reactions will come, but different types of karma seeds (actions) have different time durations after which they fructify.

Why do different actions give reactions after different time durations? To understand this, let's probe deeper into the mechanism of karma, as is illustrated through an incident from the Mahabharata.

After the bloody Kurukshetra war, Dhritrarashtra asked Krishna, "I had hundred sons and all of them were killed in the war. Why? Krishna replied, "Fifty lifetimes ago, you were a hunter. While hunting, you tried to shoot a male bird, but it flew away. In anger, you ruthlessly slaughtered the hundred baby birds that were there in the nest. The father-bird had to watch in helpless agony. Because you caused that father-bird the pain of seeing the death of his hundreds sons, you too had to bear the pain of your hundred sons dying.

Dhritarastra said, "Ok, but why did I have to wait for fifty lifetimes?" Krishna answered, "You were accumulating punya (pious credits) during the last fifty lifetimes to get a hundred sons because that requires a lot of punya. Then you got the reaction for the papa (sin) that you have done fifty lifetimes ago."*

Krishna says in the Bhagavad-gita (4.17) *gahana karmano gatih,* that the way in which action and reaction works is very complex. God knows best which reaction has to be given at what time in what condition. Therefore, some reaction may come in this lifetime, some in the next and some in a distant future lifetime.

There is a saying, "The mills of God grind slow but they grind exceedingly fine." So, every single action will be accounted for, sooner or later. The Srimad Bhagavatam gives the example: if we have a cowshed with thousand calves and if we leave a mother cow there, she will easily find out where her calf is among those thousands. She has this mystical ability. Similarly, our karma will find us among the millions of people on this planet. There may be thousands of people going on the road but only one of them meets with an accident. It is not by chance, it's by karma. Thus, the law of karma works exceedingly fine; it may be slow to act, but no one can escape.

2. Why are the ignorant not excused?

Once a person driving on a bike came across a red signal and slowed down. Then he saw a buffalo walking confidently without considering the signal. Seeing this, he also started, and immediately, the traffic policeman stopped and fined him. He asked the policeman, "You didn't fine the buffalo, why me?" The policeman replied, "Because you are a bigger buffalo!"

The buffalo does not have the intelligence to understand the law, but we human beings do. If we are driving, it is not the government's duty to educate us about the laws of the state. It is our duty to learn the state laws. Similarly, if we are living in this world taking air, water, sunlight and food from nature, we need to follow the rules laid down by God.

If one stays at a hotel, eats, sleeps and watches TV, and so on, then obviously he will have to pay for all the facilities provided by the hotel for his comfort. If the bill is not paid, a few reminders will come. And if the bill is still not paid, severe reactions are sure to come. At that time, one can't take the stance that "I did not know that I have to pay the bill for staying at the hotel."

Similarly, it is not for material nature to teach us our duties. When we take human birth, it is for us to learn the laws of karma. After jumping from the top of a 10-story building and breaking his bones, a child cannot say, "I didn't know that if I jump from a 10-storied building, I will fall down and break my bones". The law of gravity will not excuse him. Just as the law of gravity is impartial and inexorable, so is the law of karma.

Another important point to note is that ignorance is not an excuse for sin; rather, ignorance is the consequence of sin. For example, when a person commits a crime, he is put in a jail. In a standard jail, often there are reformers who give good counsel to the prisoners so that they will become good citizens. But if in the jail also, the prisoner acts criminally and starts beating the other co-prisoners, counselors and guards, then he will be taken from the normal prison cell and put in a dark dungeon where he will be given food from the window and nobody will come to give him counsel. Why is that? Because he rejected the opportunity for counseling earlier, now he is put in a place where he gets no counseling.

Similarly, if today somebody is born in a social situation or in a cultural environment where that person never gets to know about the law of karma, then that's because he has, by his past action shown God and the material energy, the superintendent, "I am not interested in knowing about your laws; I don't care. I will do whatever I want." That's why he is put in a place where he has no opportunity for getting to know about God. The current Kali yuga is actually such a dark age. The souls who are born in Kali yuga are the ones who in the previous ages of Satya, Treta and Dwapar have shown by their actions that they don't care for the laws of God and that's why many of them are born in a situation where they don't come to know about the laws of God.

Of course, God is not just a judge; he is also a loving father. Therefore, God's mercy is greater than His justice. So even in the dark dungeon of Kali yuga, where normally no prison reformers come, the Lord sends His representatives. In this particular Kali Yuga, not only did the Lord himself come in the form of Sri Chaitanya Mahaprabhu, but he also sent his representatives in the form of Srila Prabhupada and his disciples to give the knowledge of the laws of karma to even those who by their own past karma don't deserve and don't desire to know about it. That is why, all over the world people today have the opportunity to turn towards God. Actually in everybody's life, God by His grace, arranges such circumstances at least once during the human form of life when one has the opportunity to think about "what am I living for?", "what is the purpose of life?" and "what is life all about?" That time the curtains of ignorance are just opening and the stream of enlightenment is coming through. If at that time one seeks knowledge and wisdom, then God will guide him to a place where he will surely get wisdom, and that's how a person can get spiritual knowledge even from the situation where he is deprived of spiritual knowledge.

3. Why do natural calamities kill thousands of innocent people?

Let's consider a less-known incident during the tsunami disaster that happened in the Indian subcontinent a few years ago.

On the morning of that disaster, just before the tsunami struck, some scuba divers went scuba diving into the ocean to look for jewels. When they went under water, they suddenly felt a force pushing them upwards. They struggled to resist the force till it subsided. Then they went deeper under water, did their work, came back to the surface of the ocean and swam back to the coastline – only to find that there was no coast line! While they were under the water, the tsunami had devastated everything. Just consider, the tsunami killed those who were on the land, but those who were under the water were unharmed! If these Scuba divers had ventured into the ocean a little later or a little earlier, they would have been on the surface when the killer wave hit. But by their karma they were not supposed to die at that time, so although they were closest to the tsunami, they did not die.

Another even more amazing example: During an earthquake in Gujarat, there was a mother who had a small baby sucking on her breast. Suddenly the earthquake struck and a column of the roof fell on the mother. The mother died on the spot. Almost twenty-four hour later, when the rescue workers worked their way down to the debris, they found the mother dead and the infant moving his hands and legs holding on to his mother's breast. The infant is so tender that one small blow can prove fatal for him, yet there it was safe amidst a quake that proved fatal for many healthy adults.

What we learn from incidents like these is that although natural calamities kill in mass, they don't kill blindly. Only those who have the kind of karma for which they have to die at that particular time will be killed. This is an example of mass karma.

Mass karma involves a group of people who have done different kinds of bad karmas. The reaction of their karma is that they are all supposed to die. But material nature gives that reaction to many people efficiently in one stroke through a calamity. For example, all such people may be brought together in one airplane and that airplane will crash. The person who is not supposed to die will not be on that flight perhaps because his car broke down on the way to the airport and he missed the flight.

In this way, *karmana daiva netrena* – the law of karma acts under the divine supervision of the Lord. Even in a mass calamity, not one person is killed blindly; everyone gets the reactions of their own karma.

Three Types of Actions

The word karma has several connotations. The general understanding is that karma means the actions one does. Sometimes it is also used to refer to the reactions of past actions as in the phrase "one is suffering one's karma". And in other places, karma refers to the whole system of the law of karma.

But karma, in a stricter, scriptural sense, primarily means the actions done in accordance with one's prescribed duties as mentioned in the revealed scriptures. In contrast to karma, there is vikarma - viruddha rupena karma. Vikarma refers to actions done contratry to the scriptures by the misuse of one's free will. Vikarma takes one down to the lower forms of life. Kali Yuga is full of vikarma, and the four main vikarmic activities are intoxication, meat eating , gambling and illicit sex. These four main irreligious activities lead to severe karmic reactions, which come both in future and present lives. Illicit sex leads to variety of diseases. Meat eating leads to heart problems, cancer and other diseases. Gambling causes people to lose their senses and eventually lose everything. Intoxication, which people think is very enjoyable, is actually a ritual of self torture. What starts with "cheers!" often leads to cheerless repercussions. Making a big fool of themselves, sometimes drinkers are found lying in gutters.

Different from karma and vikarma, there is akarma. Akarma doesn't mean inactivity, but activity that brings no reaction, activity that frees one from the cycle of birth and death.

Is Everything Destined?

We make our destiny by our karma (and vikarma). Destiny is something like a weather forecast on a journey. A weather forecast can tell us whether our journey from one place to another is going to be snowy or sunny. But it does not determine what we do during the journey.

In the Mahabharata, Vidura explained to Dhritarastra, "Destiny determines the consequences of our actions, not our actions themselves." This means that we are not like programmed robots that have no freewill, or no choice. Our past karma does determine what will happen in our life, but it does not determine how we will react to it.

With respect to destiny, there are two schools of thought – karmavada and daivavada. Karmavada says that "By my karma I will be successful. If I just work hard enough and smart enough, then I will become the next Bill Gates. By my sweat and my muscles, I will succeed." But if you look at the reality of life, so many people work hard and not all of them are successful. Therefore karmavada, the idea that everything depends on my actions, brings frustration and the people who follow this doctrine tend to develop inferiority complex. Thus, karmavada leads to frustration because in reality it is not our action alone that determines results.

Many times, we feel sorry when we study hard but don't get good marks. But if we are honest, we will also admit that there are times in our life when we don't study very much other than the few hours before exam and still get good marks. So the law of karma works both ways, sometimes due to our past good karma we get good reactions even when we don't do proper action.

On the other hand, daivavada means to think "everything is determined by destiny, what can I do?" Dhritarastra was trying to use daivavada to justify his inaction when Duryodhana was doing atrocities on the Pandavas. Vidura told him, "Stop your son Duryodhana from waging war against the Pandavas, let him accept Krishna's peace proposal." Dhritarashtra replied, "No, if it is a will of destiny, then who am I, a tiny mortal, to stop the will of almighty destiny?" Vidura reminded him, "You have your duty; you have the freedom to choose to do your duty or not. So you should try to stop your son to the best of your capacity." Many western thinkers and many westernized Indian thinkers misunderstand the Vedic philosophy. They think that the Vedic philosophy is fatalistic because everything is supposed to be predestined and thus this notion preempts any purposeful activity. But actually, Indians were never lazy. The world's biggest poem is the epic Mahabharata which has 110,000 verses. This is seven times bigger than the world's next two biggest poems - the Illiad and Odyssey combined together. Could lazy people have composed such a massive masterpiece? Literature, architecture, art, and even science and mathematics had reached great heights in Vedic times. All this cannot be the products of lazy people. Thus, Vedic philosophy is not daivavadi.

The real Vedic understanding is that the results of our actions are determined both by our actions of this life and the reactions of the actions of past life. For example, the sowing of seeds and the ploughing of fields is the karma of the farmer. But whether it will rain sufficiently or not is the daiva. Simply by sowing the seeds and ploughing the fields there will be no harvest unless there is sufficient rain. Similarly, simply by sufficient rains, without sowing the seeds and ploughing the fields, there will be no harvest. Therefore, the Vedic scriptures explain that you must just do your duty, the right karma, and not bother about the daiva part. Not bothering about daiva means not letting our destiny discourage us from doing our duty, whatever it is. This is so because if we do our karma now, it will give fruits if daiva is favorable now. But even if daiva is not favorable now, then this right karma is still creating the favorable daiva for the future. Therefore there is no reason to get discouraged or disheartened while performing one's prescribed duty.

But it is important to note that even if a person does good karma, that good karma will bring good reactions and this means he has to still stay in the material world to enjoy those good reactions. For example, if somebody offers free water taps in charity, that is certainly good karma, but the reaction for it is that he has to take another birth in which he will never suffer from shortage of water. He might take birth near a lake or a river. Similarly, if somebody gives school textbooks in charity, then in his next life he might become the owner of a printing factory. But birth in the material world means he has to grow old, get diseased, has to die, and has to suffer the three-fold miseries of material existence.

Thus, even by good karma we don't get out of the material world, because good karma is not necessary Godly karma or akarma. As long as we are forgetful of God, we stay on in the material world. The real way to come out of this material world, which is the place of suffering, is by developing our devotional service to God, which is actually akarma.

Benefits of Knowledge of Karma:

1. Social

The understanding of karma has a lot of bearing on the present state of society. Only when we understand karma will the call to morality have any meaning. Imagine you come to a city where it reads, "Welcome to our city. There is no police force in this city; please follow the laws." Do you think anybody will follow the laws? Nobody will. Today's society has become like that. The legal system is known to be weak and corrupt. People think "If I am just clever enough, influential enough or cunning enough, then I can do whatever I want and I can get away with it." So if we want morality in society, we need to educate people to understand the law of karma. Then and then alone will the call to morality, or the call to ethics, have any meaning. That's why it is said that fear of God is the beginning of wisdom, just like for a child, fear of his father is generally the main impetus for him to study. How many of us have been chastised by our parents and forced to study? Almost everyone, sometime or the other. At that time, we didn't find it pleasant, but later on we appreciate our parents for it. If at that time we wouldn't have studied, we would have been in trouble. So here it is seen that fear is very often an impetus for doing our duty. Similarly, if there is no proper understanding of the law of karma and the fear of the karmic rections, most people will have no impetus to do good karma.

2. Individual

Perhaps even more important is that the understanding of the law of karma helps us to makes sense of our present condition and gives us the strength to face suffering. Actually, a person without spiritual knowledge is like a person who is blindfolded and is beaten from top, bottom, left, right, front and back without knowing from where the next blow is coming and why. At any moment, one can be put into such situations for which one is left groping for answers for questions like "why me, why now or why this?"

When we become well versed with the science of karma, it's like the blindfold is removed. It's a big relief.

When I was in a hospital for several months due to sickness, I was looking at other patients and talking to them. One of the things they couldn't understand and which was emotionally crushing them was, "All my relatives and friends are happy; they are in their homes, they are in their parties and enjoying life (nobody is really enjoying life actually, but that is the illusion). Why am I suffering alone here?" This thought crushes people completely when they are faced with tough situations in life. But for me as a devotee, I knew that it was just my karma, "Just let me endure it and it will get over".

In this way, the knowledge of the law of karma helps us to make sense out of our suffering and face it with calmness.

Secondly, it helps us prepare for the future with confidence. It is not that just by knowing about karma, we will become free from suffering. But we become like a sick patient who has understood what the disease is and how to cure it. The pain is still there, but it is going to decrease. But for the person who doesn't know the cure, his pain is just going to increase and, on top of that, he will be feeling helpless and dejected. But a knowledgeable person knows sooner or later all the sufferings will come to an end.

W Somerset Maugham, in his book *The Razor's edge* writes, "Has it occurred to you that transmigration is at once an explanation and justification of the evil of the world. If the evil we suffer is the result of sins committed in our past lives, we can bear them with resignation and hope that if in this one we strive towards virtue, our future lives will be less afflicted."

Thus, the science of karma is not a science of condemnation, it is science of redemption. It's message is not "You are sinful, suffer." But it's message is, "Whatever be your past karma for which you are suffering now, just surrender to God and His grace will come upon you and you will be saved."

Complete Freedom From Karma
By Devotional Service

Beyond good karma, there is akarma, devotional service, which brings the ultimate freedom from karmic entanglement. Let's see how. Devotional service provides us with four great gifts:

1. Discrimination of right and wrong

When we practice devotional service, the Lord as the Parmatma in our heart grants us the knowledge to make the right choices. All of us can, at some time or the other, hear the voice of conscience (*vivek buddhi* in Sanskrit). When we start doing something wrong, then the voice from inside warns, "Don't do this." If you want to do something right, this voice says, "Yes, do this now." So, when we chant the holy name of Krishna, when we practice devotional service, this inner voice becomes stronger and it guides us to make the right choices in life. Thus devotional service can grant us the knowledge to gradually become disentangled from all karma.

2. Determination to follow right and avoid wrong

Devotional service saves us from

a)   doing further bad karma, and

b)   the craving to do bad karma.

Chanting of the holy names gives us the inner satisfaction that enables us to say no to all the sinful pleasure of this world. Thus, we not only know the right choices, but we also get the willpower to make those right choices.

3. Minimization of sinful reactions

Certain reactions are going to come to us from past. But devotional service helps us in minimizing those reactions. For devotees, the Lord gives just a token reaction instead of the complete one. That token is given so that the devotee does not forget the miserable nature of this world.

Once, a devotee cut his finger when he was cutting vegetables. He went to Srila Prabhupada and asked why his finger got cut, even though he was cutting the vegetables for Krishna. Prabhupada told him that his neck was supposed to be cut, but since he has become a devotee, the Lord only gave him token reaction in the form of the cut finger.

4. Inner strength to face suffering

Whatever be the residual karma that comes upon us, devotional service grants us the strength to tolerate that suffering. One of the names of Krishna is Karuna-nidhi, reservoir of compassion. Our acharyas give an example of how Krishna gives us strength to endure our sufferings. When a child is going to school, the mother knows, "Today my child has not done his homework properly and the teacher is going to beat him on his hand with the stick." The mother doesn't want the child to be beaten and at the same time wants the child to be disciplined. So she sends the child to school, but gives him thick gloves to wear. When the teacher beats him, he feels the impact but he doesn't feel the pain. Similarly, when a devotee is supposed to get suffering because of his misdeeds from material nature, who is like the teacher, Krishna, who is like the mother, gives his devotees his holy name, chanting which gives them the strength to tolerate and transcend their pain. So externally a devotee may seem to be in pain, but internally because of his remembrance of the holy name, he doesn't feel the suffering. And the more advanced a devotee is, the more he can experience the reality of this protection from Krishna.

In conclusion, irrespective of whatever our past karma may be, the spiritually scientific process of devotional service is the best path to the highest happiness in this life and the next.

(The above article is a transcript of a talk given by the author to a gathering of college students)   ● ● ●

Natural Calamities – Why? What to do?

(This article was written in Jan 2005 soon after a tsunami wave struck the Indian subcontinent)

The tsunami wave that lashed several Indian Ocean countries has taken a toll of over a hundred thousand people. The magnitude of the disaster has shocked the whole world. Many countries have rushed to offer humanitarian aid. Scientists are proposing improving detection technologies to decrease casualties in future calamities.

Natural calamities are a display of an awesome power immensely and fearfully greater than the human. They jolt us out of our complacent routines and impel us to think: Why do such natural disasters occur? How should we respond to them? Can we do anything to prevent their recurrence? Does God exist? If He does, why does He not stop such calamities?

The Law of Consequences

According to the great spiritual traditions of the world, we are answerable to God for all our actions. The Vedic texts of ancient India give the most cogent and coherent understanding of this system of cosmic accountability. Known as the law of karma, this universal, infallible law of action-reaction gives all of us our due pleasures and pains according to our actions, whether right or wrong. The Vedic texts therefore contain prescriptions and proscriptions to guide us in our actions. Anyone who violates these injunctions has only himself to blame for the consequences.

To some extent we ourselves can see how the law of karma chastises transgressors. Lung and other respiratory disorders penalize smokers; liver diseases afflict alcoholics; and AIDS and other STDs punish illicit sex-mongers. We may not be able to trace the causes of all the sufferings of each person, but humility will allow us to admit the limitations of our vision. We do not and can not know about the karmic deeds and misdeeds of others – or even ourselves - in past lives. Even in this life, we cannot fully know everything that everyone – or anyone - has done. The Vedic texts give us a thorough philosophical understanding of the inherent goodness of God as our Supreme Father and the infallible benevolent nature of His jurisprudence. Therefore, they assure us that anyone suffering in any way is reaping what he has himself sown earlier.

The Price for Murder

Two activities declared to be monstrously criminal in the cosmic penal system, but which are rampant in our society are animal slaughter and abortion. From God's viewpoint, these two activities are brutal; His more powerful children – humans - are ruthlessly and systematically slaughtering His weaker and helpless children – animals and infants. And the main reason for this ghastly massacre is often the selfish hedonistic desire for the enjoyment of the tongue and the genitals. Especially despicable is the slaughter of cows. The cow is like our mother because she nourishes us with her milk. And we "scientifically advanced cultured moderns" erect factories of death to murder our bovine mothers. Not only that, nowadays human mothers, who according to poets are supposed to be "the embodiments of selfless love", murder their own children even before they have seen the light of the day. Thus we live in a civilization (maybe 'devilization' is a better word) of murderers.

Of course we have invented shrewd justifications to rationalize (rational lies) our misdeeds. A few of them with their refutations are:

* ♣ We need proteins coming from animal flesh for health (Modern scientific findings have clearly proven that meat doesn't aid, but harms, our health; and there are many other sources of proteins too).

* ♣ We need to control the population and so must encourage abortion (Then why kill only the life inside the womb? Why not the life outside? Or why not control the sexual urge?)

❖ The embryo is only a tissue; so abortion is just a tissue removal. (The embryo breathes and grows, which is what all of us do too. So if a serial killer murders us, is that also tissue removal?)

A murderer may justify his murder, but the law of the state will still punish him. Similarly we may justify or even legalize abortion and animal slaughter, but the law of karma will still punish us.

Statistics show the horrendous massacre that we cause everyday.

❖ Total cattle slaughtered in 2004 = 16500000 = 44657 /day

❖ Total annual abortions worldwide = 46 million abortions = 126027 /day.

Thus the toll of life that we take daily (170684 deaths) is far more than the toll of human life that the tsunami took. So in a karmic sense we deserve far more, we have got less than what we deserve. The tsunami disaster is not nature's cruelty; it is karmic justice.

Karma in Action

Do we have to accept the existence of the law of karma on faith? Or is there any empirical way to understand its existence? The Vedic scriptures explain that karmic punishment comes upon humanity in the form of three types of miseries called the tri-vidha tapa. If the law of karma were true, then these miseries should have increased over the last century in which karmic misdeeds have multiplied manifold.

The three types of miseries along with their status over the last century are given below:

1. Miseries caused by our own bodies and minds (adhyatmika-klesha): e.g. fever, indigestion, stress, depression

We have eradicated some diseases, but many more incurable, debilitating and excruciatingly painful diseases – AIDS, syphilis, cancer, Alzheimer's disease, to name a few - have come up. And the mind is ravaging the human race like never before in recorded human history. Psychological and psychosomatic disorders leading to stress, depression, insanity, addictions and suicides are causing havoc in the lives of many even so-called successful people

2. **Miseries caused by other living beings (adhibhautika-klesha): e.g. mosquitoes, competitors, superiors, relatives**

Crime, violence, murder and terrorism are tormenting us more than ever before. Human relationships have hit an all-time low. We proud moderns are unable to trust our own spouses, parents or children. Divorces are destroying the family, the basic building block of stable society.

3. **Miseries caused by higher natural powers (adhidaivika-klesha): e.g. extreme heat or cold, floods, storms**

Over the last century natural calamities have been increasing in both their frequency and ferocity. According to the International Society for Disaster Reduction (ISDR), there were three times as many great natural disasters in the 1990s as in the 1960s, while disaster costs increased more than nine-fold in the same period. The deaths from natural disasters have increased from 53,000 in 1990 to 83,000 in 2003.

Therefore for the intelligent, the reality of karma is not difficult to see. We can never break the law; we can only break ourselves against the law. A skeptic who jumps from the top of a hundred-story building can imagine that there is no law of gravity – but only till he hits the ground. Similarly we can go on with our godless sinful ways, imagining that there are no karmic laws – but only till the karmic reactions hit us as tsunamis or terrorism or wars or ecological disasters or in some other way.

Harmonize With God

So if we actually want to minimize the casualties due to natural calamities, better detection techniques alone will not suffice. Even if we detect a calamity in time and save ourselves from it, our karma will still detect us and give us our due suffering in some other way. Unlike the human penal system, karma is a flawless system of justice. By science or some other material means, we may alter how, when and where our karmic reactions come upon us, but we will never be able to escape them. Therefore, if we want to be saved from suffering, we have to scrupulously avoid bad karma ourselves by giving up illicit sex and meat eating, which are the root causes of abortion and animal slaughter. Further we can protect ourselves from our past misdeeds by re-harmonizing ourselves with God. This can be very easily and effectively done by adopting the non-sectarian, universal meditation on the holy names of God, especially the maha-mantra Hare Krishna Hare Krishna Krishna Krishna Hare Hare Hare Rama Hare Rama Rama Rama Hare Hare. When a criminal becomes law-abiding, the severity of punishment is often reduced. This principle is all the more true in cosmic justice, for God is our benevolent Father. Then even in this life and in this world, by harmonizing with God we can be much more peaceful and joyful than by defying God.

And if we wish to truly help our fellow citizens on this planet, humanitarian aid will not be enough. We have to offer spiritual aid by giving the enlightenment and empowerment that comes from God consciousness. That alone will equip them to protect themselves from both bad karma and its reactions.

The Shelter beyond Calamity

Of course even if we live in harmony with God, this world will still remain a place of death. Many of us may have been shocked to see the ghastly sights of so many dead bodies in the aftermath of the tsunami. But statistics tell us that the daily deaths in the whole world number 147945, which exceeds the total tsunami toll till date. If death is so rampant and universal in the world, why are we so shocked by it? Because we have specialized in hiding and forgetting the reality of death when it takes its toll gradually through "normal" ways. But when death takes a sudden and massive toll, our delusions are exposed - at least temporarily.

The Vedic scriptures urge us to not dream in vain for a happy life in this world, where death may overcome us at any moment. None of us wants to die; yet each one of us will be forced to die. This existential incompatibility indicates that we belong, not to this world of death, but to a world of eternal life. The Vedic texts explain that we are not mortal material bodies, but immortal spirit souls. We belong to an eternal spiritual world, the kingdom of God, where we live forever in a joyous harmony with God as His beloved children. When we rebel against God's authority, we are placed in the material world to experience the imagined joys and the real sorrows of living independent of Him. Equipped with material bodies – human or subhuman, we try to play God, competing and fighting to control and enjoy as much as we can. But no matter how great we become or imagine ourselves to be, nature ultimately crushes our egos through death.

The Vedic texts inform us that, during our troubled journey through this material world, we have gone through millions of lives. Therefore rather than being shocked at seeing so many deaths, we can soberly remember that we have ourselves undergone the trauma of death thousands of times. And the same ordeal awaits us again in the not-too-distant future. So the Bhagavad-gita (13.8-12) urges all intelligent persons to recognize the inevitable, inescapable evils of birth, old age, disease and death that haunt all life in this world. The Gita further urges us to re-awaken our dormant spiritual natures by living in devotion to God. Thus we can detach ourselves from material things which will be snatched away at the time of death and attach ourselves to God, with whom we will be eternally united after death.

The Vedic scriptures therefore assert that the sufferings of this world are a pointer to, a reminder of, our eternal existence. A fever impels us to take medicine to cure ourselves. The heat of the fire causes us to instantly withdraw our finger and thus save it from being burnt. Similarly, the sufferings of this world impel us to redirect our hopes of shelter and happiness from this temporary material world to the eternal spiritual world. The intelligent course of action therefore is to prepare to return back to our home, the spiritual world.

Are we ready to wake up from the dream of safety and enjoyment in this world of danger and death? Or will we sleep on till our dream turns into a nightmare, by when it may be too late to wake up? This is the ultimate question raised by the tsunami disaster, which each one of us will have to individually answer.   ● ● ●

Artificial Rains –
Imaginary Gains, Real Pains

(This article was written when the Maharashtra government. attempted to produce, with much fanfare, artificial rains through cloud seeding)

'Artificial rains soothe Maharashtra.' Headlines like these have been a frequent sight in recent newspapers. The image of a political leader and a scientist flying in an airplane, shooting a chemical spray into the clouds and rains showering down is certainly mind-grabbing. For people tormented by prolonged water scarcity, artificial rainfall seems to be a graphic demonstration of the power of technology to counter human suffering caused by the vagaries of nature

"Suitable" Clouds

A serious examination of the subject, however, reveals a picture quite different from what is made out by the hype. Firstly the extent to which the so-called artificial rains are caused by forces other than the natural is open to question. The name 'artificial rains' is misleading as the entire mechanism involved in producing rains is not replicated artificially; all that is done is the rainfall  from the naturally formed clouds is stimulated by artificial means. Sometimes, due to super-cooling, clouds, though present in the sky for a long time, do not produce rains. By cloud seeding - releasing certain hygroscopic chemicals like silver iodide into the clouds, the precipitation and hence rainfall is said to be enhanced and accelerated. Contrary to the hype, cloud seeding can therefore offer no relief to drought-affected areas as there are generally no clouds in those areas. Also ordinary cumulus clouds - the kind of clouds most often found in the sky - are too small to produce any worthwhile rains by seeding. Cloud seeding requires the presence of a "suitable" cloud. The definition of "suitable" is such that the cloud might well go on to produce precipitation even if it is not seeded at all! This is evident from the following table associated with the large-scale vertical motion of air, assuming that the potential for cloud formation (moisture and temperature distribution with height) is otherwise favorable.

Strong descent	No clouds – nothing to seed (typical drought conditions)
Strong ascent	Lots of clouds - seeding isn't needed, as natural precipitation is virtually inevitable and substantial rainfalls are likely
Weak ascent	Clouds - considered poor targets for seeding since seeded clouds usually die out and new clouds may not form at all
Moderate ascent	Isolated Best chance for seeding gains, but proper seeding strategy is needed and the chances for large total rainfall (natural + effect of seeding) are only marginal

Secondly, due to unpredictable wind motions, the area where cloud seeding will cause rains cannot be controlled. American meteorologist Chuck Doswell has explained that the rain at the ground from a seeder's typical target cloud – a fairly large cloud 10 km tall and 10 km in diameter - would be on the order of 1/100th of an inch! Not much of a result ... just about enough to wet the sidewalk. Hence it needs to be seriously examined whether the Rs 5.6 crore that the Mahararashtra government has spent on Project Varsha – money that is taken from the pocket of the hardworking taxpayer – actually leads to commensurate returns. In this connection, the Policy Statement on Planned and Inadvertent Weather Modification, issued by the American Meteorological Society is especially significant. It states, in layman's terms, that with the exception of some highly specific situations, the results of carefully controlled scientific experiments have produced essentially inconclusive results regarding the effectiveness of cloud seeding to enhance precipitation. It is clear that seeding does affect clouds, but what is not clear is that, over the long haul, economically beneficial rainfall results from the process. Does that strike you as a dazzling endorsement of cloud seeding?

Side-Effects

Thirdly, the track record of human intervention in natural processes shows that it inevitably produces some unintended harmful consequences. A typical example is the widespread soil infertility resulting from using fertilizers to temporarily increase crop yield. Moreover often the negative impact of a seemingly harmless application of technology becomes clear only after years of widespread use of that technology. And by that time replacing the harmful technology requires major social and economic changes, which are often next to impossible. A striking example is the pollution and global warming caused by the modern automobile-centered lifestyle.

Considering this track record, it requires a considerable leap of faith to believe that cloud seeding will have no side-effects. In fact, American scientist Johnny Micou, among many others, has pointed out that cloud seeding can lead to rain suppression, flooding, tornadoes and silver iodide toxicity. Those supporting cloud seeding argue that these harmful consequences have not been scientifically proven. But this is false logic because neither have the benefits of seeding been scientifically verified. This sophistry can be better understood by examining similarities from other fields. In pharmaceutical research, when drug companies want to test a new drug, they bear the expense for the research and they pay the patients on whom the drugs are tested. It is a travesty of justice that, in the case of cloud seeding, experimentation involving an unproven technology with dubious benefits and unexamined harms is done using the taxpayers' hard-earned money – with the taxpayers themselves being used as the laboratory rats!

Our Dependence on Nature

Of course the desire to reduce the sufferings of the drought-afflicted is not wrong, but the method of forcible extortion of the rains from the clouds is an invitation for disaster. The technological growth of the last few centuries has been character ized by the belief system that humans could command the forces of nature to bend to   human will if humanity could develop a proper understanding of those forces through science. The recent decades have however witnessed a growing scientific awareness that humanity would be better off trying to harmonize with nature than trying to force her into submission. This is firstly because science has started learning the hard way that human intervention in natural processes disturbs their delicate and intricate balance and leads to unforeseen counterproductive consequences, as discussed earlier. And secondly the sheer magnitude of the forces involved in nature is awesome; indeed the power of humanity as compared to that of nature is like that of a microscopic mite as compared to that of an elephant on the flea on whose back the mite lives. The extent of humanity's dependence on nature is best illustrated through the medium that is valued the most in modern society - money. In the science magazine Nature, issue dated 15 May, 1997, researchers from the University of Maryland presented the world with a "bill to nature" for $16 trillion to $54 trillion US dollars per annum for the natural resources and raw materials that humanity takes from nature: food, water, air, lumber, rocks, metals, jewels, oil and so forth. Our cosmic bill to the sun is far more staggering. American scientist Dr. Edwin Kessler has calculated that, if we had to pay 5 cents per kilowatt-hour (a relatively cheap price) for the energy provided by the sun every day over the state of Oklahoma (which covers an area of about 200 thousand km2), the cost would be around $60 billion per day!

Consciousness Controls Nature

Modern science would have us believe that these forces of nature, which so benevolently provide us with the necessities of life, are governed by cosmic chance. The Vedic texts, which are a vast body of profound knowledge coming from ancient India, consider this understanding to be naïve and uninformed. Vedic science posits the existence in the cosmos not only of physical elements and forces, but also of conscious elements. Where modern science sees only matter and its transformations, Vedic science sees the action of a supreme conscious intelligence behind everything.

The idea of a conscious intelligence orchestrating nature is much more scientifically acceptable now then it was a few decades ago. No longer do scientists feel so cocksure that the totality of nature can be explained in mechanistic terms. The more scientists have studied nature, the more they are stunned by the astounding order, the awesome energy, the incredible intricacy and the masterly harmony that characterizes every aspect of nature.

The following remark of Dr John C Cartron, emeritus Chairman of the Science and Mathematics Department at the University of Minnesota, represents the mature scientific response to the testimony of nature:" ... Hence our logical and inescapable conclusion is not only that creation occurred but that it was brought about according to the plan and will of a person endowed with supreme intelligence and knowledge (omniscience), and the power to bring it about and keep it running according to plan (omnipotence) always and everywhere throughout the universe (omnipresence). That is to say, we accept unhesitatingly the fact of the existence of the supreme spiritual being, God, the creator and the director of the universe."

More and more empiric evidence is also coming up to confirm this conclusion. 'Consciousness controls nature' is the working principle of the New Age gardeners, who seek communion with their plants and crops as a means for higher yields. A vivid example of New Age gardening is the famous Findhorn farm community in Scotland, which grows amazing flowers and vegetation on barren,

sandy soil. Dorothy Maclean, a member of the original family that started farming in Findhorn in the 1960s, explains their gardening secret: she communicates telepathically with the nature spirits and "devas" in charge of the garden and all the gardening is done exactly according to their instructions. Many people are likely to be skeptical about this sort of claims, but the miraculous abundance is well-documented and is there for everyone to see - and it continues to defy traditional scientific notions. Another successful New Age garden is Perelandra, in Virginia, USA, which was started by

Machalle Small Wright in 1976, after being inspired by Findhorn's wondrous results. These days any trendy urban bookshop can supply at least a few "deva gardening manuals" - The Deva Handbook: How to work with Nature's Subtle Energies, or Plant Spirit Medicine, or Garden Notes from the Nature Devas (helpful hints that enable you to communicate and learn on the devic level to heal the earth)

Vedic Insights

The Vedic texts go one step ahead. Not only do they assert that a Supreme Conscious Being, God, controls all the natural phenomena, but they also stress the need for harmonizing with Him. The Vedic texts assert that, just as while living in a country the citizens are duty-bound to obey the state government and pay taxes for the utilities that it provides, similarly, while living in the universe, we are expected to obey the cosmic government headed by God and pay cosmic taxes for the universal utilities of light, heat, air and water that we take from the cosmos. The method of remitting the cosmic taxes is through the medium of elaborate and intricate fire-sacrifices (yajnas) accompanied by the precise chanting of specific mantras.

On superficial examination, the yajnas may appear to be a colossal waste of resources: ghee, silk and grains are just put into fire to be reduced to ashes. But those who are intelligent enough to be not deluded by externals can, on deeper study see, the profound principles of cosmic cooperation that are activated through the  yajnas. The medium of economic exchange is known to vary greatly in accordance with the prevailing socio-cultural setting. For example, if an ancient from the Vedic age is transported through time into our society, he will be aghast to see the amount of value we ascribe to the pieces of paper that we call currency notes. Just as our medium of exchange – money – is unintelligible to an ancient, the Vedic medium of intra-universal exchange – sanctified fire and sound – is incomprehensible to us. What an intelligent person focuses on is not the medium of exchange, but the principle. We give valuable things – our time and energy – to get money and we get important things – the necessities of life – by giving money. Similarly Vedic followers offer oblations into the sacred fire to appease the Cosmic Controller and in return receive profusely all the gifts of nature. The proof of the pudding is in the eating and similarly the proof of the authenticity of the yajnas is in the resulting prosperity. The prosperity of ancient India is well-known and is almost legendary, as is described both in the Vedic literatures themselves such as the Shrimad Bhagavatam as well as by many scholars and historians including the renowned Indologist A L Basham in his world-famous 'The Wonder That Was India'. This natural prosperity of India resulting from cosmic harmonization continued till even a few hundred years ago. Indeed, the present world's most prosperous nation, USA, was discovered when explorers were searching for new navigational routes to tap the prosperity of India! Savants in Vedic science explain that the neglect and / or rejection of the Vedic principles by modern Indians has caused the present downfall of India.

Spiritual Solution

Vedic science thus reveals the root cause of the present water-crisis: non-cooperation with the cosmic government. The present attempts to forcibly extort water from the clouds to counter the drought constitute a hi-tech robbery; they are like the attempts of a recalcitrant citizen to burglarize the public water tank on finding his water supply cut off due to not having paid the water tax. The citizen may get away till he is caught, but then he will be in more trouble than what he started off with. Similarly technological attempts to extract the resources of nature by coercion may reap short-term benefits, but, in the long run, they will be counterproductive. Just as the citizen needs to pay the water tax to get his supply restored, we, modern people, as citizens in the universal state, need to harmonize with the cosmic government to have the supply of the universal utility, rain-water, restored.

In the modern times, the Vedic texts recommend a method of cosmic cooperation that is more pragmatic than yajnas. Fire-sacrifices are next to impossible nowadays due to the prohibitive costs involved as well as due to non-availability of competent priests to perform these intricate rituals. Rather in the present age of Kali, all Vedic sacrifices culminate in the sonic glorification of the Supreme Lord, as confirmed in the Bhagavad-gita (yajnananm japa yajno 'smi). Sonic control of matter should not be difficult for us to relate to; most of us have probably heard of fans that turn on and off by the clapping of hands. From the Vedic perspective, this sort of sonic technology is very crude and rudimentary. The sonic technology, or, more accurately, the mantra technology, that the Vedic texts talk about is of a level of sophistication that modern science is yet to fathom. In principle, mantras are said to be highly empowered sound vibrations that are attuned with various phenomena in nature and the predominating deity controlling them. Hence the chanting of the specified Vedic mantras, especially the maha-mantra Hare Krishna Hare Krishna Krishna Krishna Hare Hare Hare Rama Hare Rama Rama Rama Hare Hare, can harmonize modern society with the cosmic state and thus bring about sustainable prosperity.

Is it blind faith?

The idea of chanting of certain mantras causing rains may be difficult to digest for those of us who have been educated since childhood in modern matter-based scientific notions of the universe. However if we just take off the science-imposed blinkers on our intellectual vision and have an objective look at nature, we cannot but be wonder-struck. Whenever there is water scarcity in any area, water tankers are at once deployed there at a considerable expenditure to provide relief. In the earth all the land-locked areas are subject to potential water scarcity as all the water is concentrated in the oceans, rivers and lakes. Imagine millions of gallons of water being moved through the airways to provide relief. Sounds unbelievable, but that is what a cloud is – a mobile, air-borne

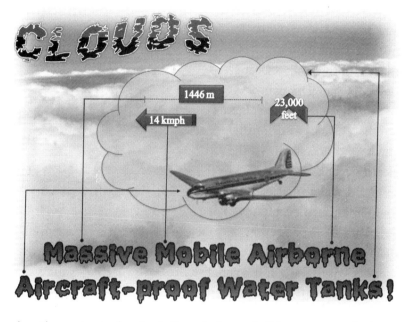

gigantic water-tank. And the design of this water tank is so astounding that an entire airplane can pass right through it and still there is not much leakage loss! Further, pressure and temperature variations cause the water vapor to form cloud droplets, which come together to form rains drops. But raindrops tend to grow only to a certain size. What if raindrops grew to huge sizes? Then the rains would, instead of sustaining life, destroy it. Experience shows that raindrops usually come down in the right size, and gently, seldom hurting even a blade of grass or the most delicate flower. Thus it certainly requires blind faith to believe that all this wondrous and benevolent arrangement is happening by itself, by chance. No wonder then that the renowned physicist Kelvin has said, "If you think deeply enough you will be forced by science to believe in God."

Once we have scaled the intellectual hurdle in understanding how God controls nature, the effect of mantras on natural phenomena becomes easier to comprehend. Imagine an illiterate villager, with no prior experience of modern medicine, coming to an allopathic doctor and complaining of severe arm pain. After due diagnosis, the doctor prescribes a painkiller and a medicine for oral administration. The villager protests, "Doctor, don't fool me. The pain is in the arm, not the mouth." Just as the uneducated rustic cannot understand the scientific connection between the oral medicine and the muscular pain, uninformed people may not be able to comprehend, with the few grams of their grey matter, the higher dimensional science by which mantra technology can activate rainfall. John Milton has therefore wisely said in his Paradise Lost, "Accuse not Nature, she hath done her part; do thou but thine." ● ● ●

Sexuality and Spirituality

The increasing availability of obscene, even pornographic, material in the media, the abortive governmental attempts to legislate it and the criticism of this moral policing by some sections of the media – all these have brought to the forefront the vexed issue of what constitutes acceptable behavior in a rapidly changing world with mutable moral standards. Alarmed at the latest onslaught on traditional cultural values, the conservatives protest vehemently, "This is against our culture; things are going too far." The radical

modernists retort, "If that's the way we find pleasure in life, what's wrong? We are not harming anyone. Why should we deprive ourselves of enjoyment just for the sake of some outdated moral norms?" Most people watch on, bemused, undecided or indifferent.

Vedic Insights

From the Vedic perspective, the current mess is no surprise. After all we are living in Kali Yuga, an age of moral anarchy and spiritual insanity. A Vedic seer would tell us that the roots of the present moral imbroglio lie in spiritual ignorance. When people addicted to material enjoyment are left to decide for themselves the subjective goals of their respective lives, how can society have a standard set of moral principles to regulate enjoyment? Without an objective purpose for life, how can there be objective moral codes? Therefore spirituality is the foundation for the edifice of morality. Without being rooted in spiritual knowledge, moral standards will inevitably be shaken and shattered by the stormy winds of changing social trends.

The Vedic texts urge us that, before plunging into a frenzied fight for enjoyment, we take time out to inquire: Who is the 'I' whom we seek to offer enjoyment? When confronted with this fundamental question of identity, most modern people can only blink in bewilderment; even the best modern philosophers can only shrug in indifference. In marked contrast, the Vedic texts clearly and confidently assert that we are not products of matter; we are souls, spiritual beings encaged in material bodies. We belong to the spiritual realm, where we rejoice eternally in a personal loving relationship with the supreme spiritual being, best known by the name Krishna (meaning the All-Attractive). By causeless misuse of our free will, when we refuse to love and serve Krishna, we are placed in the world of matter. Here we are offered a material body, which brings about a spiritual amnesia so that we can pursue unbridled our quest for happiness.

A clear white beam of a bulb, when passed through a crimson covering glass, emerges as a glaring red light. Similarly the pure selfless longing of the soul for Krishna, when passed through the covering of the material body, emerges as the perverted selfish craving of the flesh for the opposite sex. In other words, under the spell of the illusion created due to bodily misidentification, love of God distorts into lust for matter. Lust causes within all living beings the overpowering drive for gross sexual enjoyment in specific, and all forms of material enjoyment in general.

However, all material enjoyment has three inescapable characteristics: it is temporary, illusory and miserable, stated as an acronym TIME(Temporary Illusory Miserable Enjoyment). Let see how:

TEMPORARY
ILLUSORY
MISERABLE
ENJOYMENT

Temporary: The very body that promises erotic pleasure chokes that pleasure inescapably by its limited capacity for indulgence. Like a water-filled sponge, which gives out lesser and lesser water with every successive squeeze, the capacity of the body to enjoy diminishes irreversibly with indulgence, disease and age.

Illusory: The soul being like the driver of the bodily car has needs which are completely different from those of the body. Therefore, just as fuelling the car can never nourish the driver, material gratification can never bring about spiritual fulfillment; material pleasure can offer nothing more than an illusory relief to the soul.

Miserable: Sex seals the soul's misidentification with the body and consequently forces him to suffer bodily, social and environmental miseries (adhyatmika, adhibhautika and adhidaivika klesha). Further, the soul suffers due to the misidentification as nature batters the body on its distressful journey to disease, decrepitude and death. Not only that, every soul in the material world is haunted by feelings of innate dissatisfaction due to his lack of spiritual fulfillment. To mistake this innate dissatisfaction to be due to the lack of material gratification is the bane of the soul. This fundamental blunder in diagnosing the cause of his suffering propels the soul headlong into the arena of material misery, where he struggles futilely for happiness.

The Science of Sex

Through this philosophical window, let us now see how Vedic culture was systematically arranged to rescue the soul from his existential predicament of material entanglement. The Vedic social order was oriented to help every individual to progressively revert the misdirected longing of the soul back to its original pristine state. To this end, Vedic education, apart from teaching students commercial, technical and physical skills, focused on imparting them a deep philosophical understanding of their intrinsic spiritual identity so that they would not be victimized by the binding and blinding passions of sex. Sex is a basic bodily drive, which naturally results in procreation. Vedic science, being far more subtle and sophisticated than our modern matter-devoted version of science, recognized that the consciousness of the man and the woman at the time of union would determine the kind of soul that would enter the mother's womb through the father's semen. Equipped with this knowledge, a properly married couple would enter into sexual intercourse, not for bestial enjoyment, but as a sacred service to the family, society and God. The to-be parents knew that they had the grave responsibility of bringing into the world a pure soul, who would eventually grow up to be an exemplary, principled and selfless citizen and do immense good for the world. Such a sanctified union was a manifestation of the divine, as stated in the Bhagavad-gita (7.10), dharmaviruddho bhuteshu kamo 'smi bharatarashabha "I am sex life that is not contrary to religious principles." Thus, in Vedic times, sex was meant for procreation, not recreation.

Sex-addicted moderns may consider all this sentimental imagination or impractical idealism, but we would do well to remember that our so-called primitive ancestors were not brainwashed by the  maddening media blitz saturated with covert and overt sexual overtones. Almost all species of life, including so-called uncivilized tribals, have procreation as a natural consequence of copulation. Except, of course, "advanced" modern humans, for whom procreation is often scientifically suppressed through contraception and abortion in the maniac pursuit of recreation. Even when it is not suppressed, the purpose of procreation hardly ever crosses their minds, filled as they are with endless plans for sexual enjoyment. No wonder John Lennon quipped, "Most people are born on Saturday night over a bottle of wine."

Apart from sanctified procreation, the institution of marriage was meant for gratification of the bodily sexual drive in a regulated, religious way. This would gradually help both the spouses to realize the futility of all bodily enjoyment and help each other to advance together on the journey back to Krishna. Srila Prabhupada writes, "Marriage is meant to regulate the human mind so that it becomes peaceful for spiritual advancement." Thus in Vedic culture, the goal of marriage was not bodily gratification, but spiritual purification. Therefore even with marriage sex was kept the minimum. Needless to say, adultery as well as other perverted forms of sex were ruled out. These regulations were not intended to deprive people of enjoyment and force them to live a torturous life of abnegation. Rather they were meant to create a stable springboard to help catapult the soul to the transcendental platform, where he could experience unlimited spiritual happiness, which is his constitutional right. The Vedic attitude was that material enjoyment rivets the consciousness of the soul to flesh and, while offering him only a drop of pleasure, cheats him of his rightful oceanic spiritual happiness. Thus it is absence of restriction, not restriction, that deprives the soul of happiness. Continence is a universal value enjoined not just in the Vedic scriptures, but also in the scriptures of all the great religions. It is a pre-requisite for protecting the soul from material entanglement and for creating the foundation for raising his consciousness to the spiritual platform.

The Historical Degradation

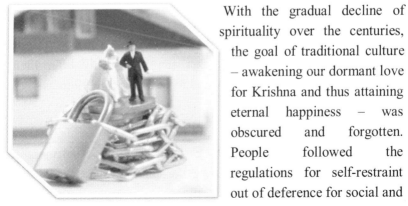

With the gradual decline of spirituality over the centuries, the goal of traditional culture – awakening our dormant love for Krishna and thus attaining eternal happiness – was obscured and forgotten. People followed the regulations for self-restraint out of deference for social and religious tradition for some time, but with the spread of Western science and its reductionistic, non-spiritual worldview, people started seeing these regulations as pointless and prohibitive. Men, using their social and physical superiority, turned towards women to exploit them as sex machines. Outraged at the male chauvinism, women retaliated by using their feminine charms to seduce men and exploit them as ATM (anytime money) machines. Hence the well-known saying, "Don't ask a woman her age and a man his salary": because both women and men use their respective strengths to exploit the other sex and so don't want the absence of that strength to be exposed. Divorces, pre-marital and extra-marital relationships became increasingly common – all in the name of enjoyment. Promiscuity – occasional forays into illicit sex - degenerated into hedonism – reckless playing with relationships for pleasure. All sorts of sexual perversions – homosexuality, bisexuality, sodomy, pedophilia – followed.

Below all this frenzy for enjoyment lies the soul longing for his original relationship with Krishna. From the spiritual viewpoint, sex is a delusion. The rubbing and squeezing of lifeless flesh and the ejection and reception of sticky, messy fluid in a rotting and dying body – whether male or female - can never satisfy the spiritual longing of the immortal soul. Sex, even within the framework of marriage, is unnatural because it takes the soul away from his natural loving relationship with Krishna and the unlimited happiness that comes naturally from serving Krishna. And the more unnatural the forms of sex that people take shelter of in their desperate search for happiness, the more they make that very happiness inaccessible to themselves. Because the spirit that can very easily offer them happiness gets shrouded by more and more layers forgetfulness.

Our Choice

But still there is hope. If the current attack on sexual morality can stir intelligent people to examine the spiritual foundation of their traditional moral principles, they can still discover the lost wealth of their heart, their forgotten Lord – Krishna. Krishna is forever waiting for us, playing on His flute, inviting us back to the sublime joys of an endless love, in His eternal abode, our original home, the spiritual world. In the current dark age of Kali, Krishna has made the channeling of our misdirected consciousness back to Him very easy by manifesting Himself as His Holy Names, especially the Hare Krishna maha mantra. When our heart is re-united with Krishna through the sublime medium of divine sound, all material enjoyment will become disdainful.

Thus Vedic insights can help us to make sense out of the current social degradation and can also equip us to confront and counter it. The onus is on each one of us to choose. Will we let ourselves be swept away by the current wave of degradation into the ocean of sin and suffering? Or will we join hands with a crew of intrepid spiritual sailors who are navigating the sturdy ship of genuine spirituality towards the safe shores of immortality and bliss? Our choice may well determine the destiny of the world.   ● ● ●

Caste System –
Material Diversity, Spiritual Equality

Caste system is probably among the most talked about and most misunderstood current social controversies; misunderstood because it is based on a false premise – caste determination by birth. .

The Social Body –
Discrimination or Cooperation?

Interestingly, the original Vedic scriptures don't consider birth – the basis of casteist discrimination in modern Hinduism – as the criterion of social classification. The Bhagavad-gita (4.13) declares that this social division, known as varnashrama, was based on qualities and activities (guna-karma). The Rig Veda (10.90.12) compares society to the human body. The brahmanas (thinkers and teachers) are compared to the head, the kshatriyas (governors and

चातुर्वर्ण्यं मया सृष्टं गुणकर्मविभागशः ।
तस्य कर्तारमपि मां विद्ध्यकर्तारमव्ययम् ॥ १३ ॥

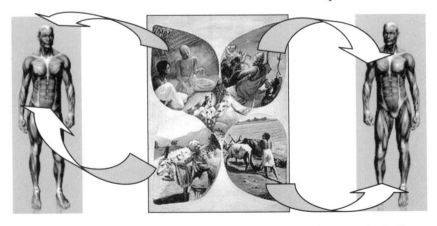

protectors) to the arms, vaishyas (producers and traders) to the belly and shudras (workers and general assistants) to the feet. In our body, one part may be positioned higher than the other, but that is just to facilitate its optimum contribution to the body. Ultimately all parts need nourishment and are necessary for proper bodily functioning. If any part is neglected or malfunctions, the whole body suffers. Similarly, in the social body, brahmanas (determined by qualities, not birth) are higher in the social hierarchy, but that is just to ensure optimum social utilization of their intellectual abilities. Ultimately, every class is valued for its contribution to society. If any class is exploited or is lethargic, the entire society is adversely affected. Importantly, these four social classes, known as varnas, are not discriminatory man-made divisions. Essentially they are four human types found in every human society. Most people exhibit qualities that reflect an overlapping of these categories, but one occupational inclination eventually predominates. Interestingly, we find similar divisions in a modern MNC – researchers, managers, financers and workers. This division is not discriminatory, but fair, because people are classified not forcibly, but as per their abilities.

Intriguingly the Greek philosopher Plato in his *The Republic* echoes this principle. Though he mentions three classes instead of four - philosopher-kings, warriors (called as auxiliaries), and merchants and workers together as one, his basis for classification is the same – natural propensities. He compares rulers to gold, auxiliaries to silver, and those in the third class to brass and iron.

Engaging people as per their psychophysical natures has several benefits:

1. Provided individual job satisfaction and security

In Vedic times, experienced elders would identify the natural inclination of a child and train him accordingly, thus empowering him to excel in his vocation and thus become emotionally satisfied and economically secure.

2. Avoided needless competition and maximized social productivity

When people are trained according to their natures, all members of society – teachers, administrators, traders, artisans – pursue their respective professions without having to compete with each other and contribute constructively to society.

Nowadays, when certain professions – engineering and medicine, for example - are glamorized, everyone chases after them. This leads to:

Students in those fields undergo intense, often maniac, competition.

Even successful students fear unemployment as too many candidates vie for too few jobs.

When students are educated contrary to their natures, they are unable to develop the competence expected of their profession, leading to harm or even havoc. Most of us have heard of incompetent doctors prescribing wrong medicines.

Dearth of talent in other fields leads to decreased overall social productivity.

3. Satisfies everyone's material needs in an efficient and uncomplicated manner.

Communities whose members specialize in different fields can trade internally and become self-sufficient, thus avoiding the complications attendant with external dependence.

Sir Sidney Low in his book, A Vision of India refutes the stereotyped portrayal of varnashrama as an elitist, exclusivist social order:

"There is no doubt that it (caste)

is the main cause of the fundamental stability and contentment by which Indian society has been braced for centuries against the shocks of politics and the cataclysms of Nature. It provides every man with his place, his career, his occupations, his circle of friends. It makes him, at the outset, a member of a corporate body; it protects him through life from the canker of social jealousy and unfulfilled aspirations; it ensures him companionship and a sense of community with others in like case with himself. The caste organization is to the Hindu his club, his trade union, his benefit society, his philanthropic society."

How Did Varnashrama Avoid Exploitation?

1. All people – irrespective of their social position – were spiritually equal as servitors of God.

The lower castes would serve the upper castes, but the upper castes would serve God – visibly. The brahmanas – the socially most powerful class before whom even the kings would bow down and offer handsome charity – would prefer voluntary material poverty to not be distracted from their absorption in  devotional service to God, studying and teaching of scriptures and performance of sacrifices. A well-known example is Chanakya Pandit, who was instrumental in installing Chandragupta Maurya as the monarch of Northern medieval India, lived in a simple hut. Similarly the kings would understand and demonstrate that the kingdom belonged to God and they were servitor-caretakers on his behalf. For example, as per time-honored traditions, many kings would personally sweep the streets in front of the processions carrying the Deities. When people would see, "Our masters are as much servants as we are, albeit serving in a different role", they would unhesitatingly execute their role, decided according to their

God-given talents. Envy and conflict arises only when people see, "I am being deprived and another is enjoying at my expense."

2. The most powerful social classes had to be the most renounced.

It was imperative for the upper castes – the brahmanas and kshatriyas – to renounce the world at around fifty and focus fully on self-realization. This not only ensured that they successfully achieved the spiritual goal of life, but also checked them from becoming exploitative.

Thus the seemingly discriminatory varnashrama system functions by enlightened cooperation. Throughout history, thinkers have tried various means to organize human society to maximize individual and social satisfaction and growth. In our times, the left attempted – at least in principle - to bring about social equality by fiat. But the differences vis-à-vis attitudes and aptitudes among people are inescapable. The communist attempt at artificial equality failed as it choked the talented by rewarding them no more than the mediocre. The right provided an open field for the resourceful, leading to industrial and economic growth – and cutthroat competition, untrammeled greed and exploitation of the needy by the wealthy. The varnashrama system ingeniously reconciled and integrated the absolute spiritual equality of all people with their relative material differences. Gerald Heard in his book *Man, the Master* calls varnashrama as "organic democracy" - "the rule of the people who have organized themselves in a living and not a mechanical relationship; where instead of all men being said to be equal, which is a lie, all men are known to be of equal value, could we but find the position in which their potential contribution could be released and their essential growth so pursued."

Mark Tully, the BBC correspondent in New Delhi, explains the superiority of varnashrama over the current seemingly equal social system in his book *No Full Stops in India*, "The alienation of many young people in the West and the loneliness of the old show the suffering that egalitarianism inflicts on those who do not win, the superficiality of an egalitarianism which in effect means equal opportunities for all to win and then ignores the inevitable losers. For all that, the elite of India have become so spellbound by egalitarianism that they are unable to see any good in the only institution which does provide a sense of identity and dignity to those who are robbed from birth of the opportunity to compete on an equal footing – caste."

Birth-Right Made It All Wrong

The caste-by-birth idea – the bane of Hindu casteism - is decidedly non-Vedic. The Vedic texts abound with examples of

qualified people, even if low-born, being elevated to respectable places in society.

The Chandogya Upanishad narrates how Gautam rsi declared a maidservant's son, Satyakama Jabali, to be a brahmana as the boy was unhesitatingly truthful – the hallmark of a true brahmana.

Furthermore, Suta Gosvami, Kanaka, Kanchipurna, Tukaram, Thiruvalluvar, Sura dasa and Haridasa Thakura were all revered as saints, despite being low-born.

A famous Vedic aphorism reiterates: *janamana jayate shudra samskarad bhaved dvijah veda-pathanat bhavet viprah brahma janatiti brahmana* "By birth everyone is a shudra, meaning everyone is unqualified. By spiritual initiation, one becomes a twice-born, that is, one begins his spiritual life. By study of Vedic scriptures, one becomes a learned scholar. By realization of the Absolute Truth alone does one become a brahmana."

Plato adds an interesting dimension to his social classification: golden parents will tend to have golden children, as silver parents will naturally have silver children, and so on. Similarly, in varnashrama often the occupation of a person would turn out to be the varna of his birth – partially due to the childhood upbringing and training. So, a child born in a brahmana family would generally become a qualified brahamana. Consequently the varna would normally be determined by birth, but it could be retained only by behavior.  So if a son of a brahmana did not develop brahminical qualities, he would no longer be accepted as a brahmana, but as a *brahma-bandhu*, unqualified relative of a brahmana. Conversely if the son of a shudra exhibited brahminical qualities, he would be accepted as a brahmana. Plato also recommends this flexibility. If an iron parent has a golden child, then, says Plato, we must acknowledge that a golden child born to an iron parent, for example, is indeed golden—his birthright should be disregarded in favor of his natural quality.

Then how did the widespread perversion of caste-by-birth originate? In medieval times, a coterie of brahma-bandhus, wanting to hold on to brahminical privileges without developing the required character, started claiming that caste was decided by birth and was unchangeable. Further they misused their social influence to deprive lower castes of access to the practices of self-realization. And thus began the unfortunate history of casteist discrimination. Genuine Vedic teachers categorically disown this caste-by-birth system as non-Vedic and label it as , the demoniacally-conceived system. Author Micheal Pym echoes in his book The Power of India: "Caste is the secret of that amazing stability which is characteristic of the Indian social structure. It is the strength of Hinduism. Naturally, it can be abused. The moment a Brahmin treats a sweeper cruelly because he is a sweeper, he departs from his Brahminhood. He becomes a usurper and a social danger. And in due course, he will have to pay for this mistake. Because men are imperfect, and because power is a deadly intoxicant, such abuses may and do occur, but they are not inherent in the institution – they are contrary to its principles, though they may be inherent in the make up of the individual.

Spirituality is the Solution

The ultimate purpose of the original varnashrama, known as daivi varnashrama, the divinely-ordained system, was not just material social organization, but systematic spiritual elevation. As eternal souls, beloved sons and servants of God, Krishna, we can attain eternal happiness only in His devotional service. This selfless divine love enables us to live as happily as is ever possible in this world and finally transports us to our original home, the spiritual world, where we live in eternal ecstasy, reciprocating love with Krishna. Varnashrama offers the best springboard to catapult us to

our spiritual birthright. Hence cultivating genuine spirituality – Krishna consciousness – and returning back to the spiritual world is the only real solution to all problems, including the problem of discrimination and exploitation.

Undoubtedly in this world, discrimination

must be prevented and redressed. But is varnashrama its cause? Untouchability and similar Hindu inequities are portrayed as the ultimate horror, yet racial groups like American Indians or Australian Aborigines in modern societies were treated worse than untouchables; they were isolated, crowded into reserves, where they could only atrophy and disappear.

Many countries today are witnessing xenophobia. And discrimination, if we may use the word, based on economic power is ubiquitous in the current consumer economy.

What causes discrimination? Almost always materialism. When people imagine that material things – wealth and comforts, power and prestige, positions and possessions – are the only way to happiness, they seek to acquire these by any means. As we live in a world of limited resources and unlimited wants, plenty for one causes scarcity for another. When the powerful become materially-minded, they encroach upon the quota of the weak, leading to social inequities. Depending on time, place and circumstances, this materialistic agenda masks itself in racial, nationalistic, religious - and casteist rationalizations.

The antidote for materialism is spirituality, which provides inner fulfillment and cures the exploitative mentality. And varnashrama is the best social order to foster spiritual enlightenment and experience. Therefore, while striving to remove the cataract of casteism, let us ensure that we don't pluck out the eye of Vedic spiritual wisdom. When the whole world is recognizing the value of ancient Indian wisdom in the form of yoga, meditation, vastushastra and chanting of holy names, let us not reject the profound and universal spiritual teachings of ancient India while correcting the social evils of Hinduism. Late British historian reminds us, "It is already becoming clear that a chapter which had a Western beginning will have to have an Indian ending if it is not to end in the self-destruction of the human race. At this supremely dangerous moment in history, the only way of salvation for mankind is the Indian way."

Srila Prabhupada, the founder of ISKCON, remarked, "Without the awakening of divine consciousness in the individual, there is no use of crying for world peace." Therefore Srila Prabhupada declared his mission to the West to be "finding brahmanas." Far from reviving the demoniac caste-by-birth perversion, he wanted to revitalize the modern social body with its missing head. He wanted to create, among the so-called lowborn Westerners as well as everywhere else, a class of genuine spiritual intellectuals, by education, culture and training. Hundreds of such spiritually transmuted intellectuals are pioneering a non-sectarian spiritual revival all over the world. When these detached devoted leaders guide society, their examples, words and policies will eradicate the material greed that causes all inequities. Hence practicing and sharing Krishna consciousness constitutes egalitarianism in its most pure, potent and practical form, the panacea for all forms of discrimination.   ● ● ●

The Complete Social Service

"Does practicing and sharing spirituality benefit society in any practical way as social service does?" Practicing spiritualists often face this question. In this article, we will address this question by analyzing a widespread social problem, starvation, and generalize the principles understood therein for other problems.

The Causes of Starvation

On seeing a beggar starving, a sensitive person will want to give some food. This will certainly offer immediate relief, but a thoughtful person will also ponder: "A few hours later he will be hungry again. What has brought this  beggar to starvation? How can *that cause* be permanently tackled?" Some of the causes of starvation relevant to our discussion are analyzed below:

1. Wanton living and self-destructive behavior (among the poor):

Many people who can and do earn enough to at least make ends meet squander their hard-earned earnings on bad habits like smoking, drinking and drugs. For example,

It is not uncommon for a social welfare worker to meet a family that is on the streets facing starvation because the head of the family has lost savings, furniture, ornaments, house, job and even health – the basis of future earning – due to his alcoholic addiction.

Regular commuters often find that many beggars refuse to accept food and want only money because they can use that money to buy, say, cigarettes.

Natural disasters like earthquakes are known to be big business opportunities for alcohol peddlers because many of the disaster-afflicted people tend to use the relief money to forget their suffering by intoxication.

Is providing material relief to addicted people not like pouring water into a bucket with a large hole at the bottom? No matter how  much they are helped materially, their situation will not be truly ameliorated till their habits are rectified. And at a material level, both governmental and non-governmental organizations have not had much success in helping people avert the tragedy of self-destruction caused by bad habits.

2. Greed and Exploitation (among the affluent):

The problem of starvation is not as much due to shortage of resources as due to mismanagement of resources. Mahatma Gandhi put it well, "There is enough in this world for everyone's need, but not for everyone's greed." In the well-researched book *Food First*, Francis Moore Lappe points out that much of the world's best land is being misused for production of cash export crops. Such misuse of precious land resources leading ultimately to starvation is largely due to greed among the affluent.

Starvation does indeed occur sometimes due to factors beyond human control such as abnormally low rains, but even then the impact of the natural calamity is compounded by the way humans respond to it. *Food First* reports a study of famines in Africa, which showed that on every occasion the affected nation had within its own boundaries the food resources to feed its starving citizens, but relief was intentionally withheld due to economic or political motives. The merchants wanted to hoard the grains, cause artificial inflation and earn more profit. Or the politicians wanted to deprive regions supporting the opposing politicians and thus settle old scores or gain the upper hand. On some occasions the food-grains would be allowed to rot in the go-downs while people all around would be starving. Or worse still the crops would be deliberately burned or grains intentionally sunk in the oceans, while the poor all around were burning in hunger and sinking to death. The same sad story of Africa often repeats itself in various parts of the world wherever natural calamities strike.

Thus greed is one of the invisible yet universal causes of starvation. Can material welfare work counter greed? A social worker may get charity from a wealthy person and use it for offering some relief. But as long as greed impels the haves to exploit the have-nots at every level – individually, socially and globally, the relief that social welfare offers will not be much more than a drop of water in a desert.

Vedic Insights

The Vedic texts of ancient India explain the root cause and the ultimate solution to suffering. Their teachings begin by unequivocally asserting that our identity is not material, but spiritual; we are eternal souls covered by temporary material bodies (Bhagavad-gita 2.13). We belong to an immortal realm, variously known as the kingdom of God or the spiritual world, where we enjoy everlasting happiness in a loving relationship with the Supreme Person, God. Known by various names such as Jehovah, Christ, Allah, Buddha and Rama in different religious traditions, God is most fully described by the name Krishna (meaning "all-attractive"). In order to enable us to fully experience the joy of love in the spiritual world, Krishna gives us free will to voluntarily choose to love and serve Him. But when we misuse our free will and desire enjoyment separate from Him, we are placed in the material world. Here we forget our spiritual identity and identify with our material body, which offers us the sensory apparatus for interacting with the foreign material environment. Within the framework of this bodily misidentification, we seek different material relationships, experiences, possessions and positions according to our dreams and schemes. But our desires for enjoyment are unlimited, whereas the resources of this world are limited. Consequently, the pursuit of enjoyment leads to an intense struggle. Worse still, being spiritual by constitution, we can never become happy by gratifying our body, just as a driver can never be nourished by fuelling his car. So, irrespective of whether we succeed or not in our plans for material enjoyment, we remain mostly dissatisfied; the difference of dissatisfaction is only a matter of degree. And ultimately all our dreams turn into nightmares as our bodies – the very basis of all our enjoyment – are battered by disease, wrecked by old age and destroyed by death. Then based on our desires and activities, we are given other suitable bodies – human or subhuman. There we continue our vain struggle for existence and enjoyment in a world of suffering and death. Thus material attempts for happiness are insubstantial – even when successful they do not offer real happiness, and futile – they inevitably fail against the inexorable force of time, which deteriorates and destroys everything material. Only the souls in the human form have sufficiently evolved consciousness and intelligence to understand and remedy their terrible predicament in material existence. Therefore, the Vedic texts urge all humans to dedicate themselves to promoting spiritual well being, a cause more complete and effective than promoting material well being.

Ending Starvation – The Spiritual Way

Let's see how promoting spiritual well being can help tackle the problem of starvation.

1. Self-restraint:

Historical studies show that most of the self-destructive addictions that haunt a large percentage of the human population today were quite rare in earlier ages, when people were naturally God-fearing. Almost everyone would be able to earn enough food to at least live because their physical and mental energy and money would not be uselessly dissipated in injurious indulgences. Therefore, except in the case of devastating natural calamities, hardly anyone would have to suffer the pangs of starvation.

Even in modern times, spiritual practices can help cure the addictions that lead to starvation. Statistical surveys have shown that the religiously committed are less likely to succumb to bad habits. Adopting religious principles also often helps addicts to free themselves. Dr Patrick Glynn writes in his book *God: The Evidence*, "It is difficult to find a more consistent correlative of mental health, or a better insurance against self-destructive behaviors, than a strong religious faith."

2. Compassion:

A spiritual vision of life increases compassion and decreases greed. Let's see how.

When a reporter once asked Mother Teresa about the secret of her compassion, which enabled her to do enormous relief work for the afflicted worldwide, in response she pointed to her rosary beads, on which she offered regular prayers. Devotion to God as the Supreme Father-Mother naturally arouses compassion for all living beings as His children, as our brothers and sisters in His family, and inspires us to selflessly work for their holistic upliftment.

When a wealthy person is God-conscious, his compassion is not restricted to an occasional act of charity; rather his whole life becomes dedicated to helping the deprived in every possible way – materially and spiritually.

When the head of state is spiritually enlightened, he cares for all the citizens like his own children – not due to political expediency, but due to spiritual love. He creates the necessary socio-economic structures to provide proper gainful employment for all of them in normal situations and adequate relief during emergencies. Thus godliness automatically engenders goodness; a godly person naturally develops good qualities like self-restraint and compassion, which are essential for any social welfare program to be effective.

3. Natural Prosperity:

The Vedic texts explain that harmonization with God leads to well being not just in the next world, but also in this world. They remind us: what to speak of our wellbeing, our very existence is dependent on God's grace. Despite our scientific progress, we still depend on God for all our fundamental material necessities – heat, light, air, water and even food. (Despite our hard work in our sophisticated factories, all our daily food is originally manufactured in God's factory, nature) When we disobey the Lord's injunctions, through material nature He withholds the supplies of life's necessities just as a father may temporarily starve his obstinate child in order to reform him. This can be seen in the steadily increasing natural calamities that have hit human society, as it has become increasingly materialistic and godless over the last few centuries. And when we live in harmony with God, He instructs Mother Nature to profusely supply all the necessities of life to His obedient children. Material prosperity through divine harmony is not a sentimental fantasy; God-centered human society in Vedic India offered a historical demonstration. The amazing prosperity of traditional India is well-documented in the Vedic texts themselves, by traveling medieval historians like Fa Hein and Hseun Tsang and even by modern Indologists like A L Basham. In fact, the wealthiest country in the world today, America, was originally discovered when Europeans were searching for a new ocean route to access the wealth of India.

Are Good Intentions Good Enough?

Srila Prabhupada illustrates the pitfalls of well-intentioned but ill-informed welfare work through an incident in his life:

Once while in Calcutta, India, he saw a neighboring lady strongly chastising her daughter. On inquiry he found that the lady's

son had been suffering from an intense bout of typhoid and the doctor had strictly forbidden him any oily foods. While the mother had been away shopping, her son had started fervently begging his sister to give his some pakoras (a fried food item). Seeing her brother's intense craving, the sister had fed him a large number of pakoras, despite the mother's strong prohibition. When the mother had returned, she had found her son's sickness alarmingly worsened and had to rush him to a hospital for emergency care. She had just returned and was scolding her daughter for her harm-causing "kindness" to her brother.

Let's consider an example from real life where good intentions turn out to be not good enough. Imagine a drunkard who routinely squanders all his earnings and abuses his family members in his drunken stupor.

When he falls sick, he is offered free medical care. His disease gets cured, but his addiction stays untreated. He goes back to his habitual intoxication and the habitual abuse of his family members and eventually has a relapse of disease. How has the free medical care done him any real good?

Therefore Srila Prabhupada would often compare social welfare efforts devoid of spirituality to the blowing of a painful boil. Even if done with sincere intention, they fail to offer any lasting solution.

In fact, the Vedic texts declare that sufferings within this world are the impetus to raise our consciousness to the spiritual plane, where we automatically re-achieve our right to eternal happiness. Srila Prabhupada writes, "The miseries of material existence serve to indirectly remind us of our incompatibility with matter." To understand this better, we need to swallow a bitter pill: this world is like a prison and everyone here is like a criminal imprisoned due to rebellion against God. Like in a prison, the hardship in this world is meant, not to penalize, but to rectify.

Imagine a welfare worker who zealously seeks to transfer a criminal from a dark dingy dungeon (a C class prison cell) to a ventilated, clean room (an A class prison cell) without trying to reform his mentality? Such a change, even if successful, serves neither the purpose of the prison – reformation of the prisoners, nor the ultimate interests of the prisoner – freedom from captivity. The Vedic texts prompt us to ponder: is offering material betterment without offering spiritual enlightenment much different? It serves neither the purpose of the material world – rectification of the rebellious mentality of the souls, nor their ultimate interests – freedom from the inevitable sufferings of material existence, repeated birth and death.

The foregoing discussion is not meant to indicate that we turn a blind eye and develop a cold heart towards the sufferings of our fellow humans. Compassion is undoubtedly a noble quality and the Vedic texts urge us to utilize it to its maximum effectiveness by becoming instruments of God's compassion.

The Complete Welfare Program

God being the most loving Father feels pain to see His children in pain, no matter what their transgressions. He creates a cosmic justice system to bring about their gradual reformation, but being much more than just a neutral judge, He also creates a mercy system to offer quick relief to sincerely repentant souls. Through His earthly representatives, the saintly devotees, He disseminates genuine spiritual knowledge. Intelligent humans, by understanding the cause of their suffering from such devotees, can voluntarily reform themselves and learn to live in loving harmony with God. Then God, out of love for them, waives their karmic punishment partly or fully according to the degree of their repentance. And ultimately God helps them to come back to their eternal home to live happily with Him forever (Bhagavad-gita 10.10-11). Therefore Vedic scriptures call upon all intelligent social workers to become agents of the Lord's compassion and do the highest good to everyone.

Srila Prabhupada would tell a story to illustrate how the agent of God's compassion provides complete welfare in one stroke.

Suppose you are the friend of a wealthy millionaire. One day you see your friend's estranged son wandering like a vagabond on the streets, drunk, disheveled, diseased, distressed and starving. Before you, somebody comes and offers him some food. He hungrily gulps down the food and continues his aimless wandering. Then someone else comes and offers him a new set of clothes. He happily wears the clothes, but still remains lost and forsaken. Then someone else gives him a few free medicines, which offer him some physical relief, but don't give any permanent solace. Then you seat him in your car, take him home, bathe and feed him and treat his ailments. When he has sobered down, you talk with him lovingly, explaining to him his father's great affection for him. Then you clarify and remove the misunderstanding that had strained his relationship with his father. And when he is ready to return back to his father, you take him back to his father's mansion where he is given the best varieties of foods, offered an entire wardrobe of clothes and attended to by a team of expert doctors. Thus his problems are permanently solved.

We are beloved children of the Supreme Lord, who is the Master of the Goddess of Fortune. Therefore we are all like princes in the kingdom of God. But due to our causeless misuse of our free will, we have left the shelter of our all-loving father and are struggling for paltry pleasure in this material world, exactly like the lost son of the millionaire in the above story. Srila Prabhupada would further state that material welfare workers are like the people who offered food, clothing and medicine to the lost son, whereas the devotee is like the father's friend who took the son back to his father.

ISKCON'S SERVICE TO SOCIETY

In our modern times, most people are so spiritually uninformed that they don't even know that they are the beloved spiritual children of the supreme father and that an eternal, joyful life is their natural birthright, if they just re-awaken their love for God. In a world bedeviled by such spiritual bankruptcy, ISKCON is:

❖ Providing systematic and scientific spiritual education free to everyone irrespective of caste, religion, nationality, gender, race etc.

❖ Offering an attractive, alternative culture that enables people to practice spirituality in a practical yet potent way in modern times and thus lead deeply meaningful and fulfilling lives.

❖ Propagating the non-sectarian, universal, time-tested chanting of the holy names of God, especially the Hare Krishna maha-mantra, and thus enabling millions of people to easily harmonize themselves with God and thus paving the way for them to return back to the kingdom of God.

❖ Helping millions of people break free from the self-destructive drives of meat-eating, intoxication, gambling and illicit sex by offering them a higher happiness and thus saving from immense karmic suffering in this and future lives.

♣ Running the world's largest vegetarian food relief program, *Food for Life*, and offering free nutritious sanctified food (*prasadam*), food that nourishes the body and awakens the soul, to millions of needy people all over the world, including in war-torn areas.

Thus ISKCON is working tirelessly at the grassroots level to help the individual return to harmony with his own true nature as a beloved child of God. Thus harmonized, he can find and distribute the treasure of love, peace and happiness that lies hidden in his own heart. Henry David Thoreau pointed out, "For every thousand hacking at the leaves of evil, there is one striking at its root." Among the various welfare measures offered by different organizations, ISKCON's propagation of pure spiritual education and culture strikes at the root cause of all suffering and helps people to become truly happy forever. ● ● ●

Think Before You Eat

Every day, several times a day, every living being, in whichever part of the world he may be, enjoys a universal ritual - eating.

Most people decide what they eat based mainly on taste, cost, habit, nutrition and convenience. But for those who are a little more thoughtful, here are some other points worth considering.

A Few Facts

Nutrition

Let us compare the nutrition values of some common vegetarian foods and some common flesh foods:

Vegetarian foods (100 gm)

Name of food stuff	Medical calories
Cashewnut	596
Coconut	444
Groundnut	549
Cheese	348
Ghee	900

Flesh foods (100 gm)

Name of food stuff	Medical calories
Egg	173
Fish	91
Mutton	194
Pork	114
Beef	114

Anatomy

Let us compare some of the physiological features of flesh eaters, plant eaters and human beings:

Features of flesh eaters	Features of plant eaters	Features of human beings
Intestinal tract only 3 times body length, so rapidly decaying meat can pass out of body quickly	Intestinal tract 10-12 times body length, fruits do not decay as rapidly, so can pass more slowly through body	Intestinal tract 12 times body length
Small salivary glands in the mouth (not needed to predigest grains and fruits)	Well developed salivary glands, needed to predigest grains and fruits	Well developed salivary glands needed to predigest grains and fruits
Acid saliva; no enzyme ptyalin to predigest grains	Alkaline saliva; much ptyalin to predigest grains	Alkaline saliva; Much ptyalin to predigest grains.
No flat back molar teeth to grind good	Flat back molar teeth to grind food	Flat back molar teeth to grind food
Features of flesh eaters	Features of Plant eaters	Features of human beings

Clearly the human body is not made for a non-vegetarian diet.

Health

Due to their unnatural diet meat-eating human beings are far more susceptible to diseases and disorders as compared to their vegetarian counterparts. Comprehensive investigations by groups such as the National Academy of Sciences have linked meat eating to cancer, and the Journal of American Medicine reports: "90-97% of heart disease could be prevented by a vegetarian diet."

Environment

Meat eating also has hazardous effects on the environment, such as forest destruction, agricultural inefficiency, soil erosion and desertification, air pollution, water depletion and water pollution.

World Hunger

Consider the following data. One thousand acres of Soyabeans yield 1124 pound of usable protein. One thousand acres of rice yield 938 pound of usable protein. One thousand acres of corn yield 1009 pound of usable protein. One thousand acres of wheat yield 1043 pound of usable protein. Now consider: this one thousand acres of Soyabeans, corn, rice or wheat, when fed to a steer, will yield only about 125 pounds of usable protein.

These and other findings point to a disturbing conclusion: meat eating is directly related to world hunger. Here are some more statistics establishing this:

* If all the Soyabeans and grains fed yearly to U. S. livestock were set aside for human consumption, it would feed 1.3 billion people.

* It takes 16 pounds of grains and Soyabeans to produce 1 pound of feedlot beef. Therefore about 20 vegetarians can be fed on the land that it takes to feed 1 meat eater.

* Feeding the average meat eater requires about 4,200 gallons of water per day, versus 1,200 gallons per day for lacto-vegetarian diet.

* While it takes only 25 gallons of water to produce a pound of wheat, it takes 2,500 gallons of water to produce a pound of meat.

* Harvard nutritionist Jean Mayer has estimated that reducing meat production by just 10 percent would release enough grain to feed 60 million people.

In summary, millions will continue to die of thirst or starvation, while a privileged few consume vast amounts of proteins wasting land and water in the process. Ironically, this same meat is their own bodys' worst enemy.

A Few Quotes

"Truly man is the king of beasts, for his brutality exceeds them. We live by the death of others. We are burial places! I have since an early age abjured the use of meat."

- Leonardo Da Vinci

"When a man wants to murder a tiger, he calls it sport; when a tiger wants to murder him, he calls him ferocity."

- George Bernard Shaw

"It is my view that the vegetarian manner of living, by its purely physical effect on the human temperament, would most beneficially influence the lot of mankind."

- Albert Einstein

"I do feel that spiritual progress does demand at some stage that we should cease to kill our fellow creatures for the satisfaction of our bodily wants. "

- M. K. Gandhi

"The flesh eating is simply immoral, as it involves the performance of an act which is contrary to moral feeling- killing. By killing man suppresses in himself, unnecessarily, the highest spiritual capacity- that of sympathy and pity towards living creatures like himself and by violating this his own feelings become cruel."

- Leo Tolstoy

"Flesh eating is unprovoked murder."

- Benjamin Franklin

"As long as man massacre animals, they will kill each other. Indeed, he who sows the seeds of murder and pain cannot reap joy and love."

- Pythagoras

"A dead cow or sheep lying in a pasture is recognized as carrion. The same sort of a carcass dressed and hung up in a butcher's stall passes as food."

- J. H. Kellogg.

The Vedic Perspective

The Bhagavad Gita states that foods such as milk products, grains, fruits, and vegetables increase the duration of life and give strength, health, happiness, and satisfaction. Conversely, foods such as, meat, fish and fowl are putrid, decomposed and unclean. They cause numerous hazards to physical health.

The Srimad Bhagavatam, the summum bonum of all Vedic literature, states that meat-eating is one of the four pillars of sinful life. Apart from bringing severe sinful reactions, meat-eating also dulls the human intellect thus rendering it incapable of understanding the higher dimensions of life. Therefore real spiritual life, nay real human life, cannot begin unless a human being stops killing his younger brothers, innocent animals, just for the satisfaction of his tongue.   ● ● ●

The Untapped Glory of India

(This article was written soon after the archaeological findings of an ancient city under water off the coast of Dwarka, India)

Once a poverty-stricken descendent of a once-prosperous clan went to a foreign land in search of better prospects in life. He struggled hard to succeed there. Meanwhile a resident of that foreign land heard about this person's ancestral wealth, came to his family estate, found a vast treasure buried there and became a millionaire.

This allegory illustrates the state of modern Indians vis-a-vis Westerners. Indians are going to the West in search of greener pastures and are struggling to make it big amidst cut-throat competition in the corporate jungles there. But Westerners are coming to India to understand the Vedic philosophy and culture. And by studying, assimilating and adopting the Vedic principles, they are finding deep fulfillment in their lives.

What is it about India that is attracting so many Western people?

Let the Evidence Speak

The June 1, 2003, issue of The Week carried the cover story 'The Legend of Dwarka'. The eleven-page article reported the archaeological discovery of a submerged city under the seabed off the coast of Dwarka in Gujarat. The team led by Dr S R Rao, one of India's most respected archaeologists, discovered a well-fortified and planned township that extended for over half a mile from the shore. The harbor found in the submerged city is the earliest clear example throughout the world of natural rock being modified to serve the needs of a harbor. The findings of stone moulds, ancient pottery with inscriptions and especially a seal with the images of a bull, unicorn and goat engraved in an anticlockwise direction, as well as the general layout of the submerged city, constitute strong evidence that this city is indeed the Dwarka described in the ancient Vedic texts. Dr Rao, an emeritus scientist at the marine archaeology unit of the National Institute of Oceanography, writes in his book, *The Lost City of Dwarka*, about his undersea finds: "The discovery is an important landmark in the history of India. It has set to rest the doubts expressed by historians about the historicity of Mahabharata and the very existence of Dwarka city."

The Glory of the Vedic Literature

When the Europeans first came across Vedic culture and literature, they were filled with amazement and admiration. Here are a few quotes of the early European scholars:

German philosopher Johann Gottfried von Herder said, "The brahmins(the spiritual intelligentsia of India) have wonderful wisdom and strength to form their people in great degrees of gentleness, courtesy, temperance, and chastity. They have so effectively established their people in these virtues that in comparison, Europeans frequently appear as beastly, drunken or mad."

The Prussian minister of education, Wilheim Von Humboldt, began published an extensive study of the Bhagavad-gita. He described the Bhagavad-gita as "the deepest and loftiest thing the world has to show."

Many of the manuscripts of the famed composer Ludwig Von Beethoven contain fragments of selections from the Upanishads and the Gita.

The philosopher Georg Hegel compared the discovery of Sanskrit to the beholding of a new continent. He further eulogized the Indian subcontinent as the **"starting-point for the whole Western world."**

Another famous German philosopher, Arthur Schopenhauer, became completely enchanted by the Upanishads. Upon reading a translation into Latin, he called them "The production of the highest human wisdom" Considering the Upanishads to contain almost superhuman conceptions, Schopenhauer said , "It is the most satisfying and elevated reading which is possible in the world; it has been solace in life and will be the solace of my death."

Frenchman Voltaire, the quintessential Enlightenment thinker, became fascinated with Vedic culture. In 1775 he asserted, "I am convinced that everything has come down to us from the banks of the Ganges: astronomy, astrology, metempsychosis, etc."

Diderot, the French philosopher and writer famed for his work on the encyclopedic, suggested in his article on India that "the sciences may be more ancient in India then in Egypt."

Jules Michelet, the French historian known for his spirited seventeen-volume Histoire de France, felt certain that India was "the womb of the world."

Biased Scholarship

Subsequently the Vedic literature became obscured by biased scholarship. Many of these Indologists all conceived of themselves as "bearers of Christian light to ignorant and superstitious Indians". Their religious convictions impelled them to study the Vedic literature, not open-mindedly to understand those texts on their own merit, but with the express objective of proving their inferiority to Christian theology. Although they superficially appreciated the Vedic literature, their overall presentation was intended to discredit those literature as incoherent and mythological. Consider the following statements of what are considered eminent Indologists:

1. **H. H. Wilson:** As the first holder of Oxford's Boden Chair for Sanskrit, H. H. Wilson delivered public lectures to promote his cause. He intended that the lectures "help candidates for a prize of two hundred pounds ... for the best refutation of the Hindu religious system." ("Horace Hayman Wilson," Eminent Orientalists, pp. 71-72.)

2. **Max Muller:** "The ancient religions of the world may have but served to prepare the way of Christ by helping through its very errors." (Vivekananda Rock Memorial Committee, India's Contribution to World Thought and Culture, pp. 167-168.)

3. **Monier Monier-Williams:** "It seems to me that our missionaries are already sufficiently convinced of the necessity of studying these works, and of making themselves conversant with the false creeds they have to fight against. How could an army of invaders have any chance of success in an enemy's country without a knowledge of the position and strength of its fortresses, and without knowing how to turn the batteries they may capture against the foe?" (Sir Monier Monier-Williams, Religious Thought and Life in India, p. 10.)

This racial bias was present not just among the intellectuals, but also among the politicians, who funded the intellectuals. Consider the statement of the governor general marquis of Hastings wrote, "The Hindoo appears a being merely limited to mere animal functions, and even in them indifferent ... with no higher intellect than a dog." (R.C. Majumdar et al., eds., History and Culture of the Indian People, vol. 10, p. 348.)

The biased scholarship was motivated not just by religious zeal, but also by political expediency. It was an essential part of the overall British political strategy to consolidate their hold of India. Since the Indians far outnumbered them, the shrewd British knew that they could rule India only with the cooperation of the Indians. And the easiest way to get that cooperation was by proving intellectually to the Indians that their own culture was pathetically inferior to what the British were offering them.

"The theories we like we call them facts and the facts we don't like we call them theories." This succinct remark of Felix Cohen summarizes the British approach to the study of India's history and heritage.

The Tragedy of Modern India

The British no longer rule India politically, but the worldview they taught continues to rule the Indian intellect. Almost all Indians suffer from feelings of national inferiority resulting from prolonged foreign subjugation and the consequent economic under-development. As a knee-jerk reaction to this inferiority complex, most modern Indians tend to reject everything Indian as primitive and irrelevant. The deep-rooted Vedic culture is treated at best as an embarrassing anachronism and at worst as a serious impediment to progress. Many Indians proudly say, "Mera Bharat Mahan" (My India is great), but they do precious little to even inquire what it is that is great about India. With their words they declare the greatness of India, but through their actions they denigrate everything that is essentially Indian by adopting wholesale Western dress, lifestyle, culture, values and goals. Of course some Indians still appreciate the greatness of traditional India, but even they feel that ancient Indian culture and philosophy can do little to help modern India. "Give up traditional religious and spiritual values, advance in science and technology, develop economically and then India will be glorious." Ideas like these have gained an unquestioning acceptance that can be compared only to what religious revelations commanded in times of yore. In the blind pursuit of materialism, the fact that citizens of nations with technological advancement and economic prosperity are battered by stress, depression, marital rupture, childhood delinquency, addiction and criminality just does not matter The fact that the Vedic literatures contain astoundingly accurate information on subjects as intricate and wide-ranging as embryology, medicine, psychology, architecture, cosmology, atomic physics, art, politics and warfare fails to prompt Indians to seriously examine their own inheritance.

The recent findings in Dwarka linking archeology and literature may mark the beginning of a new era in world history, an era of correcting the wrongs that have been perpetrated on India. If they lead to a systematic and unbiased study of India's heritage, we may still arrive at a coherent picture of "the wonder that was India". A proper understanding of her past glory will empower modern India to play her due role in the shaping of a future world. Or maybe the excitement over the findings will just fizzle out. India is too crippled by poverty to take up extensive archaeological explorations. So says the government. The political unsteadiness ensures that nothing else occupies the national mind for long. The bureaucratic delays throttle individual initiative. And most importantly few Indians have the courage to differ from the overwhelming superstition that economic development alone holds the key to India's future.

The Power of One True Indian

There was one Indian, however, who dared to differ – His Divine Grace AC Bhaktivedanta Swami Srila Prabhupada, founder-acharya of ISKCON. When Srila Prabhupada visited Britain during one of his worldwide preaching tours, a reporter inquired about the purpose of his visit. Srila Prabhupada replied that the British plundered India of all her wealth, but they forgot to take India's most precious jewel. Srila Prabhupada informed the nonplussed reporter that he had come to offer Britain that jewel – the timeless wisdom of the Vedic literature. Srila Prabhupada presented the essential Vedic conclusions with striking clarity and relevance. To a world striving for universal brotherhood, Srila Prabhupada poignantly pointed out that universal brotherhood was possible only when the people of the world accept the Universal Father, God. To individuals searching for inner fulfillment, Srila Prabhupada explained that the highest happiness can be experienced only when one lives in harmony with the will of God. To a world infatuated by technological advancement, Srila Prabhupada warned that when humanity individually, socially and globally neglects or rejects God, it courts total disaster.

Along with this revolutionary philosophy, Srila Prabhupada brought to the West a unique gift - a practical and joyful way of life, centered on selfless spiritual service to God and all His children. He also presented easy and effective mantra meditation techniques, which constituted the distilled essence of all Vedic methods for self-realization. Thousands of people, when they adopted the Vedic way of life as taught by Srila Prabhupada, experienced their lives transformed from confused despair to enlightened fulfillment. Addicts, who had been wrecked by the perverted pleasures offered by tobacco, alcohol and drugs, found themselves freed from the shackles of self-destructive behavior. Seekers, who had been disillusioned by the mindless pursuit of inane pleasures as espoused by modern society, found unlimited happiness streaming into their lives from the spiritual stratum. Intellectuals, searching for meaning and purpose to the cosmos and the life within it, discovered a body of knowledge that answered fully the deepest questions that humanity has ever pondered. Even scholars could not but appreciate Srila Prabhupada's comprehensive, coherent, cogent and potent presentation of Vedic knowledge, especially his commentary on the Bhagavad-gita, entitled Bhagavad Gita As It Is. "If truth is what works, as Pierce and the other pragmatists insist, there must be a kind of truth in the Bhagavad Gita As It Is, since those who follow its teaching display a joyful serenity usually missing in the bleak and strident lives of contemporary people." This remark of Dr Elwin H Powell, Professor of Sociology, State University of New York, is typical of the critical acclaim that Bhagavad Gita As It Is has won among the world's leading scholars. Srila Prabhupada spearheaded a cultural and spiritual revolution that continues to bring meaning and joy to the lives of millions all over the world even today. Thus the evidence that Srila Prabhupada has provided to testify to the glory of Vedic India is not just a few forms of dust dug out from some parts of the earth. His evidence is living and global: it is the vibrant lives of thousands of people, who have dedicated themselves to the selfless service of humanity and God.　　　● ● ●

The Foundation of Morality

Daily news reports of things like corruption, nepotism, favoritism, and infidelity have us fed up. Politicians say, "Education in ethics and values is the solution." But don't most people already know right from wrong? I think so. They just feel they'll fare better in life without following moral codes. And exhortation by moralists or legislation by politicians doesn't inspire them to think differently.

Living by moral principles is like following traffic laws for smooth and safe travel. The purpose of travel, however, is not to follow the laws but to reach the destination. If a traveler feels that the traffic laws delay him or obstruct his reaching the destination, he may break them if he thinks he can get away with it.

Like traffic laws, moral principles promote order, specifically orderly social interactions. But modern education doesn't teach us about the goal of social transactions or of life itself. Consequently people may stay moral out of deference to culture or tradition but give up morality when circumstances threaten or tempt them. Worse still, the incessantly glorified goals of modern consumer society— fame, wealth, luxuries, power, pleasure, prestige—encourage and even necessitate immoral behavior. The Bhagavad-gita (16.8–15) explains that a materialistic worldview leads to insatiable lust and greed, which impel corrupt actions. When people are surrounded and bombarded by materialistic allurements, they may feel that by being moral they stand to lose a lot and gain nothing tangible. Moreover, our godless education gives us no knowledge about any higher-order natural laws of cosmic accountability. And the fallibility of our penal systems is all too well known. The result? Morality appears entirely dispensable, especially for the shrewd or powerful. In such an environment, how can we expect mere platitudes to inspire people to be moral?

Love: The Basis of Morality

"Morality means lack of opportunity." This saying catches the tottering utilitarian approach to morality. The Vedic texts of ancient India assert that morality without spirituality is baseless and therefore short-lived. If we seriously want morality in society, we need to introduce systematic spiritual education centered on a positive goal of life. The Vedic texts inform us of a nonsectarian universal spiritual goal of life: to develop pure love for God. We are all spiritual beings and are meant to rejoice in our eternal loving relationship with the supreme all-attractive spiritual being, God. Being intrinsically spiritual, we find real happiness not in material acquisition but in spiritual awakening our innate love for God. The more we love God, the happier we become.

Love for God results in love for all living beings as our brothers and sisters in the one universal family of God. When we love all living beings, we will no longer desire to exploit or manipulate others for our selfish interests. Instead, our love for God will inspire us to love and serve each other. This will create a culture of warmth and trust, which engenders moral behavior. This contrasts sharply with the modern culture of alienation and suspicion, which fosters immorality.

Genuine spiritual practices, even in their preliminary stages, trigger our innate value system. We intuitively realize that God is our greatest well-wisher. Subsequently we voluntarily and lovingly choose to lead a morally and spiritually principled life, as ordained by God, knowing it to be in our ultimate interest. And as we find inner happiness by loving God, we become freed from selfish, lusty, greedy, and egoistic drives. No longer do we feel we are missing anything because of our morality. Morality ceases to be the "difficult but right" choice. Rather it becomes the easy and natural course of action for our spiritual growth.

Not Utopia, But Reality

Some may feel, "All this sounds good, but it's unscientific and utopian." In other words, we live in an age where only the scientific, practical worldview is considered reasonable and acceptable. But is the Vedic worldview really unreasonable or impractical?

We need to remind ourselves that science has never proven the non-existence of God or the soul. Rather the reductionistic approach chosen by most scientists for studying the universe just presumes the non-existence of any spiritual reality. Strikingly enough, even within this reductionistic framework, some scientists conclude that the evidence strongly suggests a super-intelligent designer of the cosmos (God) and a non-material source of consciousness within the body (soul).

Love of God will appear utopian only as long as we do not know the coherent philosophy and the clear-cut path to its attainment. Through genuine spiritual practices like prayer, meditation, and chanting the names of God, anyone can experience spiritual enrichment. Once we taste immortal love, we realize that it is the defining and unifying goal of life.

Higher Morality

Someone familiar with episodes in the lives of Krishna and his devotees might object: "But Krishna Himself sometimes acts immorally. And so do his devotees. How can worshiping an immoral God help us become moral?"

To understand this, we need to first consider the ultimate purpose of all morality. We are lost in the darkness of ignorance in the material world, not knowing what to do and what to avoid. Like a torch, moral codes light the way for us. They protect us from being waylaid by selfish desires and keep us on the way toward our ultimate objective—achieving love for Krishna and returning to him. But Krishna is the source of all morality, just as the sun is the source of all light. Because he is fully satisfied in himself, he acts only out of selfless love for us, either to reciprocate with our love or to help us rectify our errant ways. He does not need moral codes because he has not the slightest trace of selfish desires. It is we who need moral codes because we are filled with selfish desires. But if we become proud of our morality and try to examine Krishna with our moral standards, that's like searching for the sun with a torch. It's foolish and futile.

When the sun rises by its own accord, its effulgence reveals its full glory. Similarly when Krishna decides to reveal himself by his own sweet will, we can understand his pure morality and glory. Until then it is best for us to scrupulously follow moral codes to please him so that he may eventually reveal himself. And we should be careful not to become proud of our righteousness.

If we accept Krishna's position as the Supreme Lord, we can gain some understanding about how all his acts are moral. For example, Krishna steals butter from the houses of the cowherd women of Vrindavana. But how can he be considered a thief when he creates and owns everything? He takes the role of a child to reciprocate the maternal affection of his devotees. His stealing, a naughty childhood prank, enhances the sweetness of their loving exchanges. How can that be compared to our stealing, which leads to pain and punishment?

Similarly Krishna takes the role of a handsome youth to reciprocate with the devotees who desire a conjugal relationship with him. His love for the gopis (cowherd maidens) is based not on the beauty of their bodies but on the devotion of their hearts. Some people allege that Krishna's pastimes with the gopis are like the lusty dealings of ordinary boys and girls. But then why would highly renounced saints who give up the sexual love of this world, seeing it as disdainful and distasteful, worship the pastimes of Krishna with the gopis? Even today thousands of people all over the world are becoming free from the control of lusty desires by chanting Krishna's names and worshiping him. If Krishna himself were controlled by lust, how could he free his devotees from lust?

In the battle with the Kauravas, Krishna urges the Pandavas to act immorally. But that is like an authority's urging policemen to break the speed limit to catch thieves who are speeding away. The policemen are (apparently) breaking the law to serve the purpose of the law. Similarly the Pandavas break moral codes to serve a higher purpose that Krishna wants to see fulfilled: to establish the rule of morality by removing the immoral Kauravas from power.

In exceptional circumstances, Krishna's devotees may act seemingly immorally to do his will, which is meant for the ultimate good of all living beings. But generally devotees follow moral codes as an expression of their devotion to Krishna. In fact, without devotion, we will not have the inner strength to sustain lifelong adherence to moral principles.

We need to exercise caution in understanding Krishna's actions, which are above morality. Otherwise, we may misunderstand him and reject his love, condemning ourselves to staying below morality and suffering the karmic reactions for our misdeeds.

If we want lasting morality, empty exhortation and ineffectual legislation won't do. As long as people are taught to pursue material goals, they will feel morality to be impractical or even undesirable. Only when they know and pursue love for God as the goal of life will morality become desirable and practical for them. Therefore at a social level we need to introduce genuine spiritual education and practices leading to love for God and inner fulfillment. And at an individual level, recognizing the spiritual basis of morality is highly empowering. It opens for us a course of action far superior to apathy, tacit approval, helpless lamentation, or indignant self-righteousness. In a cancerous tissue, one healthy cell can activate the healing process. Similarly when the cancer of immorality afflicts modern society, each one of us can, by leading a life of spiritual and moral integrity, activate the process of social recovery.   ● ● ●

The Gita's Secret Message Of Love

Love is one of the most spoken and least understood words. Love is commonly equated with sensual enjoyment, but does such superficial titillation offer substantial satisfaction to the heart? The suffering of the stomach hungry for food is well-recognized, but the agony of the heart hungry for love is often overlooked.

In our love-starved society, the conclusion of the Gita's philosophy – its hidden message of love – is a much-needed healing balm. The Bhagavad-gita has been acclaimed as a philosophical masterpiece by intellectuals like Albert Einstein, Ralph Waldo Emerson, Henry David Thoreau, Herman Hesse and Mahatma Gandhi.

Krishna starts His message of love by enlightening Arjuna: we are all souls, spiritual beings (Gita 2.13), entitled to rejoice in eternal love with the supremely lovable and loving God, Krishna. When our loving nature is contaminated by selfishness, we start loving things more than persons – especially the Supreme Person. This misdirected love forges our misidentification with our temporary bodily coverings and impels us to exploit others for our self-centered desires. The virtuous Arjuna exemplifies the pristine loving soul, whereas the vicious Duryodhana exemplifies the perverted soul afflicted by selfishness. A well-wishing doctor who doesn't want to cause any pain to anyone may still have to carry out a painful amputation to save a patient. Similarly, Krishna exhorts, Arjuna too has to surgically heal Duryodhana and his allies on the battlefield of Kurukshetra.

In addition to the historicity, the mentalities exemplified by Arjuna and Duryodhana are present in our own hearts too. The battlefield setting of the Gita beckons all of us to become spiritual warriors and conquer the selfish lower self with the selfless higher self. Just as the wisdom of the Gita empowered Arjuna, it can empower us, too, for heralding the reign of love in our hearts — and in the world at large.

Krishna, the speaker of the Gita, is an enigma for many. The sporting, loving cowherd youth Krishna of Vrindavana seems to contrast starkly with the philosophical, analytical diplomat-warrior Krishna of Kurukshetra. Can the two be reconciled?

In the Gita, Krishna offers a concise overview of the various paths for spiritual progress – karma-yoga, jnana-yoga, dhyana-yoga and bhakti-yoga. Simultaneously throughout the Gita, he drops clues that there is a secret message; a secret that only a heart filled with love can fathom (Gita 4.3). That is why at the end of almost every chapter He emphasizes bhakti-yoga. Consider the following:

1. The sixth chapter explains dhyana-yoga quite elaborately, but concludes that the bhakti-yogi is the topmost yogi (6.47). That bhakti-yoga is the safest and the most successful form of yoga is also established through comparison at the end of the eight chapter (8.26-28)

2. The fourteenth chapter provides a systematic analysis of how all souls are trapped by the three modes of material nature – an analysis typical of jnanis, but then Krishna concludes in the penultimate verse of the chapter (14.27) that the only way to transcend the three modes is by unflinching devotional service. That the successful jnani becomes a bhakta is also stated in 7.19 and 18.54.

3. The fifth chapter presents nishkama karma-yoga, but concludes that the acceptance of Krishna as the only proprietor, benefactor and enjoyer – an implicit tenet of bhakti - is the way to lasting peace (5.29). That the devotional offering of karma to the Lord is the culmination of karma-yoga is also indicated in 3.9 and 3.30.

Finally at the climax of the Gita (18.64-66), Krishna bares his heart's love in a disarmingly sweet revelation, "Because you are My very dear friend, I am speaking to you My supreme instruction, the most confidential knowledge of all. Hear this from Me, for it is for your benefit. Always think of Me, become My devotee, worship Me and offer your homage unto Me. Thus you will come to Me without fail. I promise you this because you are My very dear friend.

Abandon all varieties of religion and just surrender unto Me. I shall deliver you from all sinful reactions. Do not fear."

Before the unequivocal finale, the message of love is both concealed and revealed. It is concealed because Krishna lovingly accommodates those not yet ready to love Him by delineating other paths for their gradual spiritual growth. All souls in this world have come here due to their envy of the Lord (7.27), due to their desire to enjoy like Him instead of with Him in the spiritual world. Indeed, Krishna reveals this most secret knowledge to Arjuna primarily because he is non-envious (9.1). If Krishna reveals His opulences to envious souls, that revelation will only increase their envy and make it more difficult for them to return back to Him. So He accommodates them by seeming to offer other paths that will make them slowly detached from material enjoyment and eventually able to become attracted to Him by hearing His glories. But, for those who are open-minded and willing to give up envy and accept the path of devotion – made easy by associating with His devotees, Krishna also reveals the supremacy of the path of love. He does so not only at the end, but also in the ninth and twelfth chapters as well as in several other places (2.61, 3.30, 11.54, 12.6-7, and 13.18). Ultimately, Krishna is longing for our love – because he knows that is the only way we can become fully and eternally happy. Srila Prabhupada makes this secret of the Gita open in his preface itself, "By the spell of illusion one tries to be happy by serving his personal sense gratification in different forms which will never make him happy. Instead of satisfying his own personal material senses, he has to satisfy the senses of the Lord. That is the highest perfection of life. The Lord wants this, and He demands it. One has to understand this central point of Bhagavad-gita. Our Krishna consciousness movement is teaching the whole world this central point"

Krishna advocates, not sectarian religious belief, but universal spiritual love. He not only teaches this love, but also demonstrates it. He happily accepts the menial role of a charioteer to assist His devotee Arjuna in the battle. The unique nature of the spiritual master-servant relationship is that just as the devotee serves Krishna,

Krishna also serves the devotee. Srila Prabhupada points out that this relationship is completely different from its exploitative mundane counterpart and is "the most intimate form of intimacy." The culmination of this divine love is revealed in the Vrindavan pastimes, where Krishna happily takes a subordinate or intimate role to reciprocate love with his servitors. Thus Kurukshetra does indeed point to Vrindavana. The Kurukshetra message, its battlefield backdrop notwithstanding, is essentially a gospel of pure spiritual love. And the Vrindavana pastimes, their pastoral romantic context notwithstanding, are a demonstration of that gospel.

This world of love is not restricted only to the pure devotees. Krishna assures the sincere aspirants of pure love that He will guide them through this world of misdirected, short-lived love back home to the world of reclaimed, endless love: "To those who are constantly devoted to serving Me with love, I give the understanding by which they can come to Me. To show them special mercy, I, dwelling in their hearts, destroy with the shining lamp of knowledge the darkness born of ignorance." (10.10-11)

Krishna is, as the Beatle George Harrison penned, the "God who loves those who love Him". When we choose the path of love revealed by Krishna, He will in turn illuminate our heart with divine wisdom and spiritual love. The easiest way to express our love for Krishna and experience his love for us is by chanting the holy names like the Hare Krishna mahamantra (10.25).

Thus the Gita is essentially a revelation of divinity's love for humanity as well as a love call for humanity's reciprocal love for divinity. Let us therefore tread the path of love revealed by Krishna. Let us love and be loved.   ● ● ●

From Adversity to Prosperity

"Man proposes, God disposes" has been the cause of immense frustration for humanity since time immemorial. The best plans are often foiled forever in a single moment by factors beyond human control. Misery can be said to be the condition in which we are unable to get what we want and / or are forced to accept that which we don't want. A thoughtful person can perceive that misery is an unavoidable, inescapable companion during the sojourn through this world (Bhagavad Gita 8.15). Everyone is put repeatedly in the unenviable position of watching helplessly all of one's cherished plans wrecked one after another, by the inexplicable and seemingly cruel will of providence.

Little Control Means No Control

Most people try to tackle this existential dilemma by trying to increase their ability to control their situations by acquiring wealth, power, knowledge, fame, beauty and even renunciation. But do these material acquisitions really solve the problem? They seem to give us control over our lives and surroundings, but actually they themselves are beyond our control. For example, a wealthy person imagines that his monetary power gives him control over his life and so wants to increase his wealth unlimitedly (16.13-15), but he can lose the wealth itself – his source of control - due to events beyond his control, such as a stock market crash. Thus wealth creates an illusion of control, while in reality it only increases one's anxiety by making one further dependent on things that are beyond one's control. Moreover money cannot bribe death, which in one moment strips one of everything (10.34). Hence the Gita asserts that these material solutions offer no actual relief (2.8). Srila Prabhupada succinctly states the futility of mundane attempts to control our lives and surroundings, "Little control means no control."

The Bhagavad-gita offers a dramatically different remedy for this existential perplexity: God proposes, man accepts. It asserts that all attempts to become happy in the material world are ultimately misdirected, as they keep us out of harmony with God. The perfection of our intelligence is when we harmonize our human will with the divine will (7.19). Accepting reversals faithfully and gracefully as the inconceivable will of the Lord is a teaching mentioned in all the major religions of the world. The prayer of Jesus the night before he was crucified, "Let Thy will be done, not mine" is a well-known example. In times of pain and grief, this prayerful surrender to the will of the Lord has the potential of bringing immediate and immense relief. However, most people are unable to muster the faith necessary for offering such a bold prayer. The Bhagavad-gita holds a unique position among all the world's scriptures in that it offers a solid intellectual springboard and a well-defined spiritual trajectory for this leap of faith. The philosophy delineated in the Gita is so cogent, coherent and comprehensive that, after understanding it, Arjuna not only accepted the will of the Lord that his relatives be killed, but went way ahead. He agreed to himself be instrumental in bringing about the execution of that divine will: karishye vacanam tava "I will do whatever You say." (18.73)

Insights From The Gita

This extraordinarily empowering perspective to the reversals of life, as explained in the Gita, can be summarized as follows:

1. We are not gross bodies or subtle minds, but are eternal souls (7.4-5). Therefore the sufferings due to the mind, the body and their extensions – relatives and friends, possessions and positions - no matter how devastating, do not deprive us of our essential spiritual identity and purpose in life – to revive our loving relationship with God. Knowing that we have a changeless core, which can never be taken away from us by any vicissitude and which can always bring us inner happiness, is in itself a source of tremendous solace and strength when everything around us seems to be falling apart.(2.13-16)

2. The Lord is our Supreme Father (14.4), and He unconditionally loves all of us - even those of us who spurn His love and even deny His very existence. The practical manifestation of His selfless, causeless love is that He creates and maintains all the background material arrangements by which we - His wayward children - can enjoy material happiness. He maintains the entire material world – the arena for material enjoyment - by arranging for all the universal necessities such as heat and light (15.12-13) He further maintains the material body – the vehicle for material pleasure - by keeping all the bodily functions such as digestion in proper order (15.14). Not only that, according to our desires to enjoy life, He gives us the corresponding inspiration and intelligence (15.15) Thus the Lord is our supreme well-wisher and benefactor (5.29)

3. All events in the material world occur as per the universal laws of action and reaction. Reversals don't come upon us by cruel chance, but are a result of our own past misdeeds – either in this or earlier lives. Acceptance of the law of karma is not fatalistic, creating feelings of helplessness and impotence, as some people misunderstand. Nor is it psychologically damaging, creating haunting feelings of guilt, as some others allege. Rather a mature understanding of the impartial law of karma is highly empowering, as we understand that we still have control over our lives. By harmonizing with the universal laws of action, as explained in the God-given scriptures, we have the power to create a bright future for ourselves, no matter how bleak the present may seem to be. (3.9)

4. For those unflinchingly devoted to the Lord, things don't go wrong just by karmic laws. The Lord personally orchestrates the events in the lives of His devotees so that they are most expeditiously elevated to the platform of unlimited, eternal, spiritual happiness. (12.6-7) Indeed for the faithful the Lord transforms material adversity into spiritual prosperity. An intelligent transcendentalist is therefore able to see a painful reversal as a spiritual catharsis performed by the Lord to free him from the shackles of the lower self and to unleash the potential of the higher

self. He sees suffering like a surgery, which, though painful, frees the body from dangerous infection and promotes the recovery of health.

Wisdom In Action

Let us see how the wisdom of the Gita empowered its original recipient – Arjuna. The setting on which the Gita was spoken – a battlefield between two huge armies poised for war - is highly intriguing. Fratricidal friction within the ruling Kuru dynasty had erupted into a massive conflagration on the sprawling plains of Kurukshetra. As thousands of soldiers, chariots, horses and elephants stood waiting for the war-cry to be sounded, Arjuna, one of the principal warriors, suffered an emotional breakdown, being overwhelmed by the prospect of killing his own relatives. In the face of extreme adversity he lost sight of his duty and turned for guidance to his friend, Krishna, who was the Supreme Godhead playing the role of a human being. Then in the midst of the belligerent armies, Krishna enlightened his friend Arjuna – and through him all of humanity for all time to come - about the temporal and eternal identity and duty of the self entrapped in material perplexities.

After hearing Krishna's message, Arjuna experienced a complete paradigm shift. He realized that Krishna was not urging him to fight the war for petty personal gains, impelled by feelings of selfish greed or mundane vengeance. Rather, he had the privileged opportunity to play a crucial role in a divine plan for re-establishing order and harmony in human society by destroying the anti-social elements who had unscrupulously grabbed power. Hence his fighting was actually necessary and beneficial service to God and to all living beings as the children of God. He realized that all the warriors assembled there – including his loved ones – were eternal souls, who would continue to live after their bodily death. But by dying in the presence of the supremely pure Lord Krishna, they would be purified of their sinful mentality and would attain spiritual emancipation. Before hearing the Gita, Arjuna had felt that he was in a lose-lose situation (2.6). If he killed his relatives he felt he would be doing a heinous sin (1.36) and if he chose to not kill them by abstaining from fighting, he would have no means of sustenance and would be disgraced for having abandoned the battle like a coward (2.33-36). After hearing the Gita, he recognized that his situation was actually win-win. He had no need to fear sin because action harmonized with divine will brings not sin and suffering, but purification and elevation (18.65-66). His killing his relatives would benefit not only himself, but also the whole world and the slain relatives too! Even if he happened to die while fighting – which he would not because the supreme will is always triumphant (18.78) – still he would attain the highest spiritual realm of everlasting happiness by laying down his perishable body in a holy war. Therefore after hearing the Gita, Arjuna confidently picked up his famed Gandiva bow, which he had dejectedly cast aside earlier, and emphatically declared his willingness to execute the all-beneficial will of the Lord (18.73). Thus the original setting of the Gita is a graphic illustration of action in accordance with spiritual wisdom transforming a disastrous reversal into a glorious triumph.

The March to Divine Harmony

The comprehensive philosophical explanation of the Gita serves as a map for the aspiring transcendentalist on his spiritual odyssey back to harmony with the Lord (16.24). Yoga – linking one's consciousness with the Lord – is the means to return to harmony. The Gita states that meditation (dhyana-yoga), speculation (jnana-yoga), detached action (karma-yoga) and devotional service (bhakti-yoga) are means by which a soul can advance on the path back to harmony. Ultimate success however comes only by devotional service (11.53-54); other paths are only stepping stones to the attainment of that devotion (6.47, 7.19, 3.9). The best method of devotional meditation for the current period in the cosmic cycle (Kali Yuga) is mantra meditation (10.25), especially the chanting of the maha mantra Hare Krishna Hare Krishna Krishna Krishna Hare Hare Hare Rama Hare Rama Rama Rama Hare Hare, which nourishes the higher self. Abstaining from the self-destructive activities of meat-eating, gambling, intoxication and illicit sex, thus starving the lower self, accelerates the return to harmony. Bhakti-yoga progressively leads to the full blossoming of our higher nature and culminates in prema, selfless love for the Supreme Lord Sri Krishna. This love leads to unconditional loving surrender to the will of the Lord and the resulting harmony of divine love makes life a joy at every moment even in this life. This divine love is the ultimate achievement of life; it conquers even death, for it continues eternally after bodily death in the highest abode, the spiritual world, the realm of pure consciousness.

Shripad Shankaracharya explains, in his Gita-mahatmaya, the unique position of the Gita within the vast Vedic library. He compares all the Vedic scriptures to a cow, Krishna to a cowherd boy milking the cow, Arjuna to a calf and the Gita to the milk of the cow. Thus the Gita is considered to be the essence of all the Vedic literature. Appreciation for the Gita is not limited to Vedic circles. Many Western scholars have found the Gita to be amazingly lucid and relevant. Ralph Waldo Emerson's remark is a sample, "I owed a magnificent day to the Bhagavad-gita. It was the first of books; it was as if an empire spoke to us, nothing small or unworthy, but large, serene, consistent, the voice of an old intelligence which in another age and climate had pondered and thus disposed of the same questions which exercise us." When Srila Prabhupada, the founder-acharya of the International Society for Krishna consciousness (ISKCON), went to the West to teach the message of the Gita and was asked in the United Kingdom about the purpose of his visit, he poignantly replied, "When you British ruled India, you plundered her off all her wealth, but you forgot to take her most precious jewel. I have come to give you what you forgot – the wisdom of the Gita."

● ● ●

DISCOVER THE POST-SECULAR SYNTHESIS

Made For Each Other

"You're saying your research proves this higher reality exists?" asks writer Vince Rause.

Prof Andrew Newberg of the University of Pennsylvania replies, "I'm saying the possibility of such a reality is not inconsistent with science."

"But you can't observe such a thing in a scientific way, can you?"

Newberg grins. He hasn't simply observed such a state; he has managed to take its picture.

Divine Findings

What you are reading is an extract from a fascinating article Searching for the Divine on pg 125 in the Jan 2002 issue of the Readers Digest. Prof Andrew Newberg is a leader in neurotheology, an emerging science which explores the links between spirituality and the brain.

Newberg and his team took pictures of the brain of the subjects in a normal waking state and in deep meditation. When they studied the scans, their attention was drawn to a chunk of the brain's left parietal lobe which they called the orientation association area. This region is responsible for drawing the line between the physical self and rest of existence, a task that requires a constant stream of neural information flowing in from the senses. What the scans revealed, however, was that at peak moments of prayer and meditation, the flow was dramatically reduced, indicating a decrease in neuronal activity. In such a brain state, the subject loses awareness of his physical self, goes to a state of complete relaxation and deep satisfaction and experiences a higher reality.

Newberg concludes that such an experience of God by the human brain is as much a reality as any perception by the brain of 'ordinary' physical reality.

This article is typical of what modern medical science is discovering (or rather rediscovering). More and more rigorous and unbiased studies are providing impeccable scientific evidence establishing the benefits, and indeed the necessity, of spirituality as an integral part of human existence.

Let the Data Speak

Consider the following data compiled by Patrick Glynn, Associate Director at the George Washington University, in his book God: The Evidence:

Suicide: A large-scale 1972 study found that persons who did not attend spiritual prayer meetings were four times as likely to commit suicide as those who attended spiritual prayer meetings frequently. A review of twelve studies of the relationship between religious commitment and suicide found a negative correlation in all twelve cases. Lack of spiritual prayer meetings attendance has been found to be the single best predictor of suicide rates, better even than unemployment.

Drug Abuse: Numerous studies have found an inverse correlation between religious commitment and abuse of drugs. One survey of nearly 14,000 youths found that substance abuse varied in inverse proportion to strength of religious commitment, with the most conservative religious youths abusing the least. The authors concluded that "importance of religion" was the single best indicator / predictor of substance abuse patterns.

Alcohol Abuse: Several studies have found that alcohol abuse is highest among those with little or no religious commitment. One study found that nearly 90% of alcoholics had lost interest in religion in youth, while among the non-alcoholic control group 48% reported an increase in religious commitment in adulthood and 32% reported no change.

Depression and Stress: Several studies have found that high levels of religious commitment correlate with lower levels of depression, lower level of stress, and greater ability to cope with stress. Religious people recover from surgery more quickly than do their atheistic counterparts.

Divorce: A number of studies have found a strong inverse correlation between attendance at spiritual prayer meetings and divorce. Spiritual prayer meetings' attendance also correlates strongly with the expressed willingness of a partner to marry the same spouse again - a measure of marital satisfaction.

Marital and Sexual Satisfaction: A study found that spiritual prayer meetings attendance predicted marital satisfaction better than any other single variable. Couples in long-lasting marriages, who were surveyed in another study, listed religion as one of the most important "prescriptions" of a happy marriage. Most strikingly, an analysis of data from a massive survey of Redbook magazine readers found that "very religious women report greater happiness and satisfaction with marital sex than either moderately religious or nonreligious women" So religious people even seem to enjoy better marital sex!

Overall Happiness and Psychological Well-being: Strong religious believers consistently report greater overall happiness and satisfaction with life. In one Gallup survey, respondents with a strong religious commitment - who agreed that "My religious faith is the most important influence in my life" - were twice as likely as those with minimal spiritual commitment to describe themselves as "very happy"

Thus Dr Glynn concludes, "Statistics show that it is difficult to find a more consistent correlative of mental health, or a better insurance against self-destructive behaviors, than a strong religious faith."

A Remarkable Revolution

That psychology and its affiliated fields have come up with these findings is remarkable, to say the very least.

Since the early twentieth century, a group of psychologists has been caustic in their condemnation of religion. They have branded faith as a form of mental disorder, a disorder that they predicted humanity would outgrow. Such thoughts have led to the predominance of the atheistic mentality in psychology and other related fields and in medical science at large.

But even in those times there were renowned thinkers who differed markedly. Consider for example what Carl Jung remarked in 1932:

Among all the patients in the second half of my life, there has not been one whose problem in the last resort was not that of finding a religious outlook on life. It is safe to say that every one of them fell ill because he had lost that which the living religions of every age have given their followers and none of them has really healed who did not regain his religious outlook.

In other words, Carl Jung firmly believed that faith was a medicine rather than a disease.

And the findings of the late twentieth century show that the atheistic challenge to religion, made under the guise of science, has collapsed - that too under the weight of scientific evidence. That this has happened in such an emphatic way in psychology itself, the field where it once gathered great momentum, is eloquent testimony to the sheer magnitude of the revolution in science vis-à-vis spirituality that we are witnessing.

The physicians are coming up with similar findings. Harvard Medical School associate professor of medicine Herbert Benson states that contemporary medical research is showing that the human mind and body are "wired for God". A Time cover story puts it in even more explicit terms. When it comes to health, "the faithful actually have God on their side." Several other fields as wide-ranging as sociology and ecology are coming up with increasing evidence showing that only a spiritual way of life is sustainable and satisfying; atheism courts disaster at every level.

Thus modern science is rediscovering what all the religious scriptures have been teaching since time immemorial: the living being and God are made for each other.   ● ● ●

When Science Points to Spirituality

Imagine a farmer who gets a Mercedes Benz as a gift. The only vehicle he has ever seen is a tractor, and the only purpose he knows for any vehicle is plowing. So he hitches a yoke to his new Mercedes and starts driving it over his field. Of course, not only does his attempt at plowing fail; his new car malfunctions. He becomes totally frustrated--with himself, his car, and his field.

Ridiculous, we might say, that somebody would use a Mercedes to plow. But could this be the story of our life? The Vedic scriptures--and the scriptures of all the great religions of the world--say that human life is meant for achieving, not material enjoyment, but spiritual fulfillment. The Vedic scriptures further explain that the human body is a precious vehicle that the soul gets after transmigrating through 8.4 million species. In all subhuman bodies, the soul has access only to material pleasure, through fulfilling the bodily demands of eating, sleeping, mating, and defending. All material pleasure is troublesome to acquire. Even when acquired, it is unsatisfying because of the body's limited capacity to enjoy. And even this paltry pleasure is inevitably curtailed by disease and old age, and terminated by death.

Only in the human body is the soul's consciousness evolved enough to access a superior source of pleasure--love of God. The Vedic scriptures explain that love of God enables the soul to attain eternal happiness in the spiritual world, his original home. Achieving this love of God is the specific and exclusive purpose for which the soul should use the human body.

We can compare the subhuman bodies, which offer flickering bodily pleasures, to tractors meant for plowing a field. And we can compare the human body, which can offer the soul everlasting happiness, to a posh Mercedes meant for a smooth ride. Using the human body for sensual pleasures is not much different from using a car for plowing.

Because we see almost everyone around us pursuing material goals--sex, wealth, luxuries, prestige, power, fame--we assume such pursuits to be the natural purpose of life. But, as the saying goes, "Do not think you're on the right road just because it's well-worn."

Let the Facts Speak

When we use a Mercedes to plow, three things result: a spoiled field, a wrecked car, and a frustrated driver. Let's see what science has discovered about using the human body only for sensual pleasure. Specifically, what happens to the environment (the field), the human body (the car), and ourselves (the driver)?

The environment: Biologist E. O. Wilson, among many other scientists, has studied the complex interdependence among various species in the biosphere. He found that every species makes some contribution to the ecology of the planet. For example, if vegetation decreases, herbivores suffer, then carnivores. But he found that one species doesn't contribute to the ecology--the human species. If the human species became extinct, there would hardly be any problems for any other species or for the ecology. In fact, human extinction would solve most ecological problems. The human species is arguably the most intelligent species on the planet. Normally in a class, the more intelligent a student, the more is his positive contribution. Then why is it that, among all species, our human contribution to the ecology is not the most positive, but the most negative? Can it be that our contribution is meant to be at a level higher than the physical?

The human body: How do activities many consider enjoyable affect the human body? Smoking causes lung disease, drinking leads to liver diseases, eating non-vegetarian and junk food ruins digestion, and illicit sex--that perpetually over-hyped carnal pleasure--brings AIDS, an epidemic for which there is no aid. Modern society, education, and media indoctrinate us into believing that material enjoyment is the goal of life. But this "enjoyment" causes our worst suffering. Could it be that we are being tragically misled into abusing the human body for activities it is not designed for?

Ourselves: And what about the effect on ourselves? Scientists are still groping in the dark about who or what the self is. But one thing is for sure: the more modern society neglects or rejects spiritual growth, the more trouble the self gets into. This is evident from our spiraling mental health problems. The World Health Organization (WHO) has declared that mental diseases--stress, depression, addiction, psychosomatic problems--will be the greatest health hazard of the current century. Worse still, WHO statistics show that over one million people commit suicide every year. That's more than the total annual deaths from wars and crimes combined. And this figure is only the reported number of suicides.

Mental disease and suicide have many causes. But the common origin is frustration in achieving one's goals, whatever they may be. When this frustration rises to an acute and hopeless degree, one feels one's very existence to be an agony. And the ending of one's existence appears to be the only solution. Why is it that we modern humans, the most "intelligent" among all species, are the only species whose members commit suicide in such alarmingly high numbers?

WHO calls suicide as "a tragic social health problem" and states that there is no proven cure for it. Could it be that the goals society sets for us are incompatible with our selves and invite the frustration that leads to mental health problems and ultimately suicide?

See and Believe

How does channeling human energy for spiritual elevation affect ecology, human health, and the self? Lets see what science says.

Ecology: Most environmental problems have arisen from the materialism and consumerism that has accompanied the decline of spirituality and its inherent self-restraint. Therefore the following quote from Alan Durning of the World Watch Institute represents what many scientists consider to be the only hope for saving the environment: "In a fragile biosphere, the ultimate fate of humanity may depend on whether we can cultivate a deeper sense of self-restraint, founded on a widespread ethic of limiting consumption and finding non-material enrichment." All forms of non-material enrichment--prayer, meditation, yoga, chanting the holy names-- clearly point to a spiritual dimension to life. And this spiritual dimension is most comprehensively explained in the Vedic scriptures. In fact the Vedanta-sutra begins with a clarion call athato brahma jijnasa: "Now therefore [now that you have a human body], devote yourself to spiritual enquiry." (Vedanta-sutra 1.1)

Human health: The current epidemic of indulgence-born diseases shows that universal scriptural injunctions for self-restraint- -sobriety (no intoxication) and continence (no illicit sex), for example--are sound health advice too. Herbert Benson of the Harvard Medical School, citing extensive research on the physical and mental benefits of spiritual living, states that the human body and mind are "wired for God." Not only that, a survey published in Reader's Digest (January 2001) stated that believers in God live an average of eleven years more than nonbelievers.

The self: And what about the self? Science has come up with a precious finding: spirituality is a sure solace for the self. Survey after survey has shown that spiritual practices protect people from self-destructive behavior and habits. Patrick Glynn of the George Washington University writes in his book God: The Evidence that surveys show that those who don't attend spiritual prayer meetings are four times more prone to suicide than those who do so. Further, the giving up of such meetings has been found to be the best predictor of suicide, better even than unemployment. These findings indicate that spirituality provides inner joy, which frees people from the uncontrollable and insatiable craving for external pleasures that leads to addictions and suicides. Such findings have inspired some modern thinkers to echo the Vedic conclusion that spirituality is not just a part of our life; it is the essence of our life. Stephen Covey, well-known author of the Seven Habits series, aptly remarks, "We are not human beings on a spiritual journey. We are spiritual beings on a human journey."

What Are We Waiting For?

Science is clearly showing that human life spent for material enjoyment is ecologically, physically, and spiritually disharmonious and disastrous. Science is also strongly indicating that when we strive for spiritual happiness, we benefit our planet and our body too. The Vedic scriptures offer us a balanced program of material regulation and spiritual growth for achieving the highest potential of human life. Bhagavad-gita (6.17) states that regulation in eating, sleeping, work, and recreation, coupled with spiritual practices, paves the way to freedom from all material miseries. The most potent and practical spiritual practice for the modern age is the chanting of the Hare Krsna maha-mantra. By chanting we can achieve a state of happiness (Bhagavad-gita 6.19) that will fully satisfy us and will never be disturbed by any material upheaval.

It's time to stop using the Mercedes for plowing. It's time to put our human vehicle into gear by chanting Hare Krsna. Then we can speed along the highway of devotional service, back to our long-lost home with Krsna.   ● ● ●

Your Cosmic Specialness

The impenetrable shell of the tortoise, the breathtaking swiftness of the leopard, the incredible color-changing ability of the chameleon: the variety in nature is amazing. Every species of life has a special gift from nature, an ability that is vital for its survival and success in the struggle for existence.

The Strange Irony

Compared to these animals, humans have no extraordinary external ability; their bodies are soft and vulnerable, they are not particularly fleet-footed and they can do little to camouflage themselves when in danger. And yet humans stand far above all other species. A puny human can tame a massive elephant and encage a ferocious lion. How? What is the special gift of nature to humans, the unique ability that makes them superior to all other species? Undoubtedly it is the advanced human intelligence. Empowered by their intelligence, humans have subjugated all the lower species. Not only that, humans have also built civilizations, developed cultures, devised languages, written literatures, come up with fine arts, inquired into metaphysics and advanced in science and technology.

Strangely enough, in the modern times, by that same intelligence, humans have created weapons of mass destruction, which threaten to wipe out all life on the planet. Furthermore, by that same intelligence, humans have developed perverted ideologies, by which they foster animosity and hatred for others of their own species. This then is the strange irony of the present condition of humanity. Intelligence has been the key to the success of humans and yet intelligence is what threatens to destroy them today. For no other species of life does its source of protection threaten to become its cause of destruction.

Advancing In Anxiety

Let's look at this situation from another perspective. All living beings are driven by a craving for pleasure. All subhuman species search for pleasure through the bodily activities of eating, sleeping, mating and defending. Humans do the same, but in more refined ways. For example, a bird lives in the same nest year after year, generation after generation, but humans try to improve their residences – from huts, to apartments, to bungalows, to villas. A cow eats the same grass lifelong, but humans choose their food from a large variety of cuisines. Modern scientific advancement has been essentially utilized for improving these four bodily pleasures. For example, humans have explored the mysteries of electrons to come up with electronics and telecommunication, which helps them enjoy erotic pleasures through television, movies and the internet. Similarly, advancement in biotechnology has been used to develop better foodstuffs. Also, worldwide, most of the funds for scientific research come from the military (which is a hi-tech arrangement for defending) and the consumer industry (which offers sophisticated methods for eating, sleeping and mating).

Humans have made these sophisticated arrangements for eating, sleeping, mating and defending, and yet they undergo far more anxiety than animals in these very activities. Animals rarely die of starvation due to artificial shortages created by others of their own species; animals rarely suffer from insomnia; animals rarely undergo the trauma of heartbreaks due to betrayed love and animals rarely live in mortal fear from others of their own species. Furthermore, animals rarely feel stressed, animals rarely struggle with depression, animals rarely fall prey to addictions and animals rarely, if ever, commit suicide. Thus we are confronted again with the strange irony that modern humans, despite their advanced intelligence and organized attempts for better enjoyment, are suffering more than their less intelligent subhuman counterparts, the animals.

The Vedic Perspective

The Vedic texts offer some interesting insights into this state of affairs. They agree that humans are endowed with a higher intelligence that makes them unique among all forms of life. They further state that this higher human intelligence is meant for a purpose far loftier than searching for better ways of obtaining bodily pleasures. Equipped with their special intelligence, humans are meant to probe into the deepest mysteries of life. The Vedic texts thus urge all humans to explore the spiritual frontier of life.

For such enterprising spiritual scientists, the Vedic texts present a comprehensive, consistent and cogent body of knowledge that answers all the fundamental questions of life. In essence, they explain that a nonmaterial self, known as the atman or the soul, animates the body and a similar non-material Supreme Being, known as the Paramatama or the Supersoul, animates the cosmos. When the soul and the Supersoul are in harmony, every moment of life becomes filled with ever-increasing joy. Sub-human species have no opportunity to achieve this fullness of life as their under-developed intelligence allows them no access to the spiritual dimension. Only when the soul gets a human body is he endowed with the intelligence to penetrate the superficial world of matter and perceive the spiritual energy within the cosmos. Humans alone can harmonize themselves with the totality of the cosmic energies - material and spiritual. When a human being achieves this harmony, he gains access to a whole new world of profound knowledge, thrilling experience and unlimited happiness. The Vedic texts also delineate a systematic program centered on meditation on divine sound, by which a spiritual scientist can experience these higher realities of life.

The Massive Blunder

In the modern times, humans have exercised their intellects tirelessly to understand the world of matter. This has resulted in significant advances in science and technology. But modern science has been dogmatically reluctant to investigate the spiritual dimension of life. A thinking person can easily perceive that life has an aspect higher than the material. Can electrons think? Can atoms have emotions? Can molecules desire? Can chemicals experience love? Obviously not. Within the framework of material science, there is no explanation whatsoever for the phenomenon of consciousness. Although the reality of consciousness is undeniable, modern science has done precious little to understand it; indeed, modern science has religiously restricted itself to the study of matter.

The Vedic texts assert that to keep the human intellect locked within the realm of matter is gross underutilization of the tremendous potential of human life. Worse still, when deprived of access to the spiritual realm, a human being cannot experience the fullness that he intrinsically longs for. He frantically searches for that fullness by manipulating matter in newer and newer ways, but to no avail. The resulting frustration causes such a human being to become stunted, throttled and distorted. Overindulgence in matter and negligence of spirit backfires and results in disharmony, distress and disaster.

The modern world is bearing the brunt of this colossal imbalance of material and spiritual values. Individually there is an increase in dissatisfaction, stress, depression, addiction and suicide and globally there is an increase in unrest, criminality, violence and terrorism.

Dare To Be Special

The essence of a living being is his desires; it is our desires that direct and determine our entire life. A human being may advance in science, technology, culture, art, literature and even religion, but if his driving desires are the same as those of the animals, if he is still interested only in eating, sleeping, mating and defending, he is not much superior to the animals. A person may have seemingly special externals – a fancy hairstyle, a fashionable dress, a hi-tech mobile, a flashy car, and so on, but if his internal desires are the same as those of the ordinary animals – to attract the opposite sex, to seek titillation of the tongue and so on, such a person is nothing more than a sophisticated animal. If his desires are not higher than those of the animals, his material advancement is but an eyewash. By such a façade, a human being succeeds only in cheating himself of the highest happiness that is due to him as a human.

A human being becomes truly special only when he makes his desires higher than those of the animals. Such a human being dares to desire the highest happiness that genuine spirituality alone can provide. Being a connoisseur of pleasure, he rejects the pleasures that the animals are seeking, considering them unworthy of his developed intelligence. He wisely refuses to tread the beaten track that all other living beings are pursuing, a path that leads to old age, disease and death. The Bhagavad-gita (7.3) declares that such a human being is very special and rare; indeed he is one among millions.

Therefore, the onus is on every intelligent person to choose his desires. Will he continue to be just another face in the crowd, another ordinary creature with the same desires of eating, sleeping, mating and defending that everyone else has? Will he continue to be just another figure in the meaningless statistics of this world? Or will he be bold enough to be special - by pursuing lofty spiritual goals in life? Will he take up the challenge of pioneering an ongoing global spiritual awakening that is the only hope for the modern misdirected civilization? The world is waiting to see.

Bhagavad-gita for the Jet-age

"We have guided missiles and misguided men." This poignant remark by Martin Luther King, Jr., about the state of the modern world rings strikingly true. In recent times there has been an amazing increase in human ability to control the outer world through science and technology. But with that has come an alarming decline in human ability to control the inner world. The resulting irrational passions lead to immorality and corruption at best, and terrorism and brutality at worst.

The current state of the world rests on the search for happiness, a quest that, Lord Krishna tells us in Bhagavad- gita, lies at the heart of all human endeavors. While asserting that happiness is our inalienable right, the Bhagavad-gita provides a clear pathway for its achievement. The fundamental teaching of Lord Krishna in the Bhagavad-gita is that our current existence has two dimensions— material and spiritual; we are spiritual beings residing in material bodies. (2.13)* Modern scientific studies in fields such as past-life memories, near-death experiences, and consciousness also strongly suggest a spiritual part of our being that exists after bodily death.

Furthermore, Lord Krishna explains that just as the soul animates the body, the Supersoul, the Supreme Being, animates the entire cosmos.

Lord Krishna tells us that material existence is temporary and troublesome because of an existential disharmony: human beings tend to neglect the spiritual dimension of their lives and focus only on material ambitions and achievements. This imbalance stunts their ability to partake of the fullness of life. The resulting dissatisfaction appears individually as stress, depression, anxiety, irritability, and so on, and socially as disunity, violence, and war. This disharmony also results in the universal and inescapable evils of birth, old age, disease, and death (13.9).

Our innate longing for immortality in a world subject to death suggests that we belong to an immortal world. Lord Krishna posits a higher-dimensional world beyond the pernicious effects of time (8.20). That realm is characterized by a sweet harmony of divine love between the innumerable subordinate souls and the Supreme. There, the Supreme Person, being all- attractive, is the pivot of all relationships and is therefore best known as Krishna, "The All-Attractive One." There, all souls enjoy an eternal life of full awareness and bliss, provided they are in harmony with Krishna's will. If they rebel, they fall to the realm of matter, where they can see the results of disharmony and eventually decide to reform themselves.

Suffering and Its Solution

During their exile in the material realm, souls occupy different bodies according to their desires and activities. Each body, whether human or subhuman, imposes on the soul the demands of eating, sleeping, mating, and defending. The soul struggles hard to try to fulfill these bodily demands, whose repetitive nature makes life a continuous hardship, with only momentary relief whenever the demands are satisfied.

Suffering, however, is good, because it provides the necessary impetus to return to harmony, just as fever provides the impetus to accept a cure. Among the 8.4 million species that inhabit the cosmos, the human form is specially gifted: only in a human body does the soul have the requisite intelligence to question his suffering and attempt to remedy it. Bhagavad-gita addresses such intelligent human beings.

Asserting that material nature is endlessly mutable (8.4), Lord Krishna advises the seeker of true happiness to not be disturbed by the dualities of heat and cold, pain and pleasure, and so on, that result from the inevitable changes in the material world (2.14). But Krishna does not recommend a life of inane fatalism; He exhorts us to direct our energies in a fruitful direction. Because our anomalous condition results from a disharmony with our spiritual nature,

Krishna recommends that attempts for improvement be directed not in the material realm but in the spiritual.

The Relevance of the Bhagavad-gita

It is here that we can see the relevance of Lord Krishna's teachings to the modern state of affairs. Over the past few centuries modern man has performed immense intellectual labor in an attempt to decrease the miseries of material existence. But all these efforts have been directed within the realm of matter, resulting in an improved ability to control material energy through science and technology. Modern man has, with almost a religious dogma, avoided applying his intellectual faculties to understanding the spiritual dimension. But all the cherished human qualities—love, compassion, honesty, selflessness—spring from the soul, the spiritual aspect of our being. Therefore negligence of spiritual life has had disastrous consequences, including a marked decline in human virtues. Hence Dr. King's observation that we live in a time of guided missiles and misguided men.

Lord Krishna systematically explains the difference between matter and spirit and provides a practical method for spiritual elevation. Lord Krishna thus helps us understand how ignorance and neglect of the spiritual dimension is the bane of modern civilization.

Returning to Harmony

Lord Krishna recommends yoga as the means to spiritual emancipation. Contrary to the general notion, Lord Krishna states that mere physical postures and breathing exercises do not constitute yoga; they are just the beginning of one type of yoga. Actual yoga involves harmonizing all energy—material and spiritual—with the original source of energy, the energetic Supreme. Lord Krishna states that meditation (dhyana-yoga), philosophical speculation (jnana-yoga), detached action (karma- yoga), and devotional service to the Lord (bhakti- yoga) are means by which a soul can advance on the path back to harmony. But ultimate success comes only by devotional service (11.53-54); other paths are only stepping stones to the attainment of that devotion (6.47, 7.19, 3.9).

The best method of devotional meditation for the current period in the cosmic cycle (Kali-yuga) is mantra meditation (10.25), especially the chanting of the maha-mantra: Hare Krishna, Hare Krishna, Krishna Krishna, Hare Hare/ Hare Rama, Hare Rama, Rama Rama, Hare Hare. A person moving forward on the path of harmony discovers in time a decrease in mental agitation from irrational passions, an unshakable inner tranquility, and finally an eternal ecstasy of love coming from the spiritual stratum (6.20- 23). Lord Krishna therefore concludes with an unequivocal call for loving harmony with the Supreme (18.66).

Lord Krishna declares the higher realities of life to be pratyaksha avagamam, directly perceivable within (9.2). Thus we see that Lord Krishna's approach to the study of the cosmos is not at all dogmatic; rather it is bold and scientific. He presents the postulates logically and systematically and provides the enterprising spiritual scientist with a practical method to verify those postulates.

Srila Prabhupada's Gift to the World

Lord Krishna's explanation of the truths of life is so cogent, coherent, and profound that, for most modern Western scholars who studied Bhagavad-gita for the first time in the seventeenth and eighteenth centuries, it was love on first reading. The remark of the famed American writer Henry David Thoreau is a sample: "In the morning I bathe my intellect in the stupendous and cosmogonal philosophy of the Bhagavad-gita, in comparison with which our modern world and its literature seem puny and trivial."

Unfortunately with the passage of time, imperial biases among Western scholars obscured the wisdom of the Bhagavad- gita from enlightening the whole of humanity. And Indian intellectuals, afflicted by feelings of cultural inferiority from prolonged foreign subjugation, did not give the Bhagavad-gita the importance it deserved.

It was only when His Divine Grace A. C. Bhaktivedanta Swami Prabhupada carried the wisdom of Bhagavad-gita to the West in the 1960s that the world started recognizing the glory of this philosophical masterpiece once again. Srila Prabhupada's Bhagavad-gita As It Is soon became the most widely read English edition of the Gita. Now translated into dozens of languages, Bhagavad-gita As It Is has transformed the lives of millions from confused despair to enlightened happiness.

East-West Synthesis

Srila Prabhupada has been acknowledged as the greatest cultural ambassador of India to the modern world. His vision was a global East-West synthesis. If a blind man carries a lame man, they can both move forward. Similarly, Srila Prabhupada understood that if the materially prosperous but spiritually blind West and the spiritually gifted but materially impoverished India joined forces, the combination would usher in an era of peace and prosperity all over the world. ISKCON is working tirelessly at the grassroots level to make this vision a reality.

The West has embraced a hedonistic way of life. And the East, especially India, enamored by the glitter of Western culture, is casting away the treasure of Vedic wisdom that is its priceless heritage. It behooves all intelligent and responsible students of Bhagavad-gita to understand, assimilate, and distribute to their fellow human beings the gift of the wisdom of Lord Krishna. ● ● ●

The Respiritualization Of Science

"For the scientist who has lived by his faith in the power of reason, the story [of the big bang] ends like a bad dream. For the past three hundred years, scientists have scaled the mountain of ignorance and as they pull themselves over the final rock, they are greeted by a band of theologians who have been sitting there for centuries." admits Astrophysicist Robert Jastrow in his book God and the Astronomers.

This statement reveals a dramatic, indeed historical, development in modern science, wherein the scientific temper is calling for inclusion of a spiritual paradigm in science. In this essay, we will analyze this amazing trend and then see the avenues that it opens for India to emerge as the spiritual leader of a post-secular world order.

History in the Making – And Remaking

Since the time Newton attempted to explain planetary orbits through the laws of gravity and motion, the scientific belief that the totality of existence can be explained through science has been gaining momentum. Correspondingly, the perception of the hand of God on the canvas of the universe has been dwindling more and more.

Prior to Newton, God was understood to be the creator and controller of the universe. Newtonian Physics relegated Him to the role of a creator, a mere clockmaker who had no power over nature, which was supposed to be governed by impersonal laws. Darwin's The Origin of Species proposed in 1859 provided the intellectual justification for removing God even from the role of the creator. The intellectual climate of that time embraced Darwinian evolution not so much because of its scientific basis, but because of its ideological implications. This covert agenda to "exile" God from the academic world was made overt by Fredrich Neitsche through his jolting "God is dead" proclamation. Subsequently, Sigmund Freud proposed that religion is a "neurosis" that humanity had been suffering from and that science would help cure it. And Karl Marx rejected religion "as the opium of the masses". Together, these four people – dubbed as "the bearded God-killers" – seemed to have effectively exiled God from the academic world.

Today almost all the academic textbooks and journals as well as commercial science fiction novels and movies portray the mechanistic notions of life as a proven fact, as an unquestionable scientific reality. Time and time again we get to hear recycled versions of the same old tale of human and universal origins: the universe originated with a big bang, unicellular life evolved fortuitously on the earth in a primordial soup, life forms evolved to increasing levels of complexity, and gradually all the flora and fauna on our planet – including we humans –came about. And concomitantly the religious worldviews of universal origins involving God are almost instantly rejected as pre-scientific superstitions.

This materialistic worldview has gained widespread acceptance not so much due to its scientific validation as due to its vigorous propagation. Moreover, the impressive technological accomplishments of science – catering to the mass demands for instant relief and pleasure – have created among people a naïve, unquestioning faith that whatever science says must be true. The extent of unquestioning faith people have in science was pointed out by Einstein himself when he said, '"Tell a man that there are 300 billion stars in the universe, and he'll believe you.... Tell him that a bench has wet paint upon it and he'll have to touch it to be sure." (also credited to Raimond Verwei).

However, over the decades, as the harmful effects of technology are being increasingly recognized, so also are the fallacies of the scientific worldview that underlies these technologies.

Most people today have been led to believe that science can explain – or will soon explain – all natural phenomena – including the origin of life and the universe. Not many of them get to know that this notion is a modern superstition, a blind belief that is only a few centuries old. Or that it is being increasingly challenged by scientific findings. All over the world, pioneering research in many different fields promises to herald a spiritual revolution within science.

The Spiritual Tidings In Science

Lets briefly see the basis of this call for the re-spiritualization of science:

1. At the macroscopic level. the "fine-tuning" of the universe – the micro-precise adjustment of almost 80 constants crucial for the formation of the universe – has led to the rise of the Intelligent Design Movement, which asserts that the tuning requires a tuner, a super-intelligent being, God, to oversee the creation and maintenance of the universe. "I saw in it (the atom) the key to the deepest secret of nature, and it revealed to me the greatness of the creation and the Creator," This remark of Noble Laureate physicist Max Born has turned out to be more prophetic then what most of his

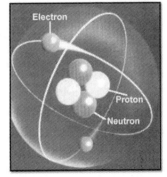

contemporaries could have imagined.

2. In the field of biology, the discovery of systems of irreducible complexity like say the bacterial flagella has posed a serious – possibly irrefutable – challenge to the Darwinian presumption that all life forms evolved gradually through natural processes from simple elements in the primordial soup. That's why Noble Laureate biologist Francis Crick had to admit that the origin of life seems "a miracle, so many are the conditions which would have had to have been satisfied to get it going."

3. The singular failure of scientists to explain consciousness – the most fundamental reality of existence – in mechanistic terms suggests that consciousness has a non-material or spiritual origin. Renowned Nobel Laureate physicist Neil Bohr states this, "We can admittedly find nothing in physics or chemistry that has even a remote bearing on consciousness. Yet all of us know that there is such a thing as consciousness, simply because we have it ourselves. Hence consciousness must be part of nature, or more generally, of reality, which means that quite apart from the laws of physics and chemistry, as laid down in quantum theory, we must also consider laws of quite a different nature."

4. The implications of Godel's theorem – the demonstration that in logic and in mathematics there must be true but unprovable statements, and that the consistency of a system such as arithmetic cannot be proved within that system – has shaken the foundations of godless rationalism, which thrived earlier on the presumption that we could one day understand

the universe in toto. This is revealed by eminent physicist Stephen Hawking as follows, "Maybe it is not possible to formulate the theory of the universe in a finite number of statements.... we and our models, are both part of the universe we are describing. Thus a physical theory, is self referencing like in Gödel's theorem. One might, therefore, expect it to be either inconsistent, or incomplete..... All the theories we have at present are both inconsistent and incomplete."

Thus despite the dazzling success of technology, science is deficient in providing a holistic framework for understanding and action. That's why eminent thinkers throughout the world, including leading scientists such as Nobel Laureate Richard R. Ernst, peace workers such as Nobel Laureates Oscar Arias Sanchez and Betty Williams, and spiritualists such as Nobel Laureate the Dalai Lama, firmly believe that only a synthesis of science and spirituality can lead the world out of the present troubled times.

Vedic Synthesis

India is renowned globally as the land of profound and peerless spiritual wisdom. Here are a few quotes of eminent Western thinkers:

1. "Whenever I have read any part of the Vedas, I have felt that some unearthly and unknown light illuminated me. In the great teaching of the Vedas, there is no touch of sectarianism. It is of all ages, climbs, and nationalities and is the royal road for the attainment of the Great Knowledge." -*Thoreau (American Thinker)*

2. "The marvel of the Bhagavad-Gita is its truly beautiful revelation of life's wisdom which enables philosophy to blossom into religion." -*Herman Hesse (1877-1962), German poet and novelist, awarded the Nobel Prize for literature in 1946.*

3. "In the great book of India,the Bhagavad-gita, an empire spoke to us, nothing small or unworthy, but large, sereneconsistent, the voice of an old intelligence, which in another age and climate had pondered and thus disposed of the questions that exercise us." -*Ralph Waldo Emerson Eminent American Thinker*

Lesser known are the accomplishments and contributions of Vedic India to the field of science. Here are a few quotes from famous Western scientists acknowledging the scientific glory of Vedic India:

1. "We owe a lot to the Indians, who taught us how to count, without which no worthwhile scientific discovery could have been made." - *Albert Einstein*

2. "After the conversations about Indian philosophy, some of the ideas of Quantum Physics that had seemed so crazy suddenly made much more sense" -*Noble Laureate W. Heisenberg , pioneer of quantum physics*

3. "The Vedanta and the Sankhya hold the key to the laws of mind and thought process which are co-related to the Quantum Field, i.e. the operation and distribution of particles at atomic and molecular levels." - *Prof. Brian David Josephson (1940 -) Welsh physicist, the youngest Nobel Laureate*

4. "It is India that gave us the ingenious method of expressing all numbers by ten symbols, each receiving a value of position as well as an absolute value, a profound and important idea which appears so simple to us now that we ignore its true merit. But its very simplicity, the great ease which it has lent to all computations, puts our arithmetic in the first rank of useful inventions, and we shall appreciate the grandeur of this achievement the more when we remember that it escaped the genius of Archimedes and Appollnius, two of the greatest men produced by antiquity." -*Pierre Simon de Laplace, French mathematician, philosopher, and astronomer.*

Whether Vedic science equals - and sometimes even surpasses - the sophistication of modern science is a debatable subject, but what is beyond debate and what makes Vedic science truly unique is its highly theistic approach. And this is why Vedic science becomes crucially important for modern humanity – because it has the potential to bridge the yawning chasm that separates science and spirituality today. Indeed, by uniting reason and faith in a higher-dimensional paradigm, it can heal the wound that has torn the human brain and the human heart far apart.

In the Vedic paradigm, science had a spiritual purpose. This is vividly stated in the Srimad Bhagavatam (1.5.22) "Learned circles have positively concluded that the infallible purpose of the advancement of knowledge, namely austerities, study of the Vedas, sacrifice, chanting of hymns and charity, culminates in the transcendental descriptions of the Lord, who is defined in choice poetry." In his purport to this, eminent Vedic scholar Srila Prabhupada, founder of ISKCON, states: "Science and philosophy also should be applied in the service of the Lord. There is no use presenting dry speculative theories for sense gratification. Philosophy and science should be engaged to establish the glory of the Lord. Advanced people are eager to understand the Absolute Truth through the medium of science, and therefore a great scientist should endeavor to prove the existence of the Lord on a scientific basis."

Thus science – the human faculty to observe and infer a rational understanding from the observation – can be used to verify and confirm spiritual truths – such as the omnipotence and superintelligence of God. This spiritual outlook to science in particular and life in general can rectify much of the exploitative and destructive use to which science is currently being put. In fact, many of the early Western scientists had a similar spiritual purpose for their scientific investigations. Eminent mathematician Johannes Kepler remarked, "I have endeavored to gain for human reason, aided by geometrical calculation, an insight into His way of creation; may the Creator of the heavens themselves, the father of all reason, to whom our mortal senses owe their existence, may He who is Himself immortal... keep me in His grace and guard me from reporting anything about His work which cannot be justified before His magnificence or which may misguide our powers of reason, and may He cause us to aspire to the perfection of His works of creation by the dedication of our lives..."

A Higher-Dimensional Science

Vedic thought considers not only science as a spiritual quest, but even spirituality as a scientific pursuit. The Vedic texts explain that genuine spirituality is meant to awaken the soul to his original spiritual identity as a harmonious unit in the supreme spiritual whole. This is affected through a harmonious combination of philosophy and religion, which constitute the two rails on which spirituality runs. The philosophy aspect of spirituality involves the study and understanding of matter, spirit and the controller of both - the Supreme. And the religion aspect involves the following of certain rules and regulations, which bring about the actual realization and experience of the spiritual realm.

The striking similarity of this understanding of spirituality with the approach of modern science to study the cosmos is worth noting. Modern science involves the formulation of hypotheses to explain the observable phenomena within the universe (similar to the philosophy aspect of spirituality). And it also involves the following of certain rules, which regulate the laboratory environment in a way by which the validity of the hypotheses can be verified (similar to the religion aspect of spirituality). Spirituality thus constitutes a higher dimensional science, in that it deals with realms of reality higher than the mundane.

The spiritual scientist, by dint of systematic practice of both philosophy and religion, realizes the actual nature of the cosmos and learns to live in harmony with it. Having realized his own identity as an eternal spiritual being and his loving relationship with the Supreme Being, such a realized spiritual scientist sees all living beings as his own brothers. His vision of universal brotherhood precipitates him to spontaneous, selfless and spiritual service towards all living beings.

Spiritual Glory Beckons Modern Indians

We modern Indians have inherited an unparalleled legacy of spiritual and scientific knowledge. Unfortunately, most Indians being unaware of their glorious legacy are disillusioned with Indian religiosity and enamored by Western technology. Since independence, India has made steady strides in scientific progress in weaponry, space research, and of course software engineering.

As far as technological advancement is concerned, we can keep improving our gadgets for a long time to come. But we need to ask a vital question: is that what the world needs today? Despite the best comforts, millions of people today are suffering from depression, stress, hypertension, addiction and suicidal urges. The technologically super-advanced West is turning to the East for spiritual solace, as is evident from the increasing popularity of meditation, yoga and chanting. And this is where India can contribute like no other country in the world. Because of our spiritual culture and scientific education, we Indians can have scientific temper in our brains and spiritual wisdom in our hearts in a way that would be impossible for anyone else in any other part of the world. Thus we are best suited to bring about the much-needed synthesis of science and spirituality that thinkers all over the world are searching for. That's why Srila Prabhupada would lament,

"Modern Indians are sitting on jewels and begging for glass." And he asserted unequivocally that spiritual harmony is indispensable for human happiness, "When the scientist, the philosopher and the medical man get the opportunity to study scientifically what is God...., then there will be paradise on the earth."   ● ● ●

A Science Of Values

Modern science operates on the principle of reductionism, that is, reducing all phenomena in the universe including human behavior, to the interactions of subatomic particles acting according to natural laws and impersonal forces.

Eminent scientists have expressed that this basic scientific methodology of reductionism is itself inadequate for understanding life in its completeness.

Consider the statements of two Nobel Laureate Scientists:

1. "I am very astonished that the scientific picture of the real world around me is very deficient. It gives a lot of factual information, puts all our experience in a magnificently consistent order, but it is ghastly silent about all and sundry that is really near to our heart, that really matters to us. It cannot tell us a word about red and blue, bitter and sweet, physical pain and physical delight; it knows nothing of beautiful and ugly, good or bad, God and eternity. Science sometimes pretends to answer questions in these domains, but the answers are very often so silly that we are not inclined to take them seriously." *-Physicist Erwin Schrodinger*

2. "I maintain that the human mystery is incredibly demeaned by scientific reductionism, with its claim in promissory materialism to account eventually for all the spiritual world in terms of patterns of neuronal activity. This belief must be classed as a superstition. ... We have to recognize that we are spiritual beings with souls existing in a spiritual world as well as material beings with bodies and brains existing in a material world." *-Brain researcher John Eccles*

Consequences On Human Values

This incompleteness of the reductionistic approach has grave consequences on the entire worldview of modern human society; it is set to erode all that we cherish as humane and valuable.

1. Consider, for example, the following statements of two eminent scientists, one spiritually-minded and the other not:

"The most beautiful and most profound emotion we can experience is in the sensation of the mystical. It is a shower of all true science…. That deeply emotional conviction of the presence of a superior reasoning power which is revealed in the comprehensible universe forms my idea of God." – *Albert Einstein*

"But now for many years I cannot endure to read a line of poetry: I have tried lately to read Shakespeare and found it so  intolerably dull that it nauseated me. I have also almost lost my taste for pictures or music… The loss of these tastes is a loss of happiness , and may possibly be injurious to the intellect, and more probably to the moral character, by enfeebling the emotional part of our nature." – *Charles Darwin*

2. Which fate do we want our children to meet?

"Man may be able to program his own cells with synthetic information long before he'll be able to access adequately the long-term consequences of such alterations, long before he'll be able to formulate goals and long before he can resolve the ethical and moral problems which will be raised." – *Noble Laureate Geneticist Marshall Nirenberg*

3. Indiscriminate scientific research in fields like genetic engineering and cloning is bound to raise far more problems than it can solve.

"The legal issue of 'responsibility' seems to imply that there is indeed, within each of us, some kind of an independent 'self' with its own responsibilities – and by implications, rights – whose actions are not attributable to inheritance, environment ,or chance." - *Physicist Sir Roger Penrose*

    4. If we accept the scientific version that we are genetically programmed machines, then will we be ready to allow a cold-blooded murderer to go scot-free on the grounds that "murder is programmed in his genes"?

"We may well reach the point in not too distant future where the parables and images of the old religions will have lost their persuasive force even for the average person; when that happens, I am afraid that all the old ethics will collapse like a house of cards and that unimaginable horrors will be perpetrated."- Noble Laureate in Physics Wolfgang Pauli. Unless one has an understanding of God as the Supreme Controller, the call to ethics has no weight. After all, what is there in an atheist's world view to impel him to stick to morality in his pursuit of pleasure? If a person does not understand his identity as an eternal soul, if he thinks that he can get away with whatever he does, provided he just does it cleverly enough, why will he not try to  maximize the pleasure that this life can offer him? "Beg, borrow, steal, kill, but enjoy" becomes the life's motto of a spiritually unprincipled person.

Paradigm Shift in Science

Due to these ominous trends, intellectual trend-setters worldwide have started questioning the validity and utility of indiscriminate scientific and technological "advancement." What is the purpose of scientific research? Human happiness. But if that is not being achieved, has science erred? Where? What can be done about it?

Maybe its time for science to set its priorities right as was recommended by Micheal Faraday centuries ago, "We ought to value the privilege of knowing God's truth far beyond anything we can have in this world." Science may add years to our life, but only spirituality will add life to our years. Without spirituality, we have no answers to fundamental questions of value, purpose and meaning – all of which are critical for satisfaction and fulfillment.

Moreover the reductionistic non-spiritual paradigm of modern science has not been proven, but presumed. This presumption was questioned by eminent scientist Louis Pasteur centuries ago "You pass from matter to life because your intelligence of today... cannot conceive things otherwise. How do you know that in ten thousand years one will not consider it more likely that matter has emerged from life?" Now in the light of devastating social ramifications, open-minded questioning has become vital for human happiness and even survival itself.

Science needs to harmonize itself with the supreme scientist God, as recommended by Albert Einstein, "I believe in God – who reveals himself in the orderly harmony of the Universe. I believe that intelligence is manifested throughout all Nature. The basis of scientific work is the conviction that the world is an ordered and comprehensible entity and not a thing of Chance. When I sit here and watch the mighty ocean, I can imagine the treasures hidden below the bed of the sea, when I see the clear blue sky above, I feel sky is the limit. When I cast my eyes around I see the wonders and beauties of Nature. Science must learn to live in Harmony with all these magnificent gifts of God to Humanity."

Vedic Value-Based Spirituality

"It is already becoming clear that a chapter which had a Western beginning will have to have an Indian ending if it is not to end in the self-destruction of the human race. At this supremely dangerous moment in history, the only way of salvation for mankind is the Indian Way." This remark of Dr Arnold Toynbee (British Historian, 1889-1975) indicates that the best contribution of India to the world should not be in the form of software engineers, but in the form of spiritual engineers.

If we want intellectually satisfying spiritual alternatives to the materialistic worldview offered by reductionistic science, India is our best hope. Many Western thinkers have acknowledged the glory of Vedic spiritual wisdom.

1. "In religion, India is the only millionaire......the one land that all men desire to see, and having seen once, by even a glimpse, would not give that glimpse for all the shows of all the rest of the globe combined." - *Mark Twain*

2. "Whenever I have read any part of the Vedas, I have felt that some unearthly and unknown light illuminated me. In the great teaching of the Vedas, there is no touch of sectarianism. It is of all ages, climbs, and nationalities and is the royal road for the attainment of the Great Knowledge." *-American Thinker Henry David Thoreau*

3. "The marvel of the Bhagavad-Gita is its truly beautiful revelation of life's wisdom which enables philosophy to blossom into religion." -*Herman Hesse (1877-1962), German poet and novelist, awarded the Nobel Prize for literature in 19.*

4. "[The Bhagavad-gita is the] Best of books - containing a wisdom blander and far more sane than that of the Hebrews, whether in the mind of Moses or of Him of Nazareth. Were I a preacher, I would venture sometimes to take from its texts the motto and moral of my discourse. It would be healthful and invigorating to breathe some of this mountain air into the lungs of Christendom." -*Amos Bronson Alcott (1799-1888) writer, philosopher, visionary.*

5. "The message of the Gita is a universal call to Democracy, liberty for the peoples, liberty for each individual. The great affirmation of the Bhagavad Gita is that every individual, whatever he may be, rich or poor, can and must raise himself on life's path and that he has a right to his emancipation, social, intellectual, and spiritual." -*Louis Revel, French author of The Fragrance of India: Landmarks for the world of tomorrow*

The glory of Vedic wisdom was seen in the caliber of its followers. When we become devoted to God, we become godly. This was the basis of the theistic Vedic social order. Moreover another cardinal principle was: real human progress is measured not by the development of technological facilities, but by the development of spiritual qualities. The glorious social order as present in India (before its spiritual foundation was destroyed by the British imperial rule) was noted by British statesman Edmund Burke, "This multitude of men (the Indian nation) does not consist of an abject and barbarous populace, much less of gangs of savages; but of a people for ages civilized and cultivated; cultured by all the arts of polished life while we (Englishmen) were yet dwelling in the woods. There have been in (India) princes of great dignity, authority and opulence. There (in India) is to be found an ancient and venerable priesthood, the depositary of laws, learning and history, the guides of the people while living and their consolation in death. There is a nobility of great antiquity and renown; a multitude of cities not exceeded in population and trade by those of the first class in Europe; merchants and bankers who vie in capital with the banks of England; millions of ingenious manufacturers and mechanics; and millions of the most diligent tillers of the earth."

Srila Prabhupada, the founder of ISKCON, taught that the foundation for real peace can be established only by spiritual wisdom, "Unless there is an awakening of divine consciousness in the individual, there is no use of crying for world peace." We need not mistake genuine devotion to be the irrational religious fanaticism seen in some parts of the world today. Srila Prabhupada analyzes the failings of such so-called religion as follows, "Religion without philosophy is sentimentalism or sometimes fanaticism, Philosophy without religion is mental speculation." If there is systematic philosophical education, then spirituality far from leading to fanaticism will lead to real harmony with nature and the master of nature.

India as a Global Spiritual Leader

The Swiss professor Dr. Richard Ernst –the 1999 Noble prize winner in chemistry – when projecting the impact of science in this millennium, took special note of India's past and her present intellectual potential for shaping humanity's future;

India has a well developed academic community with a surplus of highly creative scientists, perhaps with a special indication towards the more theoretical aspects of science and still maintain a link to the Indian culture...

I am convinced that India could become once again the cradle of a new school of thought that may significantly influence the fate of the globe during the millennium. Perhaps the contribution of India to nuclear power technology and space science will turn out to be irrelevant, but the contribution towards a new ethical foundation could be turning the wheel of history in the proper (balanced) way.

Eminent thinkers throughout the world, including leading scientists such as Nobel Laureate Richard R. Ernst, peace workers such as Nobel Laureates Oscar Arias Sanchez and Betty Williams, and spiritualists such as Nobel Laureate the Dalai Lama, firmly believe that only a synthesis of science and spirituality can lead the world out of the present troubled times.

The youth of India have a unique position in the world. By virtue of birth in the holy land of India, they inherit the priceless wealth of spiritual knowledge expounded in the Vedic texts. And by virtue of their education and training, they have developed the scientific spirit of rational inquiry. Thus they are best suited to bring about the much-needed synthesis of science and spirituality that thinkers all over the world are searching for. The late Professor Arthur Ellison, a mechanical and electrical engineer, stated, "Surely the great and unique contribution that India has made and must continue to make to the world's progress is in the field of religion--of truth and reality.... India can most certainly help the West to find the spiritual way back towards reality, which is essential for all real progress." Unfortunately, most young Indians today are enamored by the razzle-dazzle of Western culture – blue jeans, supermarkets, Big Macs, Disney "fun," rock music, Hollywood movies, and the like. But before embracing Western culture, wouldn't it be worthwhile to study the condition of those who have lived with it their whole lives? Statistics show that in the U.S.A. a thousand teenagers attempt suicide every day. Seventy percent of all high-school seniors have attempted or seriously thought about suicide. Thirty-three percent of American adults have serious mental health problems. Psychiatry and psychology are the most lucrative professions in America, and among all professionals, the highest suicide rate is found among psychiatrists and psychologists. Yet for most Indians, America is the land of their dreams. Srila Prabhupada would lament that modern Indians are sitting on jewels and begging for broken glass. Let the intelligent youth of India become selfless spiritual scientists dedicated to saving the world from its suicidal course. Let them, in the true spirit of science, study the theory of spirituality with all seriousness and at the same time perform the experiment of mantra meditation. Those who take up this challenge will become living spiritual scientists and will help usher in an era of peace, harmony, and understanding. ● ● ●

Appendix I - Atheism Refuted

Atheistic scientists like Richard Dawkins in his book The God Delusion present specious arguments to disprove the existence of God. Let's see how those arguments fall apart on proper scrutiny.

I. The designer hypothesis immediately raises the larger problem of who designed the designer. If the object in nature is complex and so improbable, the designer must be at least equally, if not more, complex and hence improbable. It is obviously no solution to the problem of improbability to postulate something even more improbable.

In order to recognize an explanation as the best, one needn't have an explanation of the explanation. This is an elementary point concerning inference to the best explanation as practiced in the philosophy of science. If archaeologists digging in the earth were to discover things looking like arrowheads and hatchet heads and pottery shards, they would be justified in inferring that these artifacts are not the chance result of sedimentation and metamorphosis, but products of some unknown group of people, even though they had no explanation of who these people were or where they came from. Similarly, if astronauts were to come upon a pile of machinery on the back side of the moon, they would be justified in inferring that it was the product of intelligent, extra-terrestrial agents, even if they had no idea whatsoever who these extra-terrestrial agents were or how they got there. In order to recognize an explanation as the best, one needn't be able to explain the explanation. In fact, so requiring would lead to an infinite regress of explanations, so that nothing could ever be explained and science would be destroyed. So in the case at hand, in order to recognize that intelligent design is the best explanation of the appearance of design in the universe, one needn't be able to explain the designer.

From the point of view of everyday logic, the origin of everything is a problem, for both science and religion. To start with a complex being may seem against the scientific principle of explaining complex things with simpler things, but science doesn't have any easy way out. Firstly, it's unscientific to say that everything came from nothing. And the alternative of a singularity as a source of everything doesn't make things any better for science. To propose as the origin of everything a singularity having infinite density, infinite temperature, infinitesimal mass, beyond all conceptions of space and time, beyond mathematical description and physical realization, begs several questions

1. Where did that singularity come from?

Some scientists propose eternally crunching and expanding universes to get around the problem of the origin of the singularity. But this is just an unproven and unprovable speculation to solve a self-created problem.

2. Something with infinite temperature and density - how simple is that? And how probable?

3. How scientific is it to talk about something beyond space and time, and beyond 'mathematical description and physical realization'?

Stephen Hawking has stated, "Any theory that predicts a singularity can be said to have broken down." So, if science necessitates postulating something beyond the realm of science, then an intelligent being is a much more logical candidate for creating the complex world we see around us than a singularity. Both are non-scientific, in the conventional sense of the word 'scientific', but we at least have experience of an intelligent being designing something, but we have no experience of a singularity and its explosion leading to design.

II. Saying that a God has designed everything is the ultimate abdication of scientific responsibility to investigate.

Scientific responsibility to investigate means the responsibility to investigate all possibilities – including the possibility that God has designed everything. To be close-minded about that possibility is also an abdication of scientific responsibility.

III. If past scientists had been satisfied with saying that God had designed everything, we would never have made all the scientific progress that we have made.

Scientific research doesn't have to be stunted by the acknowledgement of God as the ultimate designer. Science can still investigate the mechanisms by which God has designed things and utilize that knowledge for beneficial purposes. What needs to be changed is the a priori atheistic framework in which scientific research is performed.

IV. The argument for a designer stems from lack of knowledge and imagination. Just because we cannot visualize how natural selection could have led to a particular organ doesn't meant that it could never have happened. It just means that we haven't had our consciousness raised to assimilate the power of natural selection.

All of us have the knowledge that well-designed things have a designer. And all of us can imagine, if we want to, that even those well-designed things for which we never saw a designer in action must also have a designer.

There is no demonstrable proof that natural selection has led any new design at all, what to speak of any complex designs. All that has been demonstrated is that natural selection leads to variation within pre-existing designs. A dog can become bigger or smaller by breeding or perhaps by natural selection, but it remains a dog; it never becomes an elephant, as far as human observation has seen. To say that it has happened in the past when there were no humans is also not proven by the fossil record. To claim unseen evidence to prove an unproven thory; that destroys science.

And even if somebody could imagine some mechanism involving natural selection by which certain complex features in some organisms came up, that doesn't at all prove that it happened that day. That is imagination at work, not science at work.

And to say that "we haven't had our consciousness raised to assimilate the power of natural selection" is just a demand for blind faith phrased in pseudo-scientific language. When a religionist says "you haven't had your consciousness raised to assimilate the power of God," that's considered unscientific. But when a scientist says more or less the same thing, that's "scientific." Simply self-serving double standards.

There are millions of examples of designer leading to design, but none of natural selection leading to a new design.

V. To bring in God to explain the design of what science can't explain is the classic "god-of-the-gaps" fallacy. As science progresses, the place for God decreases, till ultimately he has no place left for him.

God is needed not just to explain what science cannot explain, but also to explain what science claims to have explained. For example, scientists say that earlier people thought that God moved the planets, but now we know it's gravity that moves them. But gravity is not the explanation of a phenomenon; it is just the name given to an observed phenomenon.

Newton himself stressed that his theory was only a numerical description of observable effects, and he deliberately made no hypotheses about underlying causes. He spoke of gravitation as "action at a distance," but the idea of a force acting mysteriously across empty space seemed abhorrent to Newton and other scientists, both in his day and the present. Thus the history of physics in the 18th and 19th centuries was marked by many attempts to explain gravitation through some kind of interaction of substances or particles moving through space. Unfortunately, all of these attempts were unsuccessful (Jaki, S., The Relevance of Physics (Chicago: The Univ. of Chicago Press, 1970), pp. 77-78).

So, God is the God-of-everything, and the god-of-the-gaps argument is based on misrepresenting scientific explanatory power.

References

1. Bhagavad-gita As It Is, Srila Prabhupada
2. God, The Evidence, Patrick Glynn
3. Human Devolution, Michael Cremo
4. Forbidden Archaeology, Michael Cremo and Richard Thompson
5. Life: How did it get here, Watchtower Publications
6. Origins, BBT Science
7. Searching for Vedic India, Devamrita Swami
8. 50 Nobel Laureates on God, Tihomir Dimitrov

Vedic Oasis for Inspiration, Culture & Education (VOICE)
Rekindling Wisdom, Reviving Love

VOICE offers personality development and character buildup training for thousands of youths all over India including at IITs and NITs. VOICE also has specialized wings for teenagers, children, girls and corporate executives.

VOICE Publications

'Bring out the leader in you' series
- Stress Management
- ENERGY – Your *Sutra* for Positive Thinking

'Spirituality for the Modern Youth' series
- Discover Yourself
- Your Best Friend
- Your Secret Journey
- Victory Over Death
- Yoga of Love

Pocket Books
- Art of Mind Control
- Practical Tips to Mind Control
- Can I Live Forever?
- Do We Live More Than Once?
- Tryst With Eternal Beauty
- Stress Management

Other Books
- Spiritual Scientist
- Positive Thinker

- Self-Manager
- Proactive Leader
- Personality Development
- Youth Preaching Manual
- Bhagavad-gita 7 day Course
- Value Education

The Spiritual Scientist Series
- Vol I : Selected newspaper articles
- Vol II : Selected newspaper articles
- Vol III : Science and Spirituality

Children's Books:
- My First Krishna Book
- Getting to Know Krishna
- More About Krishna
- Devotees of Krishna
- Wonderful Krishna
- Krishna's Childhood Pastime

For more information about VOICE publications, please write to publications@voicepune.com or contact Krishnakishore Das on 09822451260.